Branches & Byways
Southwest Scotland
and the Border Counties

Branches & Byways
Southwest Scotland and the Border Counties

Robert Robotham

An imprint of
Ian Allan Publishing

Half title page:
Class J39/2 No 64897 draws through Alnmouth station on 29 May 1962 to shunt more wagons to form an up freight — a railway scene that has all but ceased today.
Michael Mensing

Title page:
Ivatt Class 2 No 46482 moves on to wagons collected from the goods yard at Coldstream while working a pick-up freight from Kelso to Tweedmouth on 1 June 1962. On the down (Kelso) side at Coldstream there was a 50ft turntable used to turn the locomotives that had hauled passenger trains in from Alnwick, and latterly to turn permanent-way gangers' trolleys.
Michael Mensing

Front cover:
BR Standard Class 4 2-6-4T No 80061 is seen near Newton Stewart on 29 May 1965 with a Stranraer Town–Dumfries service, the return journey of the 08.20 Dumfries–Stranraer Town pictured on page 80. *Chris Gammell/Colour-Rail*

Rear upper:
Class J39 No 64813 is seen awaiting departure from Eyemouth with its mixed train for Burnmouth in June 1956. Beyond the crowded goods yard can be seen the harbour.
J. G. Wallace/Colour-Rail

Rear lower:
On Monday 1 August 1960, Caley 0-6-0 'Standard Goods' No 57340 waits with the thrice-weekley Whithorn branch freight at Whauphill. Although the passenger service finished 10 years previously the station still looks in good order, and has even been partly repainted. The freight service survived a further four years, being abandoned on 6 October 1964. *Chris Gammell/Colour-Rail*

Note: The 24-hour clock has been used from 1964, when introduced in BR timetables.

First published 2003

ISBN 0 86093 575 2

Published by Oxford Publishing Co

an imprint of Ian Allan Publishing Ltd, Hersham, Surrey KT12 4RG
Printed by Ian Allan Printing Ltd, Hersham, Surrey KT12 4RG

Code: 0311/A3

Contents

Introduction & Acknowledgements

My idea to put together a book covering 'Branches and Byways' in Southwest Scotland and the Border Counties came from having seen many of the remnants of the railway network that existed here while I was on exercise with my Regiment, The Royal Mercian & Lancastrian Yeomanry — formerly The Queen's Own Mercian Yeomanry, after which a Brush Type 4 (No 47528) was named at Worcester Shrub Hill station by HM The Queen in 1989. The idea was further fuelled by the availability of so many exciting photographs of trains (mainly in the British Railways era), in this area — some of them taken in quite spectacular locations.

We regularly visited Redesdale Camp at Otterburn and on the way there would pass near to the Wansbeck Valley line from Morpeth to Reedsmouth Junction, the branch from Scotsgap Junction to Rothbury, and, once there, we were close to the trackbed of the former Border Counties line from Hexham to Riccarton Junction. Being a mobile reconnaissance regiment, we often started an 'exercise' near the East Coast north of Newcastle and then advanced west covering many miles on country roads and tracks, and on numerous occasions we would cross the former routes covered in this book.

Much evidence of these routes still remains today. I remember particularly the Wansbeck Valley line at Woodburn, the Border Counties-line trackbed near the 'new' Kielder Reservoir, and the old Border Counties Railway bridge in Falstone, adjacent to a good pub where the results of a very serious leek growing competition were being announced as we enjoyed a well-earned supper between 'battles'.

The Waverley Route trackbed at Riccarton and Steele Road striding through the hills and looking ripe for reopening, the empty trackbed of the Dumfries to Stranraer line at Creetown also attracted my attention, as did the almost non-stop day-and-night procession of heavy lorries racing up and down the modernised A75. This, more than anything, made it clear to me where the transport priorities of governments since the war have been. Parking my Land Rover in Langholm on one occasion, I noticed a small mound of stones that indicated that this area had formerly been the station. How ironic that it should now be a car park.

Our exercises usually finished near Wigtown, where the Whithorn-Newton Stewart branch had run; some bridges and embankments still exist here and act as reminders of times past.

Lastly, to anyone who may accuse me of breaking away from the 'Branches and Byways' theme of this book in terms of the Dumfries-Stranraer 'Port Road' — clearly a main line — then I am sticking to what I believe is appropriate. This was a main-line byway, it passed through no large towns and was primarily a 'through route' supplemented at its eastern end by the line from Kirkcudbright, which ran an important connecting service to Dumfries. Surely this part of the line should have survived?

The main period covered by this book is British Railways days, but a few pre-Nationalisation illustrations are included where appropriate. Initially, it seemed that not much would change after World War 2, the railways continued to operate much as they always had done. However, had it not been for the war, and the inevitable growth in military and passenger traffic that it had brought, the impact on motor cars of petrol rationing in rural areas, plus the need to keep 'diversionary routes' open, then the lines covered here may have started to close much earlier than they did. Some were the subject of attempts to cut costs with railmotor services in the 1930s, while others survived just for freight. The fact that so many lasted as long as they did is amazing, the infamous Beeching Report finishing off the rest and ultimately claiming the biggest prize for the closure lobby: the Waverley Route.

As always, I am indebted to others, mainly my fellow railwaymen, now mostly in retirement, for providing me with assistance in the production of this book. This has come mainly in two ways, firstly photographically and secondly, with research and timetables, as well as local knowledge, as they were actually there!

David Holmes, whom I met while working for Railfreight Petroleum, has helped with both photographs and archive material; indeed, he spent a considerable amount of time putting together details of train workings and many key dates, for which I am most grateful. Stuart Sellar, a senior officer on the Scottish Region of British Railways, has assisted with much photographic material and other information.

Fellow author and ex-steam driver Bill Rear has assisted in my quest for Scottish and North Eastern Region working timetables, and other information. Roy Hamilton, another manager from BR's Scottish Region and an active member of the Strathspey Railway, has also taken a lot of trouble to go through his lists and provide me with prints and information to use in this book, as has W. A. C. (Bill) Smith who has produced many photographs from his extensive collection and recently produced his own excellent books entitled *The Borders' Last Days of Steam*, published by Cordfall, and *Dumfries and Galloway's Last Days of Steam*, published by Stenlake. In addition, master photographer Michael Mensing has, once again, made available to me many of his remarkable photographs.

Others too have gone out of their way to help. Alan Thompson of the J. W. Armstrong Trust has been kind enough to forward prints, as have Maurice Burns, John Langford and Richard Casserley. Colin Dickson of British Rail at York has been particularly helpful in connection with the production of track plans and other details.

Also, many thanks are due to Colin Stewart, with whom I worked at the former British Rail Telecommunications, for assisting with historical material, and Peter Waller of Ian Allan for his encouragement and advice.

Lastly, I would like to thank my wife Cheni, children Jake and Georgie and Labrador Bertie, all of whom have shown amazing patience while I have worked on this book!

Robert Robotham
Sherborne
August 2003

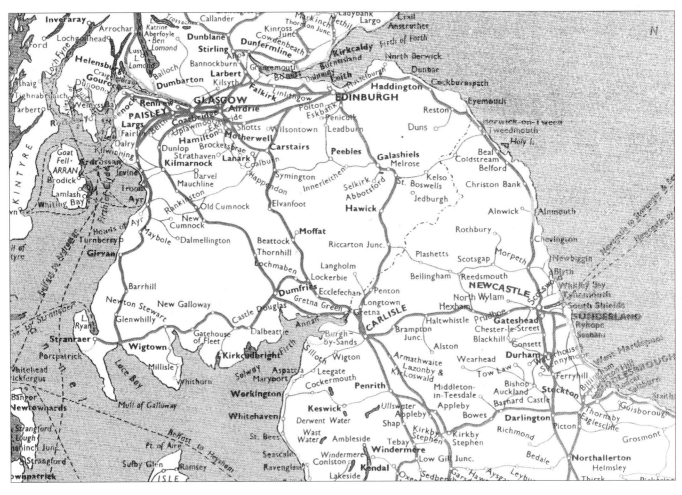

System map from BR NER timetable 1950, showing the lines covered in this book.

Southwest Scotland and the Border Counties — a summary —

Today, the railway crosses the English and Scottish Border in only two places — at Gretna on the West Coast main line and just to the north of Berwick upon Tweed at Marshall Meadows on the East Coast main line. The vast area in between can only be described as a railway wilderness, and to the west the Dumfries & Galloway Region is also now virtually devoid of the iron road.

But this was not always the case. In the period covered here, the border between Scotland and England was crossed at no fewer than six places. From west to east these were:

The Caledonian main line at Gretna
The Riddings Junction-Langholm branch at Liddel Water
The Waverley Route at Kershopefoot
The Border Counties line at Deadwater
The North Eastern line from Tweedmouth Junction to Sprouston near Carham
The North British main line from Berwick to Edinburgh at Marshall Meadows

The January 1950 edition of *The Railway Magazine* mentions that the border crossing points were to be marked and as a result, 'the erection of clear and unmistakable lineside signs has put the matter beyond all doubt'. This referred to the Border crossing points on the east and west coast main lines, but by 1950 two more signs were put up, 'at Deadwater, on the Border Counties line, from Hexham to Riccarton Junction, and at Carham, on the cross-country route from Tweedmouth to Kelso and St Boswells. The design in each case consists of a double-headed battle axe, and the words England and Scotland supported by the national emblems, the rose and thistle'. Interestingly, no sign was ever placed on the Langholm branch on the viaduct that crossed Liddel Water.

This book features the significant network of lines that existed from the Southwest of Scotland through the Border Counties to the East Coast main line in the British Railways era since 1948. To the west of Carlisle, in Southwest Scotland, the famous 'Port Road' main line from Dumfries to Stranraer still carried through express services, known as the 'Paddys', which were linked to the ferry service to and from Ireland. Two branches sprang from it, one from Castle Douglas to Kirkcudbright and the other from Newton Stewart to Whithorn. Even the line from Stranraer to Portpatrick had survived the test of time into BR days, despite its harbour — once the main ferry port linking Scotland with Ireland — being downgraded in favour of Stranraer.

The role that these lines played in supporting the agricultural industry cannot be overstated. Animal feedstuffs, fertilisers, farm machinery and other essentials were brought in by rail to the local station for farmers to collect. Their produce — dairy, beet, potatoes, grain, livestock and meat — was carried in large quantities by rail to market or final destination. Although road carriage took over much of this traffic, the farming industry relied on the railway until well into the 1960s; places such as Earlston (on the St Boswells-Greenlaw line), Duns and Kelso were 'railheads' with cattle markets built next to the stations, and closure of these lines, and others, caused much concern and change of lifestyle.

Moving to the east, the line from Dumfries to Lockerbie was still open for through services, although it lost its regular passenger services on 19 May 1952. Freight continued (mainly overnight) until closure on 18 April 1966. The former Caledonian branches from Beattock to Moffat and from Symington to Peebles West were also still open, the former closing to passengers in December 1954, although a passenger service was run on Saturdays for railway staff and their relatives. It closed to freight in April 1964.

Symington to Peebles West had its passenger services withdrawn by BR on 5 June 1950. Freight lingered on until 7 June 1954 when it ceased between Broughton and Peebles, the final stub to Symington lasting until 4 April 1966. The link from Peebles (NBR) situated on the Galashiels to Hardengreen Junction Peebles Loop line, to Peebles West (Caledonian), was finally closed on 1 August 1959.

Left:
The 'Port Road' was the direct route from Stranraer Harbour to Dumfries, the two largest places en route being Newton Stewart and Castle Douglas. Newton Stewart was the junction for the Whithorn line, and the branch to Kirkcudbright left the line at Castle Douglas. The main express service — latterly called the the 'Northern Irishman' (the 'Paddy') — from Stranraer Harbour to London Euston passed through during the night, but there were also daytime 'Paddy' services which connected with the boats to Ireland and served local stations en route. Ex-LMS Stanier 'Black Five' 4-6-0s were common performers on the line; here, No 44957 of 67E, Dumfries shed prepares to leave Castle Douglas with the 1.40pm from Stranraer Harbour to Dumfries on 24 June 1963. *David Holmes*

Above:

The BR Standard 'Clan' Pacifics were common visitors to the 'Port Road', being based at Carlisle Kingmoor and used for the overnight Euston-Stranraer service, plus other boat trains as well as military and other specials that required Class 6 power. No 72007 *Clan Mackintosh* **waits at Castle Douglas on 8 July 1961 with the 9am from Newcastle to Stranraer Harbour, which train it would have taken over at Carlisle.** *W. A. C. Smith*

Above:

The first branch off the 'Port Road' was the line from Castle Douglas to Kirkcudbright (although the 'Port Road' was actually a branch off the Kirkcudbright line!). BR Standard Class 4 Mogul No 76072 waits to depart from Kirkcudbright with the 4.51pm to Dumfries on 24 June 1963. The station once had an overall roof, but latterly the canopy was cut back, as can be seen in this view. *David Holmes*

Above:
The Whithorn branch goods is seen at Millisle Junction on 27 May 1964 where it prepares to take the short line to Garlieston. It would then set back and continue further on to Whithorn. The locomotive is BR Standard Class 2 2-6-0 No 78026 (it seems to have been positioned under some roosting pigeons overnight!), and the traffic consists of coal. Freight traffic in this part of the world was general merchandise, dairy produce and livestock, all of these being particularly susceptible to road competition, finally leaving the railway, in the main, with just coal. *J. Spencer Gilks*

Above:
'Jubilee' 4-6-0 No 45588 *Kashmir* passes Locharbriggs (between Lockerbie and Dumfries) with the SLS/SBS 'Easter Tour' on 15 April 1963. Passenger trains had ceased to operate on the route from 19 May 1952, but freight traffic lasted until 18 April 1966. *Stuart Sellar*

Left:
The Moffat branch from Beattock on the Caledonian main line had opened on 2 April 1883. Just under two miles long, it often featured mixed trains and was a stronghold of the former Caledonian Railway '431' class 0-4-4 tanks, but occasionally, one of the Beattock bankers would work the train. One of the 0-4-4Ts, No 55221, has arrived at Moffat from Beattock with the motor train service in August 1952. *Ian Allan Library*

Above:
'Black Five' No 45161 is seen at Broughton on 2 May 1962 with the local trip working No S13 on the now-truncated Symington to Peebles line. Freight services to Broughton lasted until 4 April 1966. *Stuart Sellar*

The former North British network lay largely untouched by any pre-Nationalisation closures, with branches springing from the Waverley Route to a number of small towns and villages in the Border Counties. The first of these was the branch from Riddings Junction to Langholm, and then further along the main line at St Boswells came the Tweed Valley line to the coast at Tweedmouth, which was formerly owned by the North British as far as Kelso and the North Eastern from Kelso to Tweedmouth. To the north of St Boswells, at Ravenswood Junction, came another long branch — the Berwickshire Railway — which ran through remote country to Duns, joining the East Coat Main Line at Reston.

Above:

The line from Riddings Junction to Langholm opened on 18 April 1864, having previously been open since 1862 as far as the colliery at Rowanburn near Canonbie. The town of Langholm had lobbied to be situated on a main line — indeed the Caledonian had proposed a route to Hawick from Carlisle that passed through there as an alternative to the NBR Waverley Route, but their scheme failed. Passenger services were latterly in the hands of ex-LNER 'J39' class 0-6-0s and ex-LMS 2-6-0 mixed traffic locomotives, allocated to Carlisle Canal shed. One of the latter types, No 43011, stands at Langholm station with the 3.28pm to Carlisle on 10 October 1963. Passenger services survived until 13 June 1964, freight continuing until 17 September 1967. *Hugh Ballantyne*

Right:

Coldstream station is seen on 1 June 1962 with BR Standard 2-6-0 No 78048 departing with the 9.56am from Berwick-upon-Tweed to St Boswells. Parcels have been unloaded from the train, which consists of a Gresley BCK. Coldstream was the junction for the line to Alnwick that lost its passenger service in September 1930, although freight continued as far as Wooler until 1965. The 'main' line had opened throughout from St Boswells to Tweedmouth in 1851 and at Roxburgh Junction there was a line to Jedburgh. The line was originally double track from Kelso to St Boswells, but, despite this being singled in 1933, the line proved its worth as a diversionary route for East Coast main line expresses on a number of occasions. It served a rich agricultural area and farmers relied on the railway for traffic such as animal feedstuffs and for the transportation of their produce to market, including livestock.

Michael Mensing

Above:

The line from St Boswells to Reston through Duns was severed in the floods of August 1948 and was never reconnected, thereafter being worked as two branches from either end. The passenger service ceased immediately on the western section which was truncated at Greenlaw and this then became freight only. The Duns to Reston portion continued to carry passenger traffic until 10 September 1951, following which freight was worked until 7 November 1966. The St Boswells to Greenlaw section lasted until 16 July 1965. Both ends of the line did feature railtours, but this view shows ex-NBR 'J35/4' class 0-6-0 No 64494 at Greenlaw with the goods trip from St Boswells on 15 May 1958. *Stuart Sellar*

Below:

Former NBR 'D34' class 4-4-0 No 62471 *Glen Falloch* arrives at Selkirk with a Branch Line Society railtour, the 'Scott Country', which ran on the line on 4 April 1959. The line had at one time been worked by steam railcars, but latterly, conventional steam locomotives and coaches were used. There was also freight traffic to and from the woollen mills that were close to the line. The route passed close to the home of Sir Walter Scott at Abbotsford, the station for this being at Abbotsford Ferry. Passenger services were discontinued on 10 September 1951 and all freight had gone from Selkirk by 2 November 1964, the section from Selkirk Junction to the mill at Netherfield being closed from 3 October 1966. *Roy Hamilton*

The Peebles branch opened on 4 July 1855, from Hardengreen Junction near Eskbank. By 1864 it had opened to Kilnknowe Junction at Galashiels, thus completing a single-track line that was known as the Peebles Loop. In its latter years an attempt was made to modernise the line and it became the first service in Scotland to be run regularly by diesel multiple-units, one evening service running from Edinburgh Waverley to Kelso via Galashiels. Unfortunately, this was not enough to save the line and it closed on 5 February 1962. One of the DMUs is seen here at the smart North British station in Peebles, forming the 9.58am train from Galashiels to Edinburgh Waverley on 27 November 1961. *Roy Hamilton*

At Galashiels there was a further branch to Selkirk, which passed by Sir Walter Scott's residence at Abbotsford. To the north of Galashiels was the Peebles Loop of the North British which passed close to the Caledonian station in Peebles, but there were no passenger connections — only freight traffic passed between the two companies here. At Fountainhall came the famous light railway to Lauder.

Right:
The well-known Lauder Light Railway opened from Fountainhall to Lauder on 2 July 1901. Passenger services lasted until 12 September 1932, but it lived on for freight until 1 October 1958. The last train ran on 15 November 1958 and was hauled by BR Standard Class 2 Mogul No 78049. It left Fountainhall at 2pm and called at Oxton and Lauder where crowds met the train. The train is seen during the ten-minute stop at Oxton. *Stuart Sellar*

Left:
Ex-LNER 'D49' class 4-4-0 No 62747 *The Percy*, **a long-time Blaydon engine, leaves Reedsmouth with the 11.10am from Newcastle to Hawick in 1953. Reedsmouth was the apex of lines in this part of the world, linking the Hexham to Riccarton line that this train is taking, with the line from Morpeth and Scotsgap.**
J. W. Armstrong Trust

Between Hawick and Riddings Junction came the infamous Riccarton Junction and the Border Counties branch from Hexham. This line met the Wansbeck Valley line from Morpeth at Reedsmouth Junction, the latter having a branch to Rothbury from Scotsgap. The Border Counties line allowed the North British access to Newcastle — but via a remote route! It opened on 1 July 1862 and started at Riccarton Junction where a railway community with no road access sprang up. The coal deposits around Plashetts, which it was hoped would supply the woollen mills of the Tweed Valley, produced coal that was fit only for domestic use, but there was other traffic, mainly agricultural and livestock, to and from Bellingham. A quarry on the line also saw military specials and timber traffic. Passenger services were sparse, but there were three trains a day in either direction with additional services on Saturdays for walkers and other tourists.

Below:
A special train titled the 'Wansbeck Piper' was the last passenger train to run on the Wansbeck Valley line, on 2 October 1966 and was hauled by Ivatt '2MT' Moguls Nos 43000 and 43063. The train, which was made up of 11 coaches, was organised by Gosforth Round Table and is seen climbing out of Woodburn on the 1-in-62 grade through the magnificent scenery of the area. *Maurice Burns*

The line closed to passengers on 15 October 1956, but freight survived to Bellingham until 11 November 1963, although this came via the Scotsgap line, reversing at Reedsmouth.

The Wansbeck Valley line ran from Morpeth through Scotsgap to Reedsmouth Junction; again passenger services were sparse and were withdrawn as early as September 1952. With it came a branch from Scotsgap to Rothbury — once planned to reach Kelso — and there was freight traffic in the form of stone from a quarry and coal deliveries, plus agricultural and livestock traffic. Passenger services were also withdrawn in September 1952, freight on the whole system ceasing on 11 November 1963 with the exception of the Woodburn to Morpeth section, which saw its last freight on 29 September 1966, closure taking place on 3 October 1966.

It was originally intended to run the East Coast main line through Alnwick, but in the event a double-track branch, 2¾ miles

Above:

The Alnmouth to Alnwick line saw a variety of motive power, but the 'J39s' were probably the most common performers. Here, 'J39/2' No 64924 arrives at Alnwick with the 5.35pm from Alnmouth on 29 May 1962. Note the fine gantry which controlled not only the line from Alnmouth but also the (by then) closed line to Wooler and Coldstream. *Michael Mensing*

long was constructed from Alnmouth. By 19 August 1850 passenger services had commenced, freight having started earlier that month, on the 5th. Prior to BR days, Alnwick enjoyed a through service to Newcastle, but this ceased, and passengers had to change at Alnmouth until the advent of DMUs, when they worked as through services to Newcastle once again. Originally double track, it was later singled and the signalling rationalised. It closed to passengers from 29 January 1968 and to freight on 7 October 1968, but it is now being mooted as a potential preservation scheme.

Alnwick station was rebuilt in grand style when the line from Coldstream arrived in 1887. This line was just over 35 miles long, consisting entirely of single track, and passed through Wooler. Passenger traffic was extremely light and passenger trains were withdrawn as early as September 1930. Freight finally ceased on 29 March 1965 with stations served only from the Coldstream end after the 1948 floods had damaged the line between Wooler and Ilderton. The Ilderton to Alnwick freight service was withdrawn in March 1953. This line was a true 'byway' but during World War 2 was seen as an alternative to the East Coast main line, and, as a result, some of the track was upgraded.

A three-mile branch from Burnmouth, on the East Coast main line, linked the small fishing port at Eyemouth with the rest of the railway network and carried both passengers and freight traffic. This line was lobbied for and funded partly by local people and carried fish away from the port, replacing the horse-drawn carts that had previously carried the traffic to Burnmouth. Damaged in the floods of 1948, the line was rebuilt and reopened to traffic as late as 29 June 1949. Despite ominous traffic losses to the car, lorry and bus elsewhere it was still perceived by British Railways that the line would be open for a considerable time to come, but it closed to passengers on 3 February 1962.

This network of railway lines, a complete way of life for many people, was about to change, and by 1969, with the passing of the Waverley Route, it had almost completely vanished from the railway map.

While at Nationalisation on 1 January 1948, the above comprehensive network of lines still existed in South West Scotland and the Border Counties, some other lines not yet mentioned, had closed to all traffic before that date. It is interesting to note that at this time virtually all the lines that featured on the railway map at Grouping in 1923 had survived in some shape or form with the exception of the following.

The Talla Railway

The earliest casualty of rail services in the Border Counties can certainly be described as a byway, being a line that ran from the Caledonian route from Symington to Peebles at Broughton. Work on the line began in 1895, it being built originally by the Edinburgh Water Board to carry construction materials and waste from a reservoir which was constructed to supply the Edinburgh area with water. The line was eight miles in length, laid to standard gauge and ran from Broughton to Victoria Lodge situated on the edge of where the reservoir was to be built. Also, a small halt was placed next to Crook Inn.

As well as workers on the project, passengers were permitted, but these amounted to just a few locals. Not surprisingly, once the reservoir had been completed there was no real reason to keep the line open, and, despite various requests to keep it in situ, these were ignored. Official closure came on 28 September 1905 and by 1912, the line had been dismantled, it being the first line in the Border Counties to vanish.

The Solway Junction Railway

On 13 September 1869 the Solway Junction Railway opened, linking the North British line from Carlisle to Silloth at Kirkbride across a single-track viaduct over the Solway, 1,940 yards in length, to Annan and Kirtlebridge on the Caledonian Railway main line. The line was originally supported by the Caledonian to carry, in the main, iron ore to Scotland from the Workington area, and was accessed by building another link from the Silloth branch at Abbeyholme (later Abbey Junction) to Brayton on the Maryport & Carlisle Railway. Three passenger trains per day were run on the southern section from Brayton to Annan Shawhill and then six trains per day from Annan to Kirtlebridge.

Before World War 1 an inspection had revealed that repairs were needed to the viaduct and would cost around £15,000. The war saw an increase in movements of pig iron and so there was more traffic over the viaduct with trains which included passenger coaches, pulled by light-weight locomotives. The condition of the structure deteriorated, and a further inspection in 1921 found that repair work would now cost as much as £70,000. In that year, a miners' strike saw the service on the route withdrawn, but it recommenced with only one train per day, on Tuesdays and Saturdays only, until 31 August. After a proposal to convert the bridge to road traffic, which failed, demolition began in May 1934.

By this time the northern section, from Kirtlebridge to Annan, had closed to passengers having been reduced to four trains a day

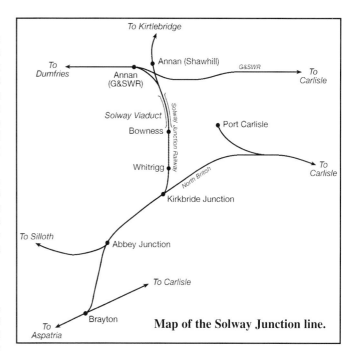

Map of the Solway Junction line.

from 27 April 1931. Freight continued twice weekly until the start of World War 2 and was then withdrawn, but the construction of a new airfield brought the section of line from Kirtlebridge back into passenger use once more. After the war had ended the line closed to passengers, while freight traffic to Annan continued until 1955 via a spur from the Glasgow & South Western main line. The freight-only link to the Maryport & Carlisle at Brayton had closed on 14 February 1933 and the track was lifted in 1937. In 1961, there was a proposal that would have reinstated the line from Kirtlebridge to Annan Shawhill and on to Chapelcross where a nuclear power station was built, but this came to nought.

The Catcleugh Reservoir Railway

The Newcastle & Gateshead Water Co created a reservoir in the valley of the Rede at Catcleugh, which was fully operational by early 1906. A dam was constructed at the southern end of the reservoir, the total capacity of which was 2,300,000 gallons. This was a 3ft gauge light railway, built, as with the aforementioned Talla Railway, to assist with the construction of the reservoir, and running from Woodburn on the Wansbeck Valley line from Morpeth to Reedsmouth Junction. It ran for 15 miles along the

Right:
Ex-Caledonian Railway 4-4-0 No 14454 has an empty stock train of cattle and sheep wagons between G&SW Junction and Shawhill Junction on the Solway Junction Railway in LMS days.
Ian Allan Library

17

valley of the River Rede through Otterburn and thence to the dam and carried construction materials that had come in at Woodburn, including pipes and stone from quarries at Woodburn and Saffronside. Clay was transported from Yatesfield with a branch built from Bennetsfield to reach this line. The railway was operated by eight locomotives, with a further seven also identified as possibly having worked there.

The line was in use until 1903, after which it was replaced by horse-drawn road transport, which was used to bring stone from the quarry at Saffronside to the dam.

The Leadhills & Wanlockhead Railway

Another early casualty, perhaps not surprisingly, was the Caledonian branch from Elvanfoot to Leadhills and Wanlockhead. The line reached a summit of 1,498ft and was the highest standard-gauge line in the country. Authorised in 1876 this line was constructed as a light railway and was opened as far as Leadhills on 1 October 1901, with the second section from Leadhills to Wanlockhead opened a year later, on 12 October 1902. This was because a new lease had been taken out on the Leadhills lead mines from 1903 (from which lead had been extracted probably since the 13th century), the smelter having been modernised along with the associated machinery.

From Elvanfoot, 50 miles south of Glasgow on the Caledonian main line, the line climbed past the former gold mines at Howkwood (where the gold for the original Scottish Crown Jewels originated) and thence over Risping Cleuch on a viaduct before arriving at Leadhills — a small mining community. A further mile and a half saw the line reach Wanlockhead, where there was a run-round loop and siding.

Despite passing through remote countryside, the passenger and freight service lasted until 2 January 1939. Closure was mainly due to the decline of the workings — one of the shafts at Leadhills closing in 1929 and a general run-down in activity following the economic difficulties of the 1920s. In 1936, the mining company went into liquidation which meant traffic was limited to tourists as freight had all but collapsed.

In recent years fortunes for the line have changed, and in 1986 the Lowthers Railway Society reopened a part of the route as a 2ft gauge railway to run from Leadhills to the summit at Hillhead. At Leadhills, a station has been constructed on the site of the former standard gauge one and the line currently terminates by the site of Glengonnar mine.

While the four lines described above did not see service in British Railways days, there were three unlikely survivors at Nationalisation. These were the Lauder Light Railway, which linked Fountainhall on the Waverley Route to Lauder via the hamlet of Oxton, the Cairn Valley Railway, from Dumfries to Moniaive, and the line from Stranraer to Portpatrick.

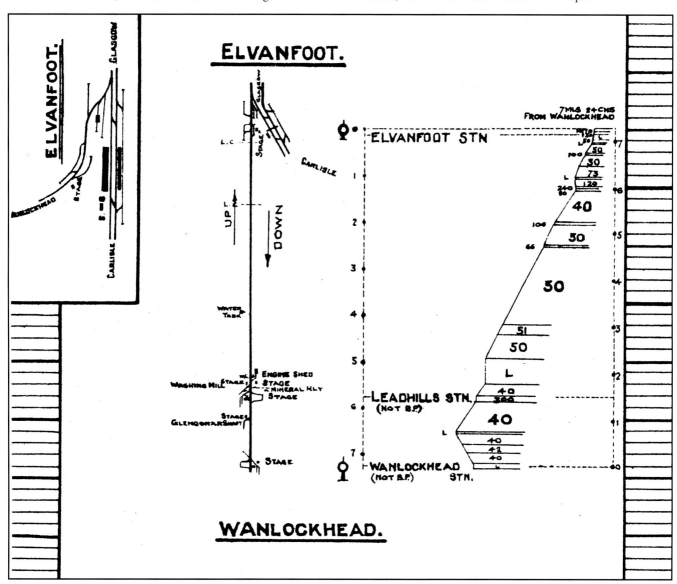

Above:
Gradient profile and diagram map — Elvanfoot to Wanlockhead.

Above:
The Leadhills & Wanlockhead Railway's first locomotive was a Caley '171' class 0-4-4T, No 172. This class was later replaced by ex-Caledonian 2P 0-4-4 tank locomotives and the LMS also tried Sentinel-Cammell steam railcars. The remoteness of the line is well illustrated in this photograph of No 172 which has just crossed the short viaduct that passed over Risping Cleuch, with a train from Elvanfoot to Wanlockhead. *Ian Allan Library*

The Lauder Light Railway

The Lauder Light Railway had lost its passenger service in September 1932, but was still open for freight in 1948. Latterly, the line was worked by ex-Great Eastern Railway 'J67' 0-6-0Ts with makeshift tenders. With water in the side tanks of the locomotive the axle load was too great for the light railway's standards and the tender allowed the weight to be spread more evenly. This line survived until 1 October 1958 carrying a daily freight service and is featured in more detail later.

The Cairn Valley Light Railway

The Cairn Valley line, a light railway, from Dumfries to Moniaive also managed to survive for freight until 4 July 1949. Passenger services had ceased on 1 May 1943, but a service of agricultural freight had continued to run between the two towns for general merchandise, parcels and coal traffic. Such was the enthusiasm for railway construction, no less that four schemes had been proposed originally to connect Moniaive to the network.

The scheme that connected the small town with Dumfries eventually won the day, but only when the Light Railways Act of 1896 had been passed and allowed the construction of such a line — more cheaply than with existing branch routes. The Cairn Valley Railway Co was created by the Glasgow & South Western, eventually opening for traffic on 1 March 1905. The line was 17½ miles long in total and could be considered a basic railway when

Miles	Chains	DOWN. STATIONS.	1† E'ty Chg. Stock	2 Pass	3 Fr'ht SO	4 Fr'ht S	5 Pass. SO	6 Pass.	7 Pass.	8 Pass. SO
			a.m.	a.m.	a.m.	a.m.	p.m.	p.m.	p.m.	p.m.
—	—	Dumfries ...dep.	5 45	8 35	11 7	11 50	12 25	2 47	5 20	9 0
1	55	Cairn Valley Jct.', „	5 48	8 38	11 12	11 55	12 28	2 50	5 23	9 3
4	79	Irongray ...... „	5 57	8 48	11 32	1215p	12 37	3 0	5 31	9 13
7	13	Newtonairds... „	6 4	8 56	11 47	12 30	12 45	3 8	5 39	9 21
8	70	Stepford......... „	6 9	9 2	11 57	12 40	12 51	3 14	5 45	9 27
10	55	Dunscore ...... „	6 14	9 8	12 14	1 0	12 57	3 20	5 51	9 33
13	53	Crossford ...... „	6 22	9 17	12 29	1 15	1 6	3 29	5 59	9 42
15	32	Kirkland ...... „	6 28	9 24	12 40	1 25	1 13	3 36	6 6	9 49
17	45	Moniaive ...arr.	6 35	9 30	12 50	1 35	1 19	3 42	6 12	9 55

Miles	Chains	UP. STATIONS.	9 Pass.	10 Fr'ht WO	11 Pass.	12 Pass SO	13 Fr'ht SO	14 Pass.	15 Pass.	16 Light Eng.
			a.m.	a.m.	a.m.	p.m.	p.m.	p.m.	p.m.	p.m.
—	—	Moniaive ...dep	7 5	7 30	9 50	1 35	2 0	3 50	6 20	10 10
2	13	Kirkland ...... „	7 12	7 43	9 57	1 42	2 10	3 57	6 27	SO
3	72	Crossford ...... „	7 18	7 55	10 3	1 48	2 20	4 3	6 33	
6	70	Dunscore ...... „	7 27	8 10	10 12	1 57	3 22	4 12	6 42	...
8	55	Stepford...... „	7 32	8 19	10 17	2 2	3 35	4 17	6†48	...
10	2	Newtonairds ... „	7 37	8 29	10 22	2 7	3 50	4 22	6†54	...
12	46	Irongray ...... „	7 45	8 52	10 31	2 15	4†10	4 31	7† 2	...
15	70	Cairn Valley Jct.„,	7 57	9 2	10 40	2 25	4 22	4†40	7 10	...
17	45	Dumfries ...arr.	8 2	9 6	10 45	2 30	4 27	4†45	7 15	10 58

LMS working timetable September 1927,
Dumfries to Moniaive.

Above:
Moniaive station is seen in 1930 with an LMS Class 2P 4-4-0 and a single coach waiting to form a service to Dumfries. At this time there were two trains either way on weekdays, with an additional service on Saturdays. The station platform had wooden edges and the building itself was made out of wood. The goods shed and station buildings are still extant here at the time of writing. Worked as a one-engine-in-steam operation, the line served quarries as well as carrying passengers and this meant that despite closing to passengers on 3 May 1943, it lasted until 4 July 1949 for freight. *Ian Allan Library*

Below:
The 3.52pm from Moniaive is seen on arrival at Dumfries, with former Caley 'Jumbo' 0-6-0 No 17452 as the train engine on 21 June 1937. *H. C. Casserley*

Above:
**Portpatrick station is seen on 21 June 1937 with the 7.5pm from Stranraer having arrived behind LMS '2P'
No 645. The line to the harbour dropped down a 1 in 35 incline, to the rear of the train, only four wagons at a
time being allowed to complete the trip. That line had been demolished by 1886, having opened just
18 years previously.** *H. C. Casserley*

compared with other branch lines, but there were three passing loops, at Irongray, Newtonairds and Dunscore, which also had goods sidings.

Passenger trains were initially in the hands of steam railcars, but these were later transferred away and more conventional power was provided in the form of 0-4-2T No 206A, which was rebuilt from an 1888-built tender locomotive by the G&SWR. In the main, G&SWR locomotives worked the line, but in latter years Caledonian 0-6-0 'Jumbos' were drafted in from Dumfries shed. At opening there were four trains to Moniaive with five returning, while an additional service ran on Saturdays.

Freight was mainly from the quarry at Morrinton as well as timber, livestock, general merchandise and coal. Moniaive had a small engine shed and the line was worked on a token system from loop to loop.

After World War 1 there was a general decline in passenger traffic which led to passenger services being withdrawn during World War 2, on 1 May 1943; they were never reinstated. Freight lasted until 4 July 1949, the main traffics being quarried stone — ironically for road building — general merchandise, agricultural traffic and coal.

Stranraer Town to Portpatrick

The third survivor was the line from Stranraer to Portpatrick, actually the stub end of the grandly titled Wigtownshire & Portpatrick Joint Railway. Built to link the through route from Dumfries — the 'Port Road' — with steamers to and from Ireland, its importance quickly declined due to the rise of Stranraer as the main port for this traffic. It was lucky to hold on to its passenger and freight services until 6 February 1950. The line survived for freight traffic as far as Colfin to serve the creamery there until 1 April 1959.

While most other lines in the area survived intact, it was clear that traffic levels in both passengers and freight would struggle to meet even direct costs as calculated at that time. The years following

the increase in business during World War 1 had seen the introduction of motor-bus and lorry services which had made significant inroads into rail traffic.

With much of their general merchandise traffic under threat, traditional forwardings such as textiles, livestock, milk, foodstuffs and other perishables and parcels were now being transferred to road because of both price and convenience, with the added advantage of same-day deliveries.

In many cases the motor bus offered a more regular and convenient service than rail, running directly into town or village centres. For instance, many stations in rural areas were far from the villages that they served, as was the case with some main line stations, an example being New Galloway on the 'Port Road' which was more than seven miles from the town of that name.

But on the other hand, while the shorter journeys were badly affected by road competition, the branches which linked to main lines providing point-to-point timings to Edinburgh and Glasgow, could not be equalled by road, and this applies to this day. Towns such as Peebles had direct services to Edinburgh and Glasgow, and provided useful feeder traffic to and from the main lines. Larger towns such as Kirkcudbright were within commuting distance from places like Dumfries, as was Langholm in relation to Carlisle. Other routes linked rural communities together and offered them services to larger conurbations that can only be dreamed of today.

The branches also provided useful diversionary routes when engineering work or other blockades affected the main lines in the area. The line from Tweedmouth to St Boswells, for example, was used to divert East Coast expresses to Edinburgh via the Waverley Route on several occasions.

Indeed, many lines had survived longer than originally anticipated because of World War 2, being used both as diversionary routes for military traffic and because they linked areas where the armed forces operated or trained. The Border Counties and Wansbeck Valley lines were two good examples of this, troop trains running to and from Woodburn and other

stations, while the 'Port Road' was an important link to Ireland and to naval and RAF bases in the area. The Alnwick-Coldstream line was also seen as a potential diversionary route in case the main line were blocked as a result of enemy action.

The harsh economics so often quoted in more modern times in relation to railways were starting to hit the lines hard, but the catastrophic floods of 1948 made an impact on routes where traffic levels had fallen and provided the opportunity to withdraw passenger services by stealth. The *Railway Magazine* of October 1950 reflects: 'The railway [the East Coast main line] was closed completely for nearly eleven weeks between Berwick and Dunbar. On the five-mile section between Grantshouse and Reston, seven bridges carrying the railway over the Eye Water were totally destroyed, and, as a temporary measure, steel bridges of a military type were built to replace them and to restore traffic as quickly as possible.'

It was not only the main line that suffered. The Berwickshire Railway from St Boswells to Duns and Reston was washed away between Greenlaw and Duns, the Eyemouth branch was severely damaged, and the Alnwick-Coldsteam line was severed between Ilderton and Wooler.

It was the use of the St Boswells-Tweedmouth line by diverted East Coast expresses that brought about the withdrawal of passenger services on the seven-mile long branch from Roxburgh Junction to Jedburgh on 13 August 1948 (due to capacity constraints between Roxburgh and St Boswells) and the closure to passengers of stations at Kirkbank, Nisbet, Jedfoot and Jedburgh.

The area suffered from heavy flooding again on 28 August 1950. The East Coast main line was blocked again at Cockburnspath and Grantshouse by the floodwater, and there was an embankment collapse. Some trains were diverted through to the Waverley Route via Kelso and St Boswells, but the Waverley became blocked itself at Melrose on the afternoon of the 28th, and the last train to be re-routed was the up 'Elizabethan'. The route was used again for diversions from the 30th, and this emphasised the importance of the Tweedmouth-Kelso-St Boswells line in keeping through Anglo-Scottish services in operation.

However, hard economics prevented lines that were convenient for diversions being retained just for that purpose and the dramatic falls in passenger traffic seen after the war had caused the Scottish and North Eastern Regions to withdraw some passenger services. None of these lines had carried more than 5,000 passengers per week and BR timetables of the time advertised replacement bus services.

So, even before Beeching and his infamous Report finally got to grips with the railway network, many branch passenger services had already gone, for example:

Coldstream to Wooler — 22 September 1930
Fountainhall to Lauder — 12 September 1932
Roxburgh Junction to Jedburgh — 13 August 1948
St Boswells (Ravenswood Junction) to Duns — 13 August 1948
Stranraer to Portpatrick — 6 February 1950
Symington to Peebles — 5 June 1950
Newton Stewart to Whithorn — 25 September 1950
Duns to Reston Junction — 10 September 1951
Galashiels (Selkirk Junction) to Selkirk — 10 September 1951
Morpeth to Scotsgap and Reedsmouth — 15 March 1952
Morpeth to Rothbury — 15 September 1952
Beattock to Moffat — 6 December 1954
Riccarton Junction to Hexham — 15 October 1956
Eyemouth to Burnmouth — 5 February 1962
The Peebles Loop (Kilnknowe Junction-Rosewell & Hawthornden) — 5 February 1962

Freight had also been withdrawn from some routes before Beeching, these being:

Ilderton to Wooler — 13 August 1948

Greenlaw to Duns — 13 August 1948
Colfin to Portpatrick — 6 February 1950
Alnwick to Ilderton — 2 March 1953
Broughton to Peebles West — 7 June 1954
Bellingham to Riccarton — 1 September 1958
Fountainhall to Lauder — 1 October 1958
Stranraer Town to Colfin — 1 April 1959
Cairnryan Junction to Cairnryan Point (WD) — 30 April 1959
Peebles Junction to Peebles West — 1 August 1959

The remaining lines also came under increasing scrutiny and suspicions of further cuts abounded in the railway press. The November 1961 *Trains Illustrated* carried a feature entitled 'Drastic cuts in Scotland?'. The article pointed out that they had received reports of extremely drastic plans to curtail passenger services. 'Local opinion is inclined to associate these reports with the recent visit to Scotland of Dr Beeching . . . The Scottish Region had no comment to make . . . The main line Waverley Route was a target with up to 15 passenger services a day being withdrawn from November and other routes are also affected. Services are also to be cut on the Dumfries to Stranraer line and the Kirkcudbright branch — all said to be poorly patronised.' The article detailed a number of minor withdrawals, naming St Boswells to Kelso (in the event, the line survived for passenger traffic until 13 June 1964), but other lines were also mentioned, including north of Inverness and Edinburgh suburban services. It continued: 'Moreover, the closure for passenger traffic of the partly outer suburban and partly rural lines to Galashiels via Peebles (see February 1962 above), also worked by diesel multiple-units, was said to be under consideration. Against closure it is being argued that after the recent dieselisation traffic increased enormously on all these lines, and that the Galashiels via Peebles line is the only railway to serve a large tract of country.'

The December issue of *Trains Illustrated* carried another article — this time entitled 'Scottish Cuts Deferred'. This piece was based on a statement issued by the Scottish Region that commented on the earlier speculation about service withdrawals. The article goes on to say: 'It [the Scottish Region] pointed out that the Government White Paper had made it abundantly clear that the Regions must act primarily as commercial concerns. Certain services are operating at a heavy loss and where it is clear that they can never be made to pay, the proposal is to cut the losses by withdrawing the least patronised trains. On these basic principles, the Board has sought the consent of the Scottish TUCC for the closure of the Burnmouth-Eyemouth branch, the Hawthornden Junction-Peebles-Galashiels lines. Since 1958, efforts have been made by the use of modern diesel traction to place the Hawthornden Junction-Peebles-Galashiels branch line on a sound financial basis but, in spite of some improvements, these efforts have not succeeded.

'On the Burnmouth-Eyemouth branch receipts have diminished over many years and alternative public transport facilities are felt to be adequate.'

The Beeching Report, published in 1963, contained various maps showing the density of both passenger and freight traffic on the remaining lines and went further. On all remaining lines covered in this book, including the 'Port Road', Beeching estimated there were less than 5,000 passengers using the advertised passenger service per week. Only Alnwick, Newton Stewart, Castle Douglas and Stranraer Harbour drew between £5,000 and £25,000 per annum, with all other stations attracting less than £5,000 per annum.

Freight traffic painted the same picture — less than 5,000 tons per week was being transported on any of the lines and forwardings were generally below 5,000 tons per annum. The exceptions, which generated up to 25,000 tons per annum, were:

Biggar	Castle Douglas	Chirnside
Coldstream	Creetown	Dalbeattie

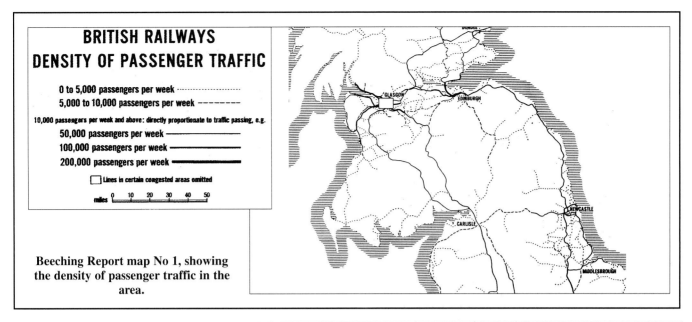

BRITISH RAILWAYS
DENSITY OF PASSENGER TRAFFIC

0 to 5,000 passengers per week ··················

5,000 to 10,000 passengers per week --------

10,000 passengers per week and above: directly proportionate to traffic passing, e.g.

50,000 passengers per week ——————

100,000 passengers per week ——————

200,000 passengers per week ══════════

☐ Lines in certain congested areas omitted

miles 0 10 20 30 40 50

Beeching Report map No 1, showing the density of passenger traffic in the area.

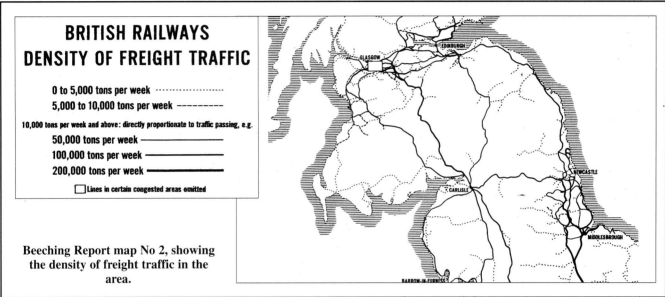

BRITISH RAILWAYS
DENSITY OF FREIGHT TRAFFIC

0 to 5,000 tons per week ··················

5,000 to 10,000 tons per week --------

10,000 tons per week and above: directly proportionate to traffic passing, e.g.

50,000 tons per week ——————

100,000 tons per week ——————

200,000 tons per week ══════════

☐ Lines in certain congested areas omitted

Beeching Report map No 2, showing the density of freight traffic in the area.

Duns	Jedburgh	Kirkcudbright
Langholm	Maxwelltown	Newton Stewart
Reedsmouth	Selkirk	Stranraer
Wigtown		

The conclusions were clear. Beeching's report recommended closing the surviving passenger services, including the Waverley Route, and freight-only services on the remaining branch services.

Although political pressure ensured the survival of the Waverley Route until 1969, the earlier closures helped put into place the conditions for its eventual demise as it was now shorn of all its connecting freight and passenger services and having to rely solely on its through route status.

Passenger services withdrawn following the Beeching Report:

St Boswells (Kelso Junction) to Coldstream — 15 June 1964
Riddings Junction to Langholm — 15 June 1964
Castle Douglas (Portpatrick Line Junction) to Kirkcudbright — 3 May 1965
Challoch Junction to Dumfries (Castle Douglas Branch Junction) — 14 June 1965
Alnwick to Alnmouth — 29 January 1968

Freight services withdrawn following the Beeching Report:

Bellingham to Reedsmouth — 11 November 1963
Woodburn to Reedsmouth — 11 November 1963
Rothbury to Scotsgap — 11 November 1963
Beattock to Moffat — 6 April 1964
Roxburgh Junction to Jedburgh — 10 August 1964
Kelso to Tweedmouth — 29 March 1965
St Boswells, Ravenswood Junction to Greenlaw — 19 July 1965
Duns to Reston Junction — 7 November 1966
Newton Stewart to Whithorn — 6 October 1964
Selkirk to Netherdale Siding — 2 November 1964
Coldstream to Wooler — 29 March 1965
Symington to Broughton — 4 April 1966
Galashiels to Netherdale Siding — 3 October 1966
Woodburn to Morpeth — 3 October 1966
Riddings Junction to Langholm — 18 September 1967
St Boswells (Kelso Junction) to Coldstream — 30 March 1968
Alnwick to Alnmouth — 7 October 1968

And today? It is a sobering thought that the only surviving part of the network covered in this book are the lines running from Challoch Junction to Stranraer Harbour (for Ayr and Glasgow), and from Dumfries to Maxwelltown for freight only. In early 2003 this line was in 'mothballed' status, although there is hope that the BP oil terminal may start receiving traffic again in the future leading to its reopening.

The 'Port Road' – a Main Line Byway – and its branches

The 1840s had seen an attempt to link Carlisle with the coast at Portpatrick. This proposal for a railway was known as the British & Irish Union Railway and was a result of Government encouragement for companies to link Ireland with other parts of the United Kingdom. This would be completed with the introduction of a steamer service across the Irish Sea. There was a post office packet station at Portpatrick and it seemed this would be the natural place for the railway to reach. The scheme foundered, however, and attention turned instead to points further east, where railways had reached the likes of Carlisle, with the Caledonian Railway's main line and the Glasgow & South Western Railway's line to Glasgow via Dumfries and Annan, which had opened in 1850.

It seemed natural that extensions to the area of Galloway would follow, and a route to Castle Douglas via Dalbeattie was authorised in July 1856, being known as the Castle Douglas & Dumfries Railway. This scheme was supported by the Glasgow & South Western Railway, which supplied half the investment in the scheme to get the line built, the rest coming from local supporters. The line left Dumfries and ran via Maxwelltown and Dalbeattie to Castle Douglas, a total of nearly 20 miles in length. Three contracts for construction saw the railway completed in October 1859, but a disagreement between the contractors and the railway company resulted in the opening date being delayed as the contractors blocked the junction with the Glasgow & South Western. The blockade was lifted following a court injunction and the line opened to all traffic on 7 November 1859.

Castle Douglas was seen as a natural point from which a further extension to the coast could be made. A Parliamentary Act incorporating the Portpatrick Railway Company had already been passed on 10 August 1857 and was seen as part of a grand scheme that would form the trunk route from England to the north of Ireland. Portpatrick was only 21 miles from Ireland at Donaghadee in Co Down, which was not too far from the important city of Belfast. Portpatrick was to be the way for passengers and mail, with the port of Stranraer being used for freight and livestock. It is interesting to note that the Portpatrick Railway's coat of arms comprised the emblems of England, Scotland and Ireland — namely a rose, thistle and shamrock.

This Act allowed for the construction of a route west from Castle Douglas to Portpatrick. The line would pass through the remote countryside of Galloway on its way to Newton Stewart, Stranraer and ultimately, Portpatrick. This was a resurrection of the original 1840s proposal, and construction work began in 1858. The line was completed to Stranraer on 12 March 1861, Portpatrick being reached on 28 August 1862. A further branch was built on a steep gradient to the harbour at Portpatrick, this being opened on 1 October 1862.

Leaving Castle Douglas, the line was 52 miles in length traversing remote countryside, passing through New Galloway and the town of Newton Stewart. It was always questionable whether the railway should really have reached Portpatrick at all. The harbour could be served only by a difficult setting-back arrangement, down the 1-in-5 gradient. In any case, it was by now clear that in fact it was to be Stranraer which was to be developed into the major port in the area, and the expected investment in Portpatrick did not materialise. And so by 1874, the harbour extension was closed and port operations were concentrated at Stranraer, leaving the line from Stranraer to Portpatrick as a branch, serving that settlement only, with a small intermediate station at Colfin, where there was a creamery.

The Portpatrick Railway was an independent line, but in 1863 the Caledonian physically arrived from the east into Dumfries with the opening of the line from Lockerbie, which they operated. The Portpatrick Railway had had a less-than-positive relationship with the Glasgow & South Western after an advance of £40,000 was offered in 1859 to assist with improvements, but this would have resulted in the G&SWR securing operating rights on the 'Port Road' of some 72% of income.

The PPR did not take up this offer and in 1863 they applied for running powers from the Castle Douglas & Dumfries Railway for Castle Douglas and Dumfries. When negotiations with the G&SWR were not successful it was the Caledonian which agreed to make the £40,000 advance in exchange for the rights to work the Portpatrick Railway, for a 43% return. This also benefited the London & North Western — the Caledonian's partner at Carlisle, where there was an uneasy relationship between these two companies and the North British and Midland railways.

The deal, as arranged, gave the operation of the 'Port Road' to the Caledonian for 21 years, much to the annoyance of the Glasgow & South Western. The eight locomotives owned by the Portpatrick Railway were taken over by the Caledonian and these were added to by some of its own. The next few years saw the Caledonian having an uninterrupted access to Stranraer, until 1877, when the line from Girvan arrived (Girvan & Portpatrick Junction Railway), and this at last let in the Glasgow & South Western for the first time.

As the steamer services linking Ireland to Scotland at Stranraer were proving to be very lucrative in 1885 (when the 21-year operating rights that the Caledonian had enjoyed had expired), the Portpatrick Railway was purchased outright by a grouping of the London & North Western, the Glasgow & South Western, the Caledonian and the Midland railways. This was to be known rather grandly as the Portpatrick & Wigtownshire Joint Railway, the G&SWR retaining primacy between Dumfries and Castle Douglas, while the Caledonian was granted running rights

in exchange for the LNWR being able to gain running powers over the line from Carlisle to Dumfries and then on the Castle Douglas.

The 'Port Road' — passenger services

From an initial three trains per day between Portpatrick and Dumfries, services expanded as the port of Stranraer grew. Belfast York Road was served by rail connections from Larne and the connections on the English/Scottish side travelled up from London on the Midland and West Coast routes departing from St Pancras at 8pm and Euston at 8.30pm respectively. There was a return working to St Pancras and Euston, together with through coaches from other services to and from Newcastle. In addition, in the summer there were many other excursion trains as well as military specials that carried troops to and from Ireland. The LMS working timetable for passenger trains for Summer 1947 shows the 'Port Road' service, complete with the Whithorn and Kirkcudbright branches, with references to mail, fish and milk — the last conveyed as 'Express' traffic.

After Nationalisation — using the Summer 1948 Scottish Region timetable as an example — British Railways continued the pattern of service inherited from the LMS and there were a good number of 'through' services that ran between Dumfries and Stranraer via Castle Douglas. The importance of the Irish boat train services was maintained, and intermingled with these boat trains were a number of long-distance local services. The first of these boat trains conveyed sleeping cars and through carriages from London Euston where it left at 6.30pm (SX). Leaving Dumfries at 2.10am, this express train called at Newton Stewart at 3.38am (leaving at 3.50am) and then ran on to Stranraer Harbour arriving at 4.33am.

The boat connection for Larne left at 6.30am (passengers were allowed to stay in their sleeper berths until 6.25), Larne being reached at 8.45 and arrival at Belfast York Road was at 10.5am (10am SO). A service that ran from Newcastle on Saturdays only in the summer departed from Carlisle at 2.3am, Dumfries at 2.52 and then ran nonstop to Stranraer Harbour arriving at 5am. Then followed a service from Carlisle at 3.14am, departing Dumfries at 4am, Castle Douglas at 4.34 and Newton Stewart at 5.25, and arriving at Stranraer Harbour at 6.2 with a sailing for Larne at 6.30am, the same ship as was served by the former trains. These three trains were known as 'Stranraer Boat Expresses'.

The 8.40am from Dumfries then ran all stations to Stranraer followed by a 2.21pm, which was all-stations to Stranraer except Parton and Palnure. On Fridays and Saturdays in the summer, there was another Stranraer boat express from Carlisle at 2.25pm, leaving Dumfries at 3.15pm, calling at Dalbeattie, Castle Douglas, Newton Stewart and Stranraer Harbour, arriving at 5.23 where the boat left for Larne at 6.15pm; arrival at Belfast York Road was at 9.30pm. The last through working of the day left Dumfries at 6.30pm, which ran all-stations (except Killywhan, Kirkgunzeon and Southwick) to Stranraer where it arrived at 9.6pm.

In the up direction, the 1948 Scottish Region timetable shows the first train leaving from Stranraer Town at 7.50am. This called at all stations to Dalbeattie, from where it ran fast to Dumfries, arriving at 10.45, with good connections made with the Whithorn and Kirkcudbright branches. A second stopper left Stranraer Town at 11.7am, although this train missed stops at Glenluce, Palnure and Parton, arriving at Dumfries at 1.50pm.

Then came, on Fridays and Saturdays only in summer, the first Stranraer boat express, the 12.35pm from Stranraer Harbour to Carlisle, arriving at Dumfries at 2.50 and Carlisle at 3.38pm. This train connected with a service that had departed from Belfast York Road at 8.55am. The next up train was the 3.40pm from Stranraer Town to Dumfries where it arrived at 6.40pm. There then followed two services which connected with the 7.15pm sailing from Larne that had arrived in Stranraer Harbour at 9.20pm. The first was the 10pm Stranraer boat express for London Euston calling at Newton Stewart, Castle Douglas, Dumfries (12.29am) and arriving at Euston at 8.5am. The second was a Fridays only service to Newcastle, departing at 10.25pm which ran in the summer only, nonstop to Dumfries, arriving there at 12.43am and Carlisle at 1.35am.

Above:
In LMS days 4-4-0 three-cylinder Compound No 916 has arrived at Stranraer Harbour with the 4.49pm from Dumfries on 21 June 1937. These locomotives had become common performers on the 'Port Road' after being displaced on the main lines by the newer LMS 4-6-0 express passenger and mixed traffic locomotives, even though some, like this one, were only 13 years old at the time. *H. C. Casserley*

DUMFRIES, CASTLE-DOUGLAS, KIRKCUDBRIGHT, WHITHORN AND STRANRAER

			WEEK DAYS																													SUNDAYS					

Miles | For continuation of Trains from Junction see pages | **WEEK DAYS** | 1 | 2 | 3 | 4 | 5 | 6 | 7 | 8 | 9 | 10 | 11 | 12 | 13 | 14 | 15 | 16 | 17 | 18 | 19 | 20 | 21 | 22 | 23 | 24 | 25 | 26 | 27 | 28 | 29 | 1 | 2 | 3 | 4 | 5 | 6

(Stations reading downward, principal stops)

DUMFRIES ... dep.
Maxwelltown
Killywhan
Kirkgunzeon
Southwick
Dalbeattie ... arr.
CASTLE-DOUGLAS ... arr. / dep.
Bridge of Dee ... arr.
Tarff ... dep.
KIRKCUDBRIGHT ... arr.
Crossmichael ... arr. / dep.
Parton
New Galloway ... arr. / dep.
Loch Skerrow ... arr. / dep.
Gatehouse of Fleet ... arr. / dep.
Creetown ... arr. / dep.
Palnure
NEWTON-STEWART ... arr. / dep.
Wigtown ... arr. / dep.
Kirkinner
Whauphill ... arr. / dep.
Sorbie
Millisle ... arr. / dep.
WHITHORN ... arr.
Kirkcowan ... arr.
Glenluce ... arr. / dep.
DUNRAGIT ... arr. / dep.
Castle-Kennedy ... arr.
Stranraer Harbour Jct.
STRANRAER HBR.
STRANRAER ... arr.

No. 1—† Advertised Dumfries depart 1.14 a.m.

No. 3—† Advertised depart Dumfries 2.0 a.m., Newton-Stewart 4.7 a.m. Arrives Killywhan 2L19 a.m. MX. On Mondays passes Killywhan 2.22 a.m. and runs five minutes earlier to Loch Skerrow arrive, thence as booked.

CROSS CHANNEL STEAMER SERVICE Th F SO
	a.m.	p.m.
Stranraer Harbour ... dep.	6 30	6 15
Larne Harbour ... arr.	8 45	8 35

A Runs June 26 to September 13 inclusive.

No. 24—Z Between Dumfries and Castle-Douglas.

Note—Line between Glenluce and Dunragit is controlled by Directional Lever and continuous track circuiting

---

STRANRAER, WHITHORN, KIRKCUDBRIGHT, CASTLE-DOUGLAS and DUMFRIES

Miles | For continuation of Trains from Junction see pages | **WEEK DAYS** | 1 | 2 | 3 | 4 | 5 | 6 | 7 | 8 | 9 | 10 | 11 | 12 | 13 | 14 | 15 | 16 | 17 | 18 | 19 | 20 | 21 | 22 | 23 | 24 | 25 | 26 | 27 | SUNDAYS: 1 | 2 | 3 | 4 | 5 | 6 | 7 | 8

(Stations reading downward)

STRANRAER ... dep.
STRANRAER HBR.
Stranraer Harbour Jct.
Castle-Kennedy ... arr. / dep.
DUNRAGIT ... arr. / dep.
Glenluce ... arr. / dep.
Kirkcowan ... arr.
WHITHORN ... dep.
Millisle ... arr. / dep.
Sorbie
Whauphill ... arr. / dep.
Kirkinner
Wigtown ... arr. / dep.
NEWTON-STEWART ... arr. / dep.
Palnure ... arr.
Creetown ... arr. / dep.
Gatehouse of Fleet ... arr. / dep.
Loch Skerrow ... arr. / dep.
New Galloway ... arr. / dep.
Parton
Crossmichael ... arr. / dep.
KIRKCUDBRIGHT ... dep.
Tarff ... dep.
Bridge of Dee ... dep.
CASTLE-DOUGLAS ... arr. / dep.
Dalbeattie
Southwick
Kirkgunzeon
Killywhan
Maxwelltown
DUMFRIES ... arr.

No. 5—On Saturdays calls at Loch Skerrow 9.37, dep. 9.38, New Galloway arr. 9.47, thence as booked.

No. 24—† F.S. Newton-Stewart depart 10.48 a.m., Castle-Douglas depart 11.50 p.m.

CROSS CHANNEL STEAMER SERVICE MFSO
	a.m.	p.m.
Larne Harbour ... dep.	9 55	7 15
Stranraer Harbour ... arr.	12 15p	9 20

A Runs June 27 to September 15 inclusive.

Note—Line between Dunragit and Glenluce is controlled by Directional Lever and continuous track circuiting.

Table 24   Dumfries, Castle-Douglas, Kirkcudbright, Newton-Stewart, Whithorn, Stranraer

St. Enoch Station		Sats only								n'n		p.m	p.m	p.m
GLASGOW . . . lev.		p.m 9†b5		p.m 9†b5	a.m .	a.m .	a.m .	a.m .	9 20	12 0			4 E 0	4 E 0
CARLISLE _ _ "		1a20	2	3 3a14	5 9	7 0	7 0	1040	1 12		2 25		—	5 P 5
EDINBURGH (Pr St.)									1040					
Dumfries _ _ _ lev.		2a10	2 52	4 a 0	6 30	8 15	8 40	1230	2 21	3 15	5 58	6 30		
Killywhan					6 45	8 29	8 55	1245	2 36		6 13			
Kirkgunzeon _ _ _					6 50	8 34	9 1	1250	2 41		6 18			
Southwick					6 56	.	9 7	1256	2 47		6 24			
Dalbeattie . . . _					7 3	8 44	9 13	1 1	2 51		6 29	6 53		
Castle-Douglas _ arr.				4 30	7 13	8 53	9 22	1 10	3 0	3 38	6 38	7 2		
Castle-Douglas lev.					7 18	8 56	1025	1 15	3 35		6 40	7 40		
Bridge of Dee . .					7 23	9 1	1030	1 20	3 40		6 45	7 45		
Tarff _ _ _ _					7 31	9 9	1038	1 28	3 48		6 53	7 53		
Kirkcudbright _ arr.					7 38	9 16	1045	1 35	3 55		7 0	8 0		
Castle-Douglas lev.				4 34		9 25		3 2	3 48		7 5			
Crossmichael . . .						9 32		3 9			7 12			
Parton _ _ _ _						9 39					7 19			
New Galloway . .						9 46		3 19			7 26			
Gatehouse of Fleet _						1011		3 39			7 49			
Creetown						1021		3 49			7 59			
Palnure _ _ _ _						1028					8 6			
Newton-Stewart _ arr.			3 38		5 19	1035		4 1	4 37		8 13			
Newton-Stewart lev.						6 25	1050		4 6	4 45	8 25			
Wigtown						6 45	11 5		4 21	4 58	8 37			
Kirkinner _ _ _						6 50	1112		4 38	5 4	8 43			
Whauphill . . .						6 54	1119		4 47	5 9	8 47			
Sorbie _ _ _ _						7 1	1129		4 53	5 16	8 54			
Millisle(for Garl'ton)						7 10	1135			5 21	8 58			
Whithorn _ _ arr.						7 19	1145			5 31	9 8			
Newton-Stewart lev.			3 50		5 25	1040		4 6	4 42		8 18			
Kirkcowan . . .						1051		4 21			8 29			
Glenluce						11 7		4 38			8 45			
Dunragit						1116		4 47			8 53			
Castle-Kennedy . .						1122		4 53	5 23		8 59			
Stranraer Harb'r arr.			4 33	5 0	6 2	—		5 0						
Stranraer _ arr.			6 30	6 3	(L37 6 30	1129			6 15		9 6			
Stranraer Harb'r lev.			8 45	8 45	8 45				8 35					
Larne Harbour arr			10X5	10 0	10X5				9 30					
Belfast (York Rd.) "														
DUNRAGIT . lev.						12h1								
GLASGOW (St. En) arr.				1021	g	3 h 7								

(Vertical column notes: "Passengers may remain in Berths until 6-25 a.m." · "TC and SC London (Euston) to Stranraer Harbour" · "To Stranraer Harb'r. Newcastle to Stranraer Harbour. Ceases after 28th August" · "TC Newcastle to Stranraer Harbour. Ceases after 28th August" · "Stranraer Boat Express" · "Fridays and Saturdays only and from 25th June until 28th August inclusive" · "Stranraer Boat Express")

St. Enoch Station	a.m	a.m	a.m	a.m	a.m inclusive	p.m	p.m	p.m	p.m	p.m
GLASGOW _ _ _ lev.							1230h		5K10	—
DUNRAGIT . . arr.							3h22		A	A
Belfast (York Rd.) lev.						8 55			5 50	5 50
Larne Harbour "						9 55			7 15	7 15
Stranraer " _ arr.						1220			9 20	9 20
Stranraer " _ lev.		7 50	11 7			1235		3 40		
Stranraer Harbour _ "		7 56	1113					3 46	10 0	1025
Castle-Kennedy . . .		8 4	1122					3 54		
Dunragit _ _ _ _		8 12						4 3		
Glenluce		8 28	1143					4 20		
Kirkcowan		8 40	1155	1 16				4 31	1041	
Newton-Stewart . arr.										
Whithorn _ _ _ lev.	7 45					3 10			7 0	
Millisle (for Garlieston)	7 53					3 20			7 8	
Sorbie	7 59					3 32			7 14	
Whauphill	8 4					3 40			7 19	
Kirkinner	8 10					3 45			7 25	
Wigtown	8 17					4 2			7 31	
Newton-Stewart . arr.	8 30					4 16			7 44	
Newton-Stewart . lev.	Stop	8 47	12 2	1 20		Stop	4 38	Stop	1049	
Palnure							4 45			
Creetown		9 6	1216				4 55			
Gatehouse of Fleet _ _		9 19	1228				5 7			
New Galloway . . .		9 45	1246				5 28			
Parton		9 51					5 35			
Crossmichael . . .		9 58	1257				5 42			
Castle-Douglas _ arr.		10 5	1 4	2 14			5 49		1146	
Kirkcudbright _ _ lev.	6 10	8 30	9 35	1235		3 10	5 10			
Tarff _ _ _ _ _	6 18	8 39	9 43	1243		3 18	5 19			
Bridge of Dee . . .	6 23	8 46	9 51	1251		3 26	5 23			
Castle-Douglas _ arr.	6 31	8 51	9 56	1256		3 31	5 33			
Castle-Douglas _ lev.	6 32	8 54	10 8	1 8	2 15	3 35	5 56	6 40	1149	
Dalbeattie . _ _ _	6d43	9 2	1018	1 18	2 24	3 44	6 7	6 49		
Southwick	6 49	9 9	.	1 24		3 51	6 15			
Kirkgunzeon . . .	6 55	9 15	.	1 30		3 57	6 20			
Killywhan	7 1	9 21	.	1 36		4 3	6 26			
Dumfries _ _ _ arr.	7 15	9 35	1045	1 50	2 50	4 17	6 40	7 16	1229a	1243a
EDINBURGH (Pr St) arr.			3 31			7 40	1050	1050		
CARLISLE _ _ arr.	9 15	1043	1159	2 49	3 38	5 48	8 15	—	1a23	1a35
GLASGOW (St. Enoch) "	10 6	.	2 17	4 8	5 27	7 45	9 36	9 36		N7a29x

(Vertical column notes right: "TC Newcastle to London (Euston) arrive 8-5 a.m." · "Fridays and Saturdays only and from 25th June until 28th August inclusive" · "Stranraer Boat Express" · "TC Stranraer Harbour to Newcastle. Fridays only and from 11th June until 3rd September inclusive" · "TC and SC Stranraer Harbour to London (Euston)" · "Stranraer Boat Express")

---

* Saturdays only	† Except Saturdays
‡ Except Mondays	§ Mondays only
A Passengers leave Londonderry 3-30 p.m	
b Sundays leave 9-20 p.m	
E Saturdays 3-50 p.m	

g Via Stranraer leave Town Station 7-20 a.m.
h Connection formed by changing at Dunragit
k Leave Dumfries for Glasgow at 4-2 a.m.
K Via Stranraer; Passengers find own conveyance from Town to Harbour Station

L Leave Stranraer Harbour 6-30 a.m.
N On Sunday mornings leave Dumfries 6-3 a.m., arriving Glasgow (St. Enoch) at 8-5 a.m.
P Saturdays 5-10 p.m
SC Sleeping Cars   TC Through Carriages
X Saturdays 10-0 a.m

Opposite page:
LMS working timetable of passenger trains — 16 June to 5 October 1947. Also showing mails and perishables.

Above:
31 May to 26 September 1948, Scottish Region timetable showing Dumfries, Castle Douglas, Kirkcudbright, Newton-Stewart, Whithorn and Stranraer.

Right:
Dumfries station is seen on 21 June 1937 with 4-4-0 Compound No 1068 having taken over the 12.25pm from Stranraer to London Euston. The locomotive carries the wrong headcode, needing to have express headlamps for this working.
H. C. Casserley

In the 1960s the motive power employed on passenger services was primarily 'Black Five' 4-6-0s from Stranraer shed 68C (1949-62) and 67F (1962-6), and Dumfries 68B (1949-62), 67E (1962-6). On 8 July 1961 'Black Five' No 44885 was on the 2.50pm from Dumfries to Stranraer, while sister engine No 45480 hauled the 3.40pm from Stranraer to Dumfries. On that day the Newcastle-Stranraer boat trains were hauled by BR 'Clan' 4-6-2 No 72002 *Clan Campbell*, 'Black Fives' Nos 44718 and 44789 double-heading with No 45152. On 2 December No 44995 from Dumfries shed hauled the 2.45 to Stranraer. However, Stanier 4-6-0s did not have all the work, Fairburn 2-6-4T No 42269 also becoming a regular performer on the Stranraer trains.

On 9 February 1963 'Black Five' No 44967 (67E) was on the 6.15pm to Stranraer Harbour, and on 20 July 1963 haulage was as follows:

Upper right:
15 June to 30 September 1959 London Midland Region timetable — the 'Northern Irishman'.

Lower right:
BR ScR timetable, 15 June to 6 September 1964 — Dumfries, Castle Douglas, Kirkcudbright, Newton Stewart and Stranraer.

Even in the early 1960s, diesels had made no impact on 'Port Road' services and the line remained the only Scottish main line worked entirely by steam.

The Summer 1964 passenger service saw the first down service away from Dumfries at 02.00, this being the 23.45 from Newcastle to Stranraer Harbour, where it was due at 04.00. The down 'Northern Irishman' left Dumfries at 03.03, having left London Euston at 19.30 the previous evening. This train called at Castle Douglas and then Newton Stewart before arrival at 05.23. The next service was a local from Castle Douglas which connected with the 08.10 from Dumfries to Kirkcudbright that left Castle Douglas at 08.50. The local departed at 08.57 calling at all stations to Stranraer Town. Another Newcastle-Stranraer boat service left Dumfries at 12.01, calling at Castle Douglas and Newton Stewart, and arriving at Stranraer Harbour at 14.06. Then there was a gap of six hours before another Dumfries to Stranraer journey could be made (there was a Kirkcudbright service via Castle Douglas at 14.50 SO), with the SX 18.00 Dumfries-Kirkcudbright, which called at Castle Douglas at 18.35. There was also a 'Port Road' stopper which left Castle Douglas at 18.45 SX, calling at all stations to Stranraer Harbour. On Saturdays only, the 18.00 to Kirkcudbright still ran, but the 'Port Road' service started from Dumfries at 18.15, running three minutes later than weekday timings to Stranraer Harbour.

In the up direction the first train left Stranraer Town at 08.05 for Dumfries, calling at all stations except Gatehouse of Fleet. There was then a gap in services until 13.40, when a train ran from Stranraer Harbour to Dumfries daily until 11 July, from which date it was extended to Newcastle Central, arriving at 18.37. Another local followed from Stranraer Town at 15.50 which also missed out Gatehouse of Fleet, which had no up services at all! This train arrived at Dumfries at 18.20. On Fridays only there was a 21.30 to Newcastle Central, calling at Newton Stewart and Castle Douglas and Dumfries at 23.59, with arrival in Newcastle at 02.18. Lastly came the up 'Northern Irishman', which left Stranraer Harbour at 22.00, calling at Newton Stewart, Castle Douglas, Dumfries and various stations to London Euston.

Steam working still dominated the route for both passenger and freight workings during the summer and on 27 June 1964 the following locomotives were seen:

12.01 Dumfries-Stranraer Harbour — No 44723 (67E)

13.40 Stranraer Harbour-Dumfries — No 44901 (12A)

15.50 Stranraer-Dumfries — No 80117 (67E)

Table 3

The Northern Irishman

EXPRESS SERVICES

between

LONDON and

BELFAST

Via STRANRAER AND LARNE

To BELFAST

		Monday to Friday nights	Sunday nights	Weekdays
		A	A	
		pm	pm	am
London Euston	dep	7 * 50	7 * 50	....
Bletchley	"	8 ‡ 51	8 h 30	..
Rugby Midland	"	9 38	9 35	....
Crewe	"	11 ‡ 17	11 ‡ 19	9 e 20
		am	am	pm
Wigan North Western	"	12 20	12 23	10 e 26
Carlisle	"	2 38	2 38	2 32
Stranraer Harbour {	arr	5 c 45	5 c 45	5 24
	dep	7 0	7 0 am (Mon.)	5 45
Larne Harbour	arr	9 15	9 15 "	8 30
Belfast York Road	"	10 5	10 5 "	9 20

From BELFAST

		Monday to Saturday nights	Weekdays
		pm	am
Belfast York Road	dep	5 50	8 0
Larne Harbour	"	6 50	9 0
	arr	8 55	11 45
Stranraer Harbour {			pm
	dep	10 * 0	12 17
		am	
Carlisle	arr	1 21	3 9
Crewe	"	4 37	6 d 21
Nuneaton Trent Valley	"	6 b 1	8 f 57
Rugby Midland	"	6 17	9 f 21
Bletchley	"	7 b 1	10 g 48
London Euston	"	8 10	9 k 10

*—Seats may be reserved in advance on payment of a fee of 2s. 0d. per seat.
b—Stops only to set down passengers.
‡—Stops only to take up passengers.
A—Passengers from London desiring meals should travel as far as Rugby or Crewe by the 7.25 pm train on which restaurant facilities are available.
SC—1st and 2nd Class Sleeping Cars.
TC—Through Carriages.
b—Stops when required to set down Sleeping Car passengers only on notice being given to Attendant before arrival at Crewe.

c—Sleeping Car passengers may remain in berths on arrival at Stranraer Harbour until 6.25 am.
d—Change at Carlisle.
e—Change at Carlisle. Saturdays departs 5 minutes later.
f—Change at Carlisle and Crewe.
g—Saturdays only. Change at Carlisle, Crewe and Blisworth.
h—Change at Rugby.
k—Change at Carlisle and on Saturdays arrives Euston 9.20 pm.

For details of Cabins and Berth Charges and addresses to which applications should be made for accommodation on the vessels—see page 59. For details of Steamer Reservation Tickets and general arrangements—see separate folder, to be obtained at Stations and Agencies.

Table 8 — DUMFRIES, CASTLE DOUGLAS, KIRKCUDBRIGHT, NEWTON-STEWART and STRANRAER

Week Days only

[Complex down-direction timetable: stations listed with mileage columns — London (Euston), Glasgow (St. E.), Carlisle, Dumfries, Dalbeattie, Castle-Douglas, Tarff, Kirkcudbright, Crossmichael, Parton, New Galloway, Gatehouse-of-Fleet, Creetown, Newton-Stewart, Kirkcowan, Glenluce, Dunragit, Castle-Kennedy, Stranraer Harbour, Stranraer (Town)]

[Complex up-direction timetable: Stranraer (Town), Stranraer Harb, Castle-Kennedy, Dunragit, Glenluce, Kirkcowan, Newton-Stewart, Creetown, Gatehouse-of-Fleet, New Galloway, Parton, Crossmichael, Kirkcudbright, Tarff, Castle-Douglas, Dalbeattie, Southwick, Dumfries, Carlisle, Glasgow (St. E.), London (St. Pancras), (Euston)]

A Also runs on Saturdays until 27th June and from 29th August
B Fridays and Saturdays only
b On Sundays arr 3 55 am
D Diesel service
d Arr London (Marylebone) On Sundays arr 5 32 am
E or E Except Saturdays
f Arr 2 28 am on Sundays
G Saturdays excepted. Does not apply on 31st July and 3rd August
H Dep 4 45 pm on Sundays
J Arr 8 20 am on Sundays
K Except Saturdays but runs on Sunday nights

M Mondays only
N Sleeping Car passengers may remain in their berths until 6.25 am
P On Fridays arr 6 22 pm
Q pm
Q Saturdays only. Runs 4th July to 22nd August inclusive. (TC Newcastle dep 9 32 am) Stranraer-Larne Boat Train
R On Sunday nights dep 9 0 pm
S or S Saturdays only

SC Sleeping Car
T On Saturdays arr 8 37 pm
TC Through Carriages
U Mondays and Saturdays only
V Arr 5 45 pm on Saturdays
W Saturdays only. Commences 11th July. TC to Newcastle arr 6 37 pm (Larne-Stranraer Boat Train)
X Sunday nights
Y or Y Except Mondays
Z Also runs on Saturdays until 4th July inclusive

22 August 1964:
09.32 Newcastle-Stranraer Harbour — Nos 45247 (12A), 44975
18.15 Dumfries-Stranraer Harbour — No 80009 (67A)

27 August 1964:
15.50 Stranraer-Dumfries — No 80117 (67E)

This was the last complete summer the 'Port Road' carried such traffic, for there was less than a year to go before the withdrawal of both passenger and freight services. This had been approved for July 1964 but was then deferred for another 11 months due to the 1965 General Election and a possible reprieve should a Labour Government be elected. Although the Labour Party was voted into power, the reprieve was not forthcoming.

Until closure, the overnight services to and from Euston were mostly double-headed over the 'Port Road' as far as Dumfries by two 'Black Fives', with the up service pilot locomotive then returning with the 02.20 parcels from Dumfries. BR Standard 'Clans' also made regular appearances and on 9 February 1965 the up 'Northern Irishman' was hauled by Nos 44999 (67F) and 72005 *Clan Macgregor* (12A) with the down service on the morning of 22 February hauled by No 72009 *Clan Stewart*, while the 00.50 up parcels was hauled by No 72005. By March 1965, Stranraer crews were road learning the Dumfries route via Ayr and Mauchline in preparation for the diversion of services when the 'Port Road' closed, although no official closure date had even been announced!

Workings on 1 May 1965 saw the following power:

08.00 Stranraer-Dumfries — No 45013 (12A)
15.50 Stranraer-Dumfries — No 44723 (67E)
18.15 Dumfries-Stranraer — No 45235 (12A)

The last passenger trains

A special to Castle Douglas from Lincoln was hauled as far as Dumfries by preserved 'A3' Pacific No 4472 *Flying Scotsman* on 15 May 1965. No 4472 did not run down the 'Port Road', the train being worked forward by Nos 76073 and 45463. When the special arrived back, departure was made for the south via the Lockerbie branch, which neatly turned the 'A3', as the turntable at Dumfries was not long enough to take the 4-6-2.

Despite closure at last being set for 14 June 1965, there was a last fling for the 'Clans' on some military specials to see out the line with some Class 6 power. On Sunday 16 May three trains carrying TA regiments ran through to Woodburn from Stranraer. These were hauled by ex-LMS 'Jubilee' 4-6-0 No 45573 *Newfoundland*, and 'Clans' Nos 72006 *Clan Mackenzie* and 72008 *Clan Macleod*.

Two weeks later, on the 30th, the back workings of these military specials were hauled by three 'Clan' locomotives, Nos 72006 *Clan Mackenzie*, 72007 *Clan Mackintosh* and 72008 *Clan Macleod*. 'Black Fives' Nos 45463 and 45467 were provided as pilots on two of the trains, one assisting to Loch Skerrow and the other as far as Castle Douglas. Nos 72006 and 72008 had also been in action the day before on two other military specials. All these 'Clans' were based at Carlisle Kingmoor (12A).

The last day of services on 12 June 1965 saw:

08.00 Stranraer-Dumfries — No 80117
08.20 Dumfries-Stranraer — No 76074
12.01 Dumfries-Stranraer — No 45480
13.40 Stranraer-Middlesbrough — No 45115
15.35 Stranraer-Dumfries — No 76074
18.20 Dumfries-Stranraer — No 45469
22.00 Stranraer-Euston — Nos 45480 and 44689

The end for the Portpatrick line

Despite Portpatrick not developing as a major port as had been hoped, the line from Stranraer carried on until 6 February 1950, when it closed to passenger traffic.

Freight traffic survived as far as Colfin until 1 April 1959. In the summer of 1948 there were three trains a day, leaving Stranraer at 6.45am, 12.15pm and 4pm, returning from Portpatrick at 7.30am, 2.35pm and 5.15pm, with an intermediate stop at Colfin. The following year before closure the service was reduced to only two services a day, and eventually Stranraer Town station was to close too, on 7 March 1966, with all services being diverted into the Harbour station. The replacement bus service was operated by Western SMT of Portland Street, Kilmarnock.

There were five journeys from Stranraer, some of which for convenience started from Harbour and Town stations. An extra service ran on Saturdays, while in the opposite direction there were four services, with two extras on Saturday evenings.

The 'Port Road' — freight services

Perishable and goods traffic to and from Ireland grew to significant levels before World War 1 and had almost doubled, from 6,913 tons per annum in 1901 to 12,828 tons in 1915. There was significant traffic in Irish cattle, while the Galloway area was itself the source of cattle, which were despatched regularly from Galloway station and others along the route. The dairy industry prospered in the long term, and a number of creameries were established in the area and were located at:

Whithorn — Scottish Co-operative Wholesale Society
Bladnoch (Wigtown) — Scottish Co-operative Wholesale
 Society
Sorbie — United Creameries
Dunragit — United Creameries
Colfin — Wigtownshire Creameries Co
Stranraer — Wigtownshire Creameries Co
Maxwelltown — Carnation

They produced milk, butter, cheeses and cream for transportation out of the area, but needed fuel to power them, thus the railway also had inward traffic, such as coal.

Stranraer was also a port where fish from western Scotland and the north of Ireland was consolidated for onward transportation. This culminated in an evening fish train to Carlisle from the harbour where the fish traffic was loaded. Coming into the area was coal — Wigtownshire and Galloway having no supplies of their own — and this was sent to local merchants for domestic and light-industrial purposes, industry such as the creameries and for the steamers on the Irish Sea.

Passenger trains also conveyed what could be called 'freight' traffic in the form of mails, parcels and other 'smalls', but other goods, usually perishable traffic or livestock, were carried by these services in vans attached to passenger trains.

Table 59   Glasgow, Ayr, Girvan, Stranraer and Portpatrick

		a.m	a.m	p.m				a.m	p.m	p.m
GLASGOW (St. Enoch)	—	—	8 55	1230	Portpatrick — — — —	lev.	7 30	2 35	5 15
Paisley (Gilmour St.)	.	—	9 11	1243	Colfin	"	7 39	2 53	5 24
Ayr	— — — — —	.	—	10 3	1 30	Stranraer —	arr.	7 47	3 3	5 32
Girvan	. . . .	.	—	1044	2 11	Dumfries v Castle Douglas	"	1045	6 40	1229B
Dumfries via C. Douglas	4 0	8 40	—			Girvan — — . — —	"	1 8	5 35	1030B
Stranraer . . . lev.	6 45	1215	4 0		Ayr	"	1 46	6 16	11B9
Colfin — — — — "	7 3	1233	4 11		Paisley (Gilmour St.)	"	2 52	7 15	12B1
Portpatrick . . arr.	7 11	1241	4 19		GLASGOW (St. Enoch) .	arr.	3 7	7 30	12 15B

Above:

31 May to 26 September 1948 Scottish Region timetable showing Stranraer to Portpatrick.

Above:
Working timetable of passenger trains between Stranraer and Dumfries 15 June to 13 September 1959, showing (left) overnight parcels from Stranraer to Carlisle; (right) overnight Newcastle and Euston services; and (opposite) down Newcastle to Stranraer, ECS, parcels, Euston and postal services.

An examination of the freight records of the LMS in 1927 shows, for instance, that the 3.27 and the 3.59am from Dumfries to Stranraer Harbour included horseboxes for livestock traffic to and from Ireland. (See also the Summer 1947 working timetable above.)

Mail, newspapers and parcels traffic for Ireland came overnight on the Euston service. There were also dedicated parcels services. In BR days, in the summer of 1959, for example, there was a 12.25am Parcels MX (it ran on Sunday mornings) from Stranraer Harbour to Carlisle which ran fast to Dumfries. The 3.45pm passenger train from Stranraer Town to Dumfries also carried vans for mail traffic, and mails from Ireland were conveyed on the 10pm 'Northern Irishman' for Euston.

In the down direction, there was one dedicated parcels service, the 12.22am from Carlisle, which called at Dumfries at 2.50 and then at Castle Douglas and Newton Stewart before arriving at Stranraer Harbour at 5.9am. Other mails came via the down 'Northern Irishman' which started from Euston at 7.50pm and left Dumfries at 3.25am.

In LMS days, when the line was the prime carrier of freight traffic between Northern Ireland and the rest of the United Kingdom, there was an express freight from Stranraer Harbour at 12.33pm for Carlisle Kingmoor Yard which conveyed traffic to other destinations on the network. Like the expresses, this train was limited-stop, calling only at Newton Stewart, Loch Skerrow (to cross the 12-noon freight from Dumfries) and Castle Douglas.

Dairy products figured greatly in the line's traffic and as a result, the 3.10pm from Stranraer Town was booked as a daily milk train that picked up at stations to Dumfries Yard and if the traffic was heavy, was extended to Carlisle. A further milk train even ran on Sundays from Kirkcudbright to Castle Douglas where it connected into the Sundays only express freight from Stranraer Harbour, departing at 3.35pm for Dumfries.

At 10.32pm came another important departure on the 'Port Road', this time 'The Fish' from Stranraer Harbour for Carlisle and thence to other destinations.

Supplementing these were two general freights from Stranraer, at 7.50am and 4.35pm. The 7.50am called at most stations to Castle Douglas and also supplied Loch Skerrow signalbox with provisions every Wednesday. The 4.35 arrived at Dumfries Yard at 9.50pm, but on Saturdays the train was held

(Main timetable: Kilwinning to Stranraer Harbour — Weekdays)

Mileage	Station									
	KILWINNING arr / dep									
	Byrehill Jn.									
	Bogside Racecourse									
	IRVINE arr									
	Dreghorn dep									
	Springside									
	Crosshouse									
	KILMARNOCK arr									
	Gailes									
	KILMARNOCK dep									
	Gatehead									
	Drybridge									
	Barassie									
	Troon Goods									
	Troon arr / dep									
	Prestwick									
	Newton-on-Ayr									
	AYR arr									
	Alloway Jn. dep									
	HEADS OF AYR arr / dep									
	Dalrymple Jn.									
	Hollybush									
	Holehouse Jn.									
	Patna									
	Waterside									
	DALMELLINGTON arr / dep									
	Maybole									
	Kilkerran									
	Dailly									
	GIRVAN arr									
	Pinmore dep									
	Pinwherry									
	Barrhill									
	Glenwhilly									
	New Luce									
	DUMFRIES dep									
	Maxwelltown									
	Killywhan									
	Southwick									
	Dalbeattie									
	CASTLE DOUGLAS arr / dep									
	Tarff									
	KIRKCUDBRIGHT arr									
	Crossmichael									
	Parton									
	New Galloway									
	Lochskerrow									
	Gatehouse of Fleet									
	Creetown									
	Newton Stewart arr / dep									
	Kirkcowan									
	Glenluce arr / dep									
	DUNRAGIT arr									
	Castle Kennedy dep									
	Stranraer Harbour Jn.									
	STRANRAER TOWN dep									
	STRANRAER HBR. arr									

Table 61   STRANRAER and PORTPATRICK
WESTERN S.M.T. CO., LTD., PORTLAND STREET, KILMARNOCK

			Week Days					
Inward from Stranraer	H		pm		pm		S	H
Stranraer Town Scn... dep	6 30	..	1210	..	3 40	.. ..	5 30	.. 6 30 .. 8 32
Stranraer Port Rodie	6 35	..	1215	..	4 5	5 30	..	.. 6 30 .. 8 37
Portpatrick .. .. arr	7 5	..	1245	..	4 35	6 0	..	.. 7 0 .. 9 7
Outward to Stranraer	am		am		pm		S	S
Portpatrick .. .. dep	6 50	..	11 0	..	3 0	.. 7 0	8 0	.. 9 5
Stranraer Port Rodie	7 20	..	1130	..	3 30	.. 7 30	8 30	.. 9 35
Stranraer Town Scn... arr	7 30	..	1135	..	3 35			

* Operates via Stranraer Harbour   H Starts from Harbour Station   S Saturdays only.

Above:
15 June to 6 September 1964 Scottish Region timetable — Stranraer to Portpatrick bus service.

Port No 2 (Faslane was Port No 1) — which was being built at Cairnryan. This was to be used for warship construction should the Clyde yards and Liverpool be damaged by enemy action. The line left the main line at Cairnryan Junction (a mile out from Stranraer), where there were exchange sidings. Construction started on 1 January 1941 and the line was opened by July 1943. It ran for 6¼ miles to Cairn Point, to the north of Cairnryan, but there were no proper stations, trains calling where necessary for passengers and for freight as there were wharves alongside the loch at Innermessan, Leffnoll, Cairnryan, Cairn Point and Old House Point. There was also a passenger service to Stranraer which actually terminated at a temporary station at London Road, from where personnel could get into Stranraer. At Leffnoll there was a small locomotive depot and more sidings to handle shipbuilding traffic.

After the two World Wars, trains of gas shells (up to 64 wagons each) ran to Cairnryan for dumping at sea. There was one report of a heavy train hauled by an 'Austerity' 2-8-0 that ran through the loop at Creetown where it was scheduled to cross the up Euston passenger service. After having run through the points at the end of the loop the train set back, the driver believing that the road was set for the up express. Four wagons of gas shells promptly derailed, but luckily no more than that happened! Cairnryan was closed for military traffic in 1950, but the junction and box were not taken out of use until 1962. This was because the area was used for scrapping surplus ships, and this continued beyond the closure of the railway, the most notable casualty being the former aircraft carrier HMS *Ark Royal*, later to be replaced by a through-deck cruiser of the same name. However, that was not the end of the story as Cairnryan is now a port for ships to and from Larne.

At the other end of the line there was an ammunition factory and storage facility at Southwick. As with Cairnryan, this was considered to be well out of the way of enemy air attack, and also had a number of sidings and a small internal network.

By 1948 the pattern of freight services had changed as traffic had started to decline. The dedicated milk and express fish services were withdrawn, the former traffic being handled by the pick-up general freight services although the through freight services had survived, leaving Stranraer Town at 1.5pm. Livestock forwardings by rail were particularly in decline — this was one of the commodities on which road transport had had a major impact. There had also been a limited amount of meat traffic — this too had dwindled, but wagon loads still featured on the perishables trains. The working timetables between 1948 and 1962 illustrate this decline as the number of freight services gradually diminish, notably perishables and fish which vanish altogether as far as dedicated services, although pick-up services that delivered coal and other commodities continued to run to serve local destinations.

---

longer in various loops to let other trains pass, not arriving until 10.41pm.

In the down direction in 1927, there was a general freight from Dumfries Yard at 4.58am MX for Stranraer, where it arrived at 11am. On Mondays, this train departed at 4.40am (having come from Kingmoor at 3.20), as the 4.58 went to Kirkcudbright on MO — this train left at 5.40 on MX. There was another general freight arriving at 7.55am MO (8.50 MX) from Kingmoor at 7.20am for Stranraer, where it arrived at 15.03. A third followed from Dumfries Yard at 12 noon arriving at 6.45pm. This working shunted the cattle sidings at Castle Douglas for the 7.50am freight ex-Stranraer to pick-up for Dumfries and other destinations. There was no down through express freight, as there was no perishable traffic coming into the area, with wagons and vans being returned on the normal down services. The last weekday freight ran on Saturdays only from Dumfries to Castle Douglas and arrived at 7.51pm.

The line was always an important carrier of military traffic and during the two World Wars carried a large number of troops and a sizeable quantity of equipment. In World War 2 there was also work in connection with the secret port — known as Military

UP

Mileage M C M C	Station		K85	K88	K94	K88	K87		K89	K86	K 94	K81	K94		K77	K78	K79	K83			K97	
			am SX	am	am	am SX	am		am	am PM	am	am PM	am PM		PM	PM SX	PM SO	PM SX		PM SO SX		am am	
0 00 0 00	STRANRAER TN. dep		5 10							6 25		7 15			12 25			4 40				
0 24 0 79	Stranraer Harbour dep									6 28		7 18			12 28			4 44				
1 24	Stranraer Hbr. Jn. arr		5 13									7 23										
	Cairnryan Jn. arr		5 18									7 34										
	dep		5 38									7 40										
2 47	Castle Kennedy arr									6 38		7 45			12 34			4 50				
	dep			5 45						6 55			7 56		12X42			4X58				
5 34	Dunragit arr		5 53							7 7					12X55			5X18				
	dep		6 5							7 30												
8 60	Glenluce arr									7 45					1 6			5 30				
17 14	Kirkcowan arr									7 55					1727			5 51				
	dep									8 23												
										8 55												
0 00	WHITHORN dep														1 45	2 40	3 10					
3 76	Millisle arr														2X5	3X 5	3 42					
5 72	Sorbie arr														2X13	3X 5						
8 26	Whauphill arr														2 25	3 17						
	dep														2 35	3 25						
9 74	Kirkinner arr														2 40	3 30	4					
	dep														2 50	3 40	4 10					
12 17	Wigtown arr															3 46	4 16					
	dep															3 50	4 40					
23 33 19 18	NEWTON STEW'RT arr								9 14						1 41	3 15	4 35	4 50		6 5			
															9 40	9 40	1 57			6 35			
26 55	Palnure dep											10X 6	10X 6	2 28								
29 61	Crectown dep											10X22	10X22	2 35			6 56					
34 29	Gatehouse of Fleet dep											10 48	10 48	2 46			7 14					
40 30	Loch Skerrow dep											10 56	10 56				7X30					
44 29	New Galloway dep											11 14	11 14	3X 0			7X48					
46 38	Parton arr											11 24	11 24	3X10			7 59					
49 52	Crossmichael dep											11 37	11 37	3X26								
												11 47	11 47				8 10					
0 00	KIRKCUDBRIGHT dep					9 55			11 40		11R55	11R55				8 0	8 0			9 30		
3 39	Tarff arr					10 9						12 4	12 4				8 14	8 14				
7 38	Bridge of Dee arr					10 30						12 14	12 14									
53 23 10 20	Castle Douglas arr					10 50	11 30		12 7		12X27	12 27	3 50			8 34	8 34			9 52	10 50	
	dep				10 30	11 5	11 45				12X29		4 15			8 18	8 44	8 54			11 1	
58 43	Dalbeattie arr			10 25	10 42	11 20	11 38		12 5		2 18		4 29				8 27	8 59	9 9			11 20	
60 43	Southwick arr			10 37																		
62 53	Kirkgunzeon arr								12 2														
64 67	Killywhan arr						12 2		12 27	12 45		2R42		4 51			8 45	9 17	9 27		11 35		
	dep								12 45		3 2						9 2	9 35	9 45			11 46	
71 17	Maxwelltown arr			7 30	10 50	11 16	11 20		12 28		3 32		5 17			9 5	9 42	9 50			11 50	
72 71	Dumfries No. 1 arr				10 57	11 25			1 6		3 40		5 22			9 10	9 47	9 55			11 55	
73 05	DUMFRIES arr				11 2		11 29		1 10		3 45											

H—Until 26th June and from 10th September will pass New
Galloway 3.8 p.m., Crossmichael arrive 3X22 depart 3X35, Castle
Douglas arrive 3.48 p.m.

DOWN

Mileage M C M C	Station		K89	K85	K77		K84		K88		K78	K94	K 94		K88		K81		K79		K94			
			am	am	am SX	am		am	am		am SO	am SX	PM SO		am		am PM		noon SX	am SX	am SX	PM SO		
0 00	DUMFRIES dep		4 15	5 0					5 20	5 40	7 38	7 38		8 22			8 55		10 55					
0 14	Dumfries No. 1 arr		4 20	5 6					5 25	5 44	7 42	7 42					8 59		10 59					
1 68	Maxwelltown arr		4 25	5 11					5 32		7 47	7 47					9 5		11 5					
8 18	Killywhan arr		4 44	5 30						5 49	8 4	8 6					9 26		11 24					
10 32	Kirkgunzeon arr																9 40							
12 42	Southwick arr																9 45							
	dep																9 55							
14 42	Dalbeattie arr			5 3	5 50				6 26		8 25	8 25							11 12					
	dep			5 18	6 5				6X44			9 55							11 24					
19 62 0 00	Castle Douglas arr			5 37	6 44				6X55			10 15		10 15			11 29		11 57		1 25		1 25	
	dep			5 50	7 38												1 25		12X28		1 25			
2 62	Bridge of Dee arr				7 46																			
6 61	Tarff arr				7 54							10 31												
	dep											10 52												
10 20	KIRKCUDBRIGHT arr			6 15	8 4							11 5												
23 33	Crossmichael arr								7 6										12X40	1X35	1X35			
26 47	Parton arr								7 20										12X55	1X52	1X52			
28 56	New Galloway arr								7 38								1 10		2 9	2 9				
	dep								7 55								1 57		2 36	2X56	2X56			
32 52	Loch Skerrow arr								8X15								1X37		3X 2	3X 2				
	dep								8X28								2 2							
38 56	Gatehouse of Fleet arr								8 46								2 31		3 10	3 10				
43 24	Creetown arr								9L 0								2L17			RU	RU			
46 30	Palnure arr								9X15								2X26			RU	RU			
49 52 0 00	NEWTON STEW'RT arr								9N35								2 45		3 5	3 54	3 54			
7 01	Wigtown arr				9 25		10 55		1 0		10 40						12 0		3 5					
	dep				9NSO						10 50						12 30							
9 24	Kirkinner arr				10K 6						11N15						12 45							
10 72	Whauphill arr				10 45		10 55				11 55						1 0							
	dep				10 55						12 10						1 10							
13 26	Sorbie arr				11 22						12 30						1 25							
15 22	Millisle arr				11 32						12 50						1 45							
	dep				11N57						1 5						2X10							
19 18	WHITHORN arr				12N10						1N15						2 30							
					1 25						1 25													
55 71	Kirkcowan arr						11 15		1X20								3 24							
64 25	Glenluce arr						11 38		1X30								3 32							
67 51	Dunragit arr		7019		10X*57		12 40		1 53						2 35		4 13							
	dep		80 5		11X*20										2 45		4 23							
70 38	Castle Kennedy arr						11 29		1 30						2 56		4 56							
71 61	Cairnryan Jn. arr		8 14						2 35						2 59		5 2							
	dep								2 52						3 5		5 32							
72 61 0 00	Stranraer Hbr. Jn. arr		8 20						2 59								5 42							
0 79	Stranraer Harbour arr				11 35				1 45						3 10		5 50							
73 05	STRANRAER TN. arr		8 25		11 40				1 48		3 5				2 30	3 15								

Working timetables of freight trains, Summer 1955.

31 May to 26 September 1948

up trains

am

7.20 MX Maxwelltown to Dumfries Yard — traffic from the Carnation siding

7.55 Stranraer Town to Newton Stewart — general pick-up/set down freight train

8.45 Kirkcudbright to Dumfries Yard — traffic was general merchandise and coal empties

10.15 Newton Stewart to Dumfries Yard — general pick-up/set down

10.30 SX Castle Douglas to Dumfries Yard — as well as general merchandise this train conveyed meat and ran as an 'express freight'

12.00 TThO Dalbeattie to Dumfries Yard — general pick-up that also shunted at Maxwelltown

pm

1.00 SO Dalbeattie to Dumfries Yard — general pick-up — no Maxwelltown shunt

1.5 Stranraer Town to Dumfries Yard — express freight

2.20 MWFO Maxwelltown to Dumfries Yard — shunts private siding

2.35 Portpatrick to Stranraer — mixed train, served the creamery at Colfin

5.00 Stranraer Town to Dumfries Yard — pick-up/set-down freight

am

10.30 SuO Kirkcudbright to Dumfries Yard — perishables and milk

pm

2.55 SuO Stranraer Town — express freight

down trains

am

4.55 Dumfries Yard to Kirkcudbright — general pick-up/set-down

5.35 Dumfries Yard to Stranraer Town — general pick-up/set-down

6.5 Dumfries Yard to Maxwelltown — traffic for the creamery

7.35 TThO Dumfries Yard to Dalbeattie — general pick-up/set-down

8.50 Dumfries Yard to Newton Stewart — pick-up/set-down freight

11.00 Dumfries Yard to Stranraer Town — pick-up/set-down freight

pm

12.20 Stranraer Town to Portpatrick — mixed, general merchandise, Colfin creamery

1.00 MWFO Dumfries Yard to Maxwelltown — shunts Maxwelltown

2.30 SuO Dumfries Yard to Stranraer Town — through freight

15 September 1958 to 14 June 1959

up trains

am

6.25 Class H from Stranraer Town to Newton Stewart — pick-up/set-down

9.40 SX Class H from Newton Stewart to Dumfries Yard — pick-up/set-down

9.40 SO Class H from Newton Stewart to Dumfries Yard — pick-up/set-down

10.40 Class D from Castle Douglas to Dumfries Yard — traffic from Kirkcudbright

pm

12.30 SX Class F from Stranraer Town to Dumfries Yard — limited-stop

12.30 SO Class F from Stranraer Town to Dumfries Yard — limited-stop

1.15 Class K from Stranraer Town to Colfin — coal for the creamery

4.40 SX Class F from Stranraer Town to Dumfries Yard — pick-up/set-down

7.20 Class H from Kirkcudbright to Dumfries Yard — branch freight

down trains

am

4.23 Class H from Dumfries Yard to Kirkcudbright — pick-up/set-down

5.40 Class E from Dumfries Yard to Stranraer Town — pick-up/set-down, shunts as required

8.55 Class H from Dumfries Yard to Newton Stewart — pick-up/set-down as required

10.46 SX Class H from Newton Stewart to Stranraer Town — shunts at Kirkcowan, Glenluce and Dunragit

10.55 SO Class H from Newton Stewart to Stranraer Town — shunts at Kirkcowan, Glenluce and Dunragit

10.50 Class H from Dumfries Yard to Stranraer Town — pick-up/set-down as required

pm

2.15 Class K from Colfin to Stranraer Town — traffic from the creamery

11 September to 17 June 1962

up trains

am
6.20 SO Class E Stranraer Town to Dumfries Yard
6.20 SX Class E Stranraer Town to Dumfries Yard

pm
12.25 SX Class E Stranraer Town to Dumfries Yard
12.25 SO Class E Stranraer Town to Dumfries Yard
7.20 Class H Kirkcudbright to Dumfries Yard

down trains

am
4.35 Class E from Dumfries Yard to Kirkcudbright
5.43 SX Class D Dumfries Yard to Stranraer Town
5.43 SO Class D Dumfries Yard to Stranraer Town
9.00 Class H Dumfries Yard to Castle Douglas
10.40 SX Class H Dumfries Yard to Stranraer Town
10.40 SO Class H Dumfries Yard to Stranraer Town

In latter days these freight services were regularly hauled by ex-LMS types and traditionally these were the Hughes Fowler 'Crab' 2-6-0s which had dominated freight services on the 'Port Road' together with the Caley 0-6-0 'Jumbos'.

20 July 1963
No 42919 — 10.40am Dumfries-Stranraer
No 42906 — 6.20am Stranraer-Dumfries

By 7 December 1963 the majority of sightings were of 'Black Fives', No 44885 (67E) being seen on the 06.20 Stranraer-Dumfries; on 2 May 1964 the 06.20 goods from Stranraer to Dumfries was hauled by No 45082 (12A).

27 June 1964
No 44702 (64C) — 12.25pm Stranraer-Dumfries
No 76073 (67E) — returning from Newton Stewart to Dumfries Yard with brake van

22 August 1964
No 45053 (64C) headed the 6.20am Stranraer-Dumfries service

As with the passenger services, the existing through freight services were 'divertable' via Ayr. So it was the pick-up services that served local businesses which were badly missed when closure came on 14 June 1965, thus consigning the area to become yet another railway 'desert' where the railways just 'gave up' and no longer provided a service.

The last freights ran on 12 June 1965, all with 'Black Five' power:

am
6.50 Stranraer to Dumfries Yard — No 45469
11.10 Dumfries Yard to Stranraer — No 44721
12.42 Stranraer to Dumfries Yard — No 44707

There was no reprieve for any stations on the route except Maxwelltown, where the oil sidings remained open well into Railfreight Speedlink days. They are now mothballed pending possible reopening. The line is still open from Stranraer Harbour to Challoch Junction where it forks north to Ayr and Glasgow.

'Port Road' — locomotive allocations

Dumfries, 1950 (68B)

Class	3MT	2P	4P	6P5F	3P	2P	2F	3F
Type	2-6-2T	4-4-0	4-4-0	2-6-0	4-4-0	0-4-4T	0-6-0	0-6-0
	40170	40576	40902	42908	54443	55124	57302	57563
		40577	40904	42909	54444	55164	57329	57600
		40614	40912	42915	54507		57337	57601
			41109	42918			57344	57602
			41135	42919			57349	57621
			41171				57362	57623
			41175				57378	
			41179				57391	
							57397	
							57405	

Dumfries, 1959 (68B)

Class	3MT	2P	6P5F	5MT	3P	2P	3F	2F	3F	4MT
Type	2-6-2T	4-4-0	2-6-0	4-6-0	4-4-0	0-4-4T	0-6-0	0-6-0	0-6-0	2-6-0
	40151	40576	42908	44995	54502	55124	56310	57302	57600	76072
	40170	40577	42909	45169	54507	55232	56327	57329	57601	76073
		40614	42913	45432				57349	57602	
			42915	45480				57362	57621	
			42918					57378	57623	
			42919							

Dumfries, 1965 (67E)

Class	5MT	5MT	5MT	2MT	4MT	2MT	4MT
Type	4-6-0	4-6-0	4-6-0	2-6-0	2-6-0	2-6-0	2-6-4T
	44699	45115	45471	46450	76073	78051	80023
	44701	45432	45480	46479	76074		80061
	44723	45463			80117		
	44995	45467			80119		

Stranraer, 1950 (68C)

Class	2P	4P	2P	3F	2F
Type	4-4-0	4-4-0	0-4-4T	0-6-0	0-6-0
	40600	41092	55125	56234	57375
	40611	41099		56372	57445
	40616	41127			57478
	40623				

Stranraer, 1965 (67F)

Class	5MT	4MT	2MT
Type	4-6-0	2-6-0	2-6-0
	44999	76112	78016

Stranraer, 1959 (68C)

Class	2P	'Crab'	5MT	4MT
Type	4-4-0	2-6-0	4-6-0	2-6-0
	40566	42749	45125	76112
	40611			
	40616			
	40623			

Above:
BR Standard Class 4 No 76112 of Stranraer, and an unidentified 'Black Five', leave Stranraer Town with the 8.5am service for Dumfries on 8 May 1959. The train would travel on the original route of the Portpatrick & Wigtownshire Joint Railway, a distance of 53 miles from Portpatrick to Castle Douglas, where there was an end-on junction with the Castle Douglas & Dumfries Railway. The station here has survived, and there are still a number of sidings, including a carriage shed and goods loading bank. Traffic though bears no relation to the volumes that were carried when the 'Port Road' was open, and even in the years following its closure. Stranraer still attracted Motorail services and considerable freight traffic and there were a number of private sidings. The 1990s saw a dramatic decline in all of this business with the earlier demise of Speedlink and Motorail, as well as rail foot passengers, many of whom now fly to and from Ireland. To the right of the train is also the small locomotive shed and turntable. Stranraer Town was the terminus for the Portpatrick train service and acquired the addition 'Town' in March 1953 to differentiate it from Harbour station. It closed officially on 7 March 1966, the 'Port Road' having closed on 14 June 1965. *John Langford collection*

CASTLE DOUGLAS TO KIRKCUDBRIGHT

Historical perspective

Pressure to construct a branch line to Kirkcudbright came to fruition in August 1861, when a 10-mile extension was granted Parliamentary powers — the Kirkcudbright Railway. This took the form of a single-track line, and work was completed in time for it to open by 17 February 1864. It was refused permission to introduce passenger traffic, as the Board of Trade inspectors insisted that the track layout at Castle Douglas be modified to accommodate the new service. Thus, a new station had to be built short of the junction at St Andrew Street. By August, work was completed and passenger trains were able to serve the main station in Castle Douglas, with St Andrew Street closing three years later.

Train services

Services from Kirkcudbright to Castle Douglas and Dumfries were generally interwoven with services from Stranraer. As a continuation of services that had run on the line in LMS times the service in 1948 comprised six trains from Kirkcudbright to Dumfries which left at 6.10, 8.30, 9.35am (changing at Castle Douglas), 12.35 (changing at Castle Douglas) 3.10 and 5.10pm (changing at Castle Douglas). The through services called at all stations from Castle Douglas to Dumfries and all had reasonable connections from there to Carlisle. In the down direction there were departures from Dumfries at 6.30, 8.15, Castle Douglas at 10.25am, Dumfries at 12.30, Castle Douglas at 3.35, Dumfries at 5.58 and a final departure from Castle Douglas at 7.40pm. The Castle Douglas departures connected with trains from the 'Port Road' Dumfries to Stranraer workings, although some of the waiting times were not 'friendly' as trains had to wait for connections from the Stranraer direction as well.

The Kirkcudbright branch was worked by a variety of motive power and an example of this can be seen on 31 May 1958. The 1.53pm from Kirkcudbright arrived in Dumfries behind ex-LMS 4-4-0 '2P' No 40577 (64B) running tender first. The 4.51pm from Kirkcudbright was hauled by ex-LMS Class 3 2-6-2T No 40151 (68B) and the 6.2 to Kirkcudbright was hauled by BR Standard 2 6-0 No 76072 — three different types of locomotive.

On 22 April 1961 the 1.53pm from Kirkcudbright was hauled by 2-6-2T No 40152 and the 2.50pm Dumfries-Stranraer was in the charge of 4-6-0 No 45169. On 8 July 1961 the line was worked by Nos 76072 and 76073 which had the 12.22pm to Castle Douglas and Kirkcudbright. On 2 December 1961 the 1.53pm Kirkcudbright-Dumfries was hauled by 'Black Five' No 44885 (68B), with the usual load of two LMS corridor coaches on the train. Fairburn tank No 42269 also worked the line, featuring on both freight and passenger services.

From 4 December 1961, service cuts were introduced on the line. The 12.22pm from Dumfries to Kirkcudbright was withdrawn along with its balancing working, the 1.53pm from Kirkcudbright to Dumfries. The 'Port Road' suffered too, with the withdrawal of the 10.58pm SO from Stranraer to Dumfries and the 2.45pm SO from Dumfries to Stranraer, both of which connected at Castle Douglas with the 12.22 SO from Kirkcudbright to Castle Douglas, and this meant that the train was retimed to 12.40pm and extended to Dumfries. The 3.30pm SO from Castle Douglas to Kirkcudbright also started from Dumfries, which it left at 2.50pm.

'Crab' 2-6-0 No 42699 (67E) was seen on the 12.40pm from Kirkcudbright on 9 February 1963, and No 76073 (67E) worked the 2.50pm to Kirkcudbright. By December 1963 BR Standard tanks were taking over from the Fairburn tanks, but these did not have a complete monopoly of the Kirkcudbright services. On the 7th, No 80119 (67E) worked the 2.50pm from Dumfries to Kirkcudbright and No 76073 (67E) hauled the 12.40pm from Kirkcudbright to Dumfries.

On weekdays in 1964 there were four passenger services, and a daily freight service, usually hauled by a Standard Class 4 2-6-4T of the 80xxx series or a BR Standard Class 4MT 2-6-0 of the 76xxx series. These locomotives had by now replaced the earlier LMS types, the '2P' 4-4-0s and the inevitable Caledonian 'Jumbo' 0-6-0 tender engines. 'Black Fives' were also common performers on the Kirkcudbright services, all these locomotives being shedded at Dumfries. Standard Class 4 tank No 80023 hauled the 14.50 Dumfries to Kirkcudbright on 2 May 1964, and on 27 June 1964 the 14.50 Dumfries-Kirkcudbright was headed

Left:
31 May to 26 September 1948 Scottish Region timetable — Dumfries, Castle Douglas, Kirkcudbright, Newton Stewart, Whithorn, Stranraer.

by No 80119 (67E). On 22 August 1964 the following workings took place:

12.40 Kirkcudbright-Dumfries — No 76072 (67E)
14.50 Dumfries-Kirkcudbright — No 80117 (67E)
16.51 Kirkcudbright-Dumfries — No 80117 (67E)
18.00 Dumfries-Kirkcudbright — No 80117 (67E)

In the summer of 1964 a passenger train left Dumfries at 06.38, leaving Castle Douglas at 07.19 and arriving at Kirkcudbright at 07.39. Here it formed the 08.00 back to Dumfries, where it arrived at 08.56. Before the 08.00 had gone, an earlier departure, at 06.10, arrived at Dumfries at 07.04. An 09.30 departure from Kirkcudbright then ran as far as Castle Douglas only, arriving at 09.49 and connecting with the 08.05 from Stranraer Town to Carlisle. On Saturdays only there was a 12.40 service to Dumfries, arriving at 13.42, and then a long gap to the last departure of the day to Dumfries, leaving at 16.51. From Dumfries came the 08.10 through service, arriving at Kirkcudbright at 09.11, and a 14.50 SO arriving at 15.48, this train starting at Castle Douglas at 15.30 on weekdays. The final service of the day left Dumfries at 18.00, with a weekday arrival of 18.58 at Kirkcudbright, three minutes earlier on Saturdays.

All services called at Dalbeattie, and the 08.10 from Dumfries, the 12.40 (SO) and the 16.51 from Kirkcudbright called at Southwick as well. Mondays to Fridays the two evening trains from Dumfries to Stranraer and Kirkcudbright were combined as far as Castle Douglas. The Stranraer portion was worked forward at 18.45 by a locomotive that had run light from Dumfries to Castle Douglas an hour beforehand. This light engine also carried the guard to work the 15.50 Stranraer Harbour to Dumfries, joining the train at Castle Douglas and relieving the Stranraer guard to work back on the 18.00 from Dumfries.

In February 1965 the service was dominated by Nos 76073 and 76074, along with BR Standard Class 4 2-6-4Ts Nos 80117, 80119, 80023 and 80061. On 22 February No 80061 had hauled the 18.00 to Kirkcudbright, this train having a Stranraer portion which was taken over by No 80119, which had earlier run light, leaving Dumfries at 17.00 and carrying the guard for the 15.50 from Stranraer, as mentioned above.

The following day saw Nos 80117 and 80023 double-heading the 08.07 to Kirkcudbright. The train split at Castle Douglas, with No 80117 going on to Stranraer. The final day of operation of passenger services was 1 May 1965, the early diagram being worked by No 80117. This locomotive hauled the 12.40 back from Kirkcudbright to Dumfries, but No 76073 worked the afternoon and evening services. All services were discontinued from 3 May 1965. Today, with commuting to Dumfries and Carlisle having increased substantially in recent years, the trains are badly missed and would be well patronised.

Freight services
A mixed freight service for perishables, general merchandise and coal ran daily on the branch, and to cater for perishables an up train even ran on Sundays, although this was later withdrawn as much of this traffic was lost to road competition. The down train ran from Dumfries early in the morning so that customers could get their goods at the start of the working day, and there was a return working early on in the day, this down train being retimed to an evening departure in latter years. There was also a daily trip to and from Castle Douglas for connection with the Stranraer-Dumfries through freights. At Castle Douglas there were a number of sidings for freight traffic, including livestock, plus a loading dock to the rear of the down platform. Other roads led to the goods shed and there were coal staithes to the south of those that supplied the local merchants.

In latter days the freight services were dominated by BR Standard Class 4 2-6-0s and 2-6-4Ts, but ex-LMS 'Black Fives' were common and Nos 44723 (19 April), 45471 (27 April), 45467

Above:
15 June to 6 September 1964 Scottish Region timetable — Dumfries, Castle Douglas, Kirkcudbright, Newton Stewart and Stranraer.

(28 April) and 45432 (29 April) were all seen on these workings in 1965.

31 May to 26 September 1948
up trains
8.45am Kirkcudbright to Dumfries Yard
9.55am SuO Kirkcudbright to Dumfries Yard
down trains
4.55am Dumfries Yard to Kirkcudbright

15 September 1958 to 14 June 1959
up trains
11.40pm SX Class H Kirkcudbright to Castle Douglas
7.20pm Class H Kirkcudbright to Dumfries Yard
down trains
am
4.23 Class H Dumfries Yard to Kirkcudbright
10.15 Class H Castle Douglas to Kirkcudbright

11 September 1961 to 17 June 1962
up trains
11.40pm SX Class H Kirkcudbright to Castle Douglas
7.20pm Class H Kirkcudbright to Dumfries Yard
down trains
am
4.35 Class E Dumfries Yard to Kirkcudbright
10.15 Class H Castle Douglas to Kirkcudbright

NEWTON STEWART TO WHITHORN

Historical perspective

With the Portpatrick Railway coming to Newton Stewart, a scheme known as the Machars Railway, later known as the Wigtownshire Railway, was started in 1871. By July 1872 Parliamentary powers were received and a line to Whithorn via Garlieston was born. The Caledonian Railway was contracted to work the line, but saw it as a risky enterprise and extracted harsh terms from the railway, expecting receipts not to cover operational costs. The Wigtownshire Railway found it impossible to work the line itself; an offer from the North British Railway was received to work the line for 65% of the income — much better than the Caledonian deal — but eventually a locomotive superintendent, Thomas Wheatley, formerly of the NBR, was recruited to run the line after leaving the NBR following a disagreement.

Train services

Services started with freight on 2 March 1875 and passenger services commenced from 7 April as far as Wigtown. An extension to Garlieston was opened on 2 August 1875, with a harbour extension being added on 3 April 1876, ostensibly for traffic to and from the Isle of Man. Garlieston was the nearest Scottish port to the Isle of Man, but no regular steamer service was introduced as the port was tidal and it was limited to excursions. On one occasion a train even missed the steamer, and Thomas Wheatley had to pay the passengers' compensation himself, such were the terms of his contract! On 9 July 1877 the line reached Whithorn, where the station consisted of one single-face platform and building, with three sidings for goods traffic. Apart from passengers, traffic consisted of livestock, coal and mails, and there were creameries at Sorbie, Wigtown and Whithorn which generated dairy traffic. There was also limited traffic, such as grain to and from Garlieston, as well as other agricultural products.

Wheatley died in 1883, whereupon his son replaced him, but this arrangement lasted only until the creation of the joint committee in 1885. The Railways Act of 1921, which grouped the independent lines into the 'Big Four', saw the end of the Portpatrick & Wigtownshire Joint. Ownership was transferred to the London Midland & Scottish Railway by the end of 1923, and it was for the new company to run services on both the main line and branches for the next 25 years.

The Wigtownshire line had always seemed to have the air of a rather run-down branch line. The branch off it, from Millisle Junction to Garlieston, was a particularly poor earner of passenger income, it being down to £1 per week in 1900. There were even two mail services which had been withdrawn by 1903, with the bags being wheeled to and from Millisle Junction on a cart!

Whithorn itself was the most southerly station in the whole of Scotland and had opened after the original terminus of the line had been transferred from Garlieston via Millisle Junction.

In 1948, two years before they were withdrawn, passenger services consisted of four trains from Newton Stewart to Whithorn, with only three returning. These left the junction at 6.25, 10.50am, 4.45 and 8.25pm and took roughly 35 minutes for the 19-mile trip, calling at Wigtown, Kirkinner, Whauphill, Sorbie, Millisle (for Garlieston) and Whithorn. In the opposite direction, services calling at all stations left Whithorn at 7.45am, 3.10 and 7pm.

Passenger services ended on 25 September 1950. Freight services continued and a pick-up train ran three days a week on Mondays, Wednesdays and Fridays, shunting the Garlieston branch as required. This freight service also succumbed to road competition and was withdrawn on 6 October 1964, eight months before the 'Port Road' itself closed.

A number of railtours worked over the line in its latter years. There was the SLS 'Wigtownshire Railtour' which ran from Glasgow St Enoch to Whithorn and Garlieston on 2 September 1961. The train was hauled by restored GNSR 4-4-0 No 49 *Gordon Highlander* and ran to Ayr and Girvan before arriving at Dunragit, from where Caley 'Jumbo' No 57375 took the train on to Newton Stewart. The train then travelled over the line to Whithorn before returning to Glasgow at 9.13pm. The tour was organised by W. A. C. Smith, one of the main photographic contributors to this book but then Scottish Area Secretary of the SLS, and cost 33 shillings (£1.65).

The RCTS/SLS 'Scottish Railtour' travelled on the line on 23 June 1962. Restored Caledonian Single No 123 piloting No 49 departed from Stranraer for Newton Stewart 57 minutes late as the two locomotives had struggled on the outward run on the Ayr to Stranraer line. The train had been banked out of Girvan by 'Crab' No 42879 as far as the tunnel at milepost 4, but after this the train brakes had leaked on (making the train come to a stand). The locomotives recovered to climb over the summit, but at a cost in time. The two locomotives worked the train to Whithorn and returned to Newton Stewart before leaving to head for Castle Douglas, whereafter they performed much better, until at Palnure the tablet was dropped, requiring an emergency stop to pick it up. The train was then hauled from Castle Douglas to Kirkcudbright by Fairburn tank No 42699, Nos 123 and 49 having run light to Dumfries, where they took over for the run to Carlisle and the end of the tour.

Another notable excursion ran along the branch on 15 April 1963. Ex-LMS 'Jubilee' 4-6-0 No 45588 *Kashmir* had hauled the train from Carlisle to Stranraer, and at Newton Stewart a connection was made with the Whithorn line. A former Millisle-shed locomotive, Caledonian 0-6-0 No 57375, then proceeded, with the enthusiasts travelling in a number of open mineral wagons topped-and-tailed by two brake vans. Restored Highland Railway 4-6-0 No 103 and No 49 then took the train on from Stranraer to Glasgow.

Following closure to passenger services on 25 September 1950, buses catered for the passengers, and the replacement bus service on the Whithorn branch continued to be shown in Scottish Region railway timetables while the 'Port Road' remained open. Some buses even ran to and from the railway station at Newton Stewart. On weekdays in 1964 there were seven departures, and, of the seven, the 06.00, 10.40 16.35 and 20.35 started at Newton Stewart station. The other three started from the Square in Newton Stewart and departed at 13.25, 17.35 and 19.15. The buses, operated by Western SMT of Kilmarnock, called at Wigtown, Kirkinner, Garlieston, Sorbie and Whithorn. The service was supplemented on Saturdays. In the return direction there were departures from Whithorn at 07.35, 09.25, 17.50 and 20.50. All except the 17.50 ran to the railway station at Newton Stewart. Another service, departing at 14.55, ran to the station at Newton Stewart on Saturdays only. In terms of frequency, this was a better service than the trains had provided.

Freight services

31 May to 26 September 1948

up trains

12.00   Whithorn to Millisle — locomotive to shunt traffic at Garlieston

3.50pm   Whithorn to Newton Stewart — pick-up

9.35pm   Whithorn to Newton Stewart — pick-up

down trains

9.15am   Newton Stewart to Whauphill

12.30pm   Newton Stewart to Whithorn

1.20pm   Millisle to Whithorn — locomotive having shunted at Garlieston

In latter years, the branch freight was worked as a trip and did not feature in the working timetable. Instead, the line was worked on Mondays, Wednesdays and Fridays only, calling for traffic as required as well as working the Garlieston branch as necessary. Regular engine, Drummond Caledonian 'Standard Goods' 0-6-0 No 57375 worked the branch freight on 21 August 1963 — probably one of its last outings — but the remainder of the services were hauled in the main by BR Standard Class 2, 2-6-0 tender locomotives.

The 'Port Road' and its branches — an epitaph

Despite their forming part of an important link between Ireland, England and Scotland, for through services as well as those linking together some rural communities, all lines in the area soon became candidates for closure. The general idea was that local services, certainly west of Castle Douglas, were poorly used and sparse in any case. Trains from Kirkcudbright and Castle Douglas to Dumfries could easily be substituted by buses and road hauliers, and the 'boat trains' could likewise be re-routed via Ayr and Mauchline Junction.

These ideas were put forward even in the pre-Beeching closure era and were proposed by BR Scottish Region which planned to discontinue services to Stranraer altogether. This absurd idea was rightly rejected as politically unacceptable, as it would have left the busy port of Stranraer without a rail connection. The compromise was finally settled four years later, with closure from Castle Douglas to Challoch Junction being sanctioned by the Government in July 1964. However, worse was to come and the impending General Election of that year put the decision on hold. With local people hoping that the new Labour Government would reverse the decision, a hammer blow was to follow as the closure of the line from Dumfries to Castle Douglas and Kirkcudbright was also included in the post election bill. In the event, this service ceased first on 3 May 1965, and six weeks later the 'Port Road' itself was closed on the night of 12 June 1965 — authorisation having been given in early 1965 — and, fittingly, the last train was the up 'Northern Irishman'.

Today the 'Port Road' is extant only as far as Maxwelltown for freight traffic, although this is currently 'mothballed', while the section from Stranraer Harbour to Challoch Junction still survives for trains to Ayr. A visit to the area today reveals a busy A75 road, now upgraded and full of articulated lorries constantly plying their way to and from Stranraer. The railway route remains intact in many places, apart from in the main towns of Castle Douglas and Newton Stewart. The most impressive reminder is the viaduct at Big Water of Fleet — it now remains as a discarded piece of transport infrastructure, but it is extremely unlikely that it will ever carry a train again. By December 1965 all the telegraph poles had been cut down, some even being left lying across the line. November 1965 had seen track-lifting taking place on the Kirkcudbright line, while the second track of the double-track section from Castle Douglas to Dumfries was being taken out. Lifting of the track was done by rail, the train actually being propelled along the former down line to where work was being carried out. By the middle of May 1966, the lifting gang had removed the up line from Castle Douglas to halfway between Dalbeattie and the Urr Water bridge.

With the demise of the 'Port Road', steam duties from Dumfries shed were much diminished, and by 30 April 1966 the steam allocation had officially gone, although some locomotives were still in store or under repair, these being:

Class	'5MT'	'Clan'	2MT	4MT
Type	4-6-0	4-6-2	2-6-0	2-6-0
	44699	72006	78051	76102
	44995			
	45120			
	45177			
	45463			
	45480			
	45489			

Steam had also vanished from the 'Port Road' demolition train, BRCW Type 2 diesel No D5353 being used in May 1966. Demolition was still proceeding on the Castle Douglas to Maxwelltown section in September, only a short stretch at Killywhan remaining double. Track panels were being stored at Maxwelltown. At the Stranraer end of the line demolition started as late as 11 December 1967, working from Challoch Junction. This was despite opposition, as by this time local people felt that a restored service from Newton Stewart would be justified.

Table 63		NEWTON STEWART and WHITHORN										
		WESTERN S.M.T. CO., LTD., PORTLAND STREET, KILMARNOCK										

Week Days

Outward from Newton Stewart	am		am	S pm	pm		S pm		pm		pm	E pm	✱ pm	pm					
Newton Stewart Stn. dep	6 0	....	1040	...	...	1 25	...	2 40	...	4 35	...	5 35	7 15	7 15	8 35	...	...	...	...
Newton Stewart Square ..	6 5	....	1045	1215	...	1 45	...	3 0	...	4 40	...	5 55	7 35	7 35	8 55	...	...	...	...
Wigtown	6 25	...	11 5	1235	...	1 57	...	3 12	...	5 0	...	6 7	7 47	7 47	9 15	...	...	...	...
Kirkinner	6 37	...	1117	1245	...	2 15	...	3 30	...	5 12	...	6 25	...	8 5	9 27	...	...	...	...
Garlieston	6 55	...	1135	...	...	2 23	...	3 38	...	5 30	...	6 33	...	8 13	9 45	...	...	...	...
Sorbie	7 3	...	1143	...	...	2 35	...	3 50	...	5 38	...	6 45	...	8 25	9 53	...	...	...	...
Whithorn arr	7 15	...	1155	...	...	...	...	...	...	5 50	...	...	...	...	10 5	...	...	...	...

Inward to Newton Stewart	am		am	S pm	pm		pm												
Whithorn dep	7 35	...	9 25	2 55	...	5 50	...	8 50	..	..	..	..	...	...	...	...	...	...	...
Sorbie	7 47	...	9 37	3 7	...	6 2	...	9 2	...	...	...	...	...	...	...	...	...	...	...
Garlieston	7 55	...	9 45	3 15	...	6 10	...	9 10	...	...	...	...	...	...	...	...	...	...	...
Kirkinner	8 13	...	10 0	3 32	...	6 28	...	9 28	...	...	...	...	...	...	...	...	...	...	...
Wigtown	8 25	...	1010	3 45	...	6 40	...	9 40	...	...	...	...	...	...	...	...	...	...	...
Newton Stewart Square ..	8 45	...	1030	4 5	...	7 0	...	10 0	...	...	...	...	...	...	...	...	...	...	...
Newton Stewart Stn. arr	8 50	..	1033	4 10	..	...	...	10 5	...	...	...	...	...	...	...	...	...	...	...

E Saturdays excepted   S Saturdays only   ✱ Saturdays only but daily during July and August

Left:
**ScR timetable,
15 June to
6 September 1964 —
Newton Stewart-
Whithorn bus service.**

STRANRAER TO NEWTON STEWART

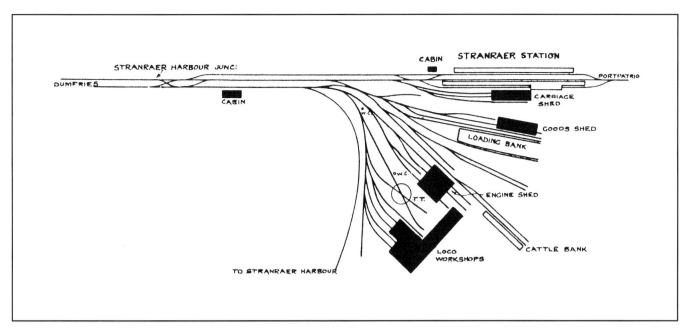

Above:
Track plan of the Stranraer area.

Above left:
'Black Five' No 45432 has arrived at Stranraer Town on 12 July 1963 with the 8.57am from Castle Douglas, this train having a connection with the 8.10am from Dumfries to Kirkcudbright. By this time the freight service to Colfin on the Portpatrick line had ceased — the stub end of this can be seen in the foreground, now forming the headshunt for the run-round loop and complete with a new buffer stop. Between Stranraer Town and Stranraer Harbour were the locomotive shed/workshops and the cattle dock. The former was a combination of Joint, Caledonian and Girvan sheds and closed in October 1966. Note the signal which was 'repeated' to allow good siting from the Portpatrick line — not really required now — but the small shunt arm to the platform loop has been removed. *Michael Mensing*

Below:
The 12.1pm from Dumfries, hauled by 'Black Five' No 45061, is seen approaching Stranraer Harbour on 12 July 1963 a few minutes earlier than in the previous photograph. This was the almost standard formation for most 'Port Road' services at this time; others would have vans attached for perishables and other traffic such as newspapers and parcels.
Michael Mensing

Lower left:
Further to the north on Loch Ryan is Stranraer Harbour station. 'Black Five' No 45061 arrives with the 12.1pm from Dumfries on 12 July 1963. The train is signalled into the station and to the left of this can be seen the steamer *Stranraer Princess* at the pier, waiting to sail for Larne. The sidings to the right have now all gone; they once accommodated much freight traffic, coaching stock and Motorail services, but the only regular passenger services today are operated by 'Sprinters'. The cattle dock, which once handled cattle imported from Ireland, can also be seen adjacent to the harbour approach road. *Michael Mensing*

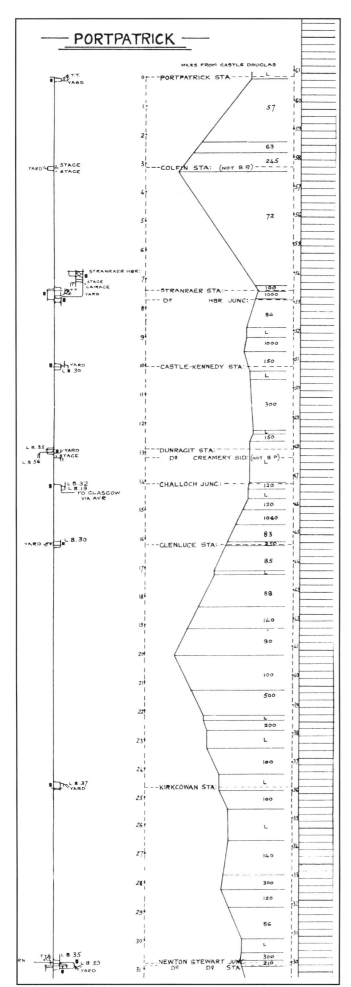

PORTPATRICK

MILES FROM CASTLE DOUGLAS

0	PORTPATRICK STA.
1	57
2	63
3	COLFIN STA: (NOT B.P.) 245
4	
5	72
6	
7	STRANRAER STA: 100 / 1000
8	D? HBR. JUNC: 86
9	1000
10	CASTLE-KENNEDY STA. 150
11	300
12	150
13	DUNRAGIT STA: D? CREAMERY SID: (NOT B.P.)
14	CHALLOCH JUNC: 120
15	120 / 1060
16	GLENLUCE STA: 83 / 250
17	85
18	88
19	140
20	90
21	100
22	500 / 200
23	
24	100
25	KIRKCOWAN STA: 100
26	
27	140
28	300
29	120 / 86
30	
31	NEWTON STEWART JUN? D? D? STA: 300 / 210

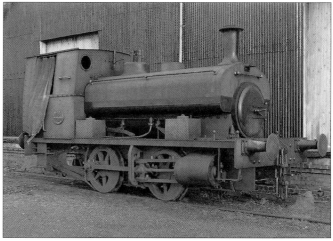

Above:
Two industrial locomotives were based at Cairnryan by Pounds (Shipowners & Shipbreakers). One of these, an 0-4-0 saddle tank, built in 1945 by Andrew Barclay & Co (No 2200) is seen there on 16 December 1962. The other was an 0-6-0 pannier tank built by Bagnall of Stafford (No 2614) in 1940. Both locomotives were scrapped on site after relatively short careers. *W. A. C. Smith*

Upper right:
The interior of Stranraer Harbour station, opened in 1862, is seen on 15 April 1963, with Caley 0-6-0 'Standard Goods' No 57375 having arrived with a special from Whithorn. *John Langford collection*

Lower right:
The lines from Stranraer Harbour and Stranraer Town met at Stranraer Harbour Junction. From there towards Castle Kennedy, a run of approximately two miles, the line ran up a 1-in-86 climb before a descent at 1 in 150 into Castle Kennedy and then, further down, 1 in 300 to Dunragit, passing Cairnryan Junction, which was opened in November 1942 to serve the naval facilities along Loch Ryan. 'Black Five' No 45483 is seen near Castle Kennedy on the way to Stranraer with a tiny down freight. The double-track formation can clearly be seen, the line being doubled from Castle Kennedy to Dunragit in World War 2. Trains to Ayr still run through here today, but the station is closed and single track suffices again for today's traffic levels.
Michael Mensing

Left:
Gradient profile — Stranraer to Newton Stewart.

Above:
Stanier 4-6-0 No 45463 passes the smart-looking station at Dunragit with a mixed freight from Stranraer to Dumfries on 29 May 1965. To the west of the station were a number of sidings, and to the east of Dunragit was another creamery siding. *W. A. C. Smith*

Below:
Fourteen miles from Portpatrick was Challoch Junction where the line to Glasgow via Ayr joined the Portpatrick & Wigtownshire Joint. Originally there was a signalbox here, but this was taken out at the start of World War 2 and the junction was operated from Dunragit. From Challoch Junction the 'Port Road' climbed through Glenluce for roughly six miles — in places as severe as 1 in 83 — crossing Glenluce Viaduct, a stone structure of eight arches. The 'Port Road' is visible to the left as 'Black Five' No 45127 and pilot locomotive BR Standard 2-6-0 No 76112 begin the 16½-mile climb to Chirmorie on the Ayr line with an empty coaching stock train on 29 May 1965. *W. A. C. Smith*

Right:
BR 'Clan' 4-6-2 No 72008 *Clan Macleod* **passes Dunragit with the 06.20 troop train from Woodburn to Stranraer Harbour on 16 May 1965. These troop trains brought welcome Class 6 power to the route in its final months of operation — and would have reached Woodburn via the Newcastle & Carlisle and Morpeth, the more direct line from Hexham to Reedsmouth Junction and Woodburn having been finally closed on 1 September 1958.** *W. A. C. Smith*

Centre right:
BR Standard Class 4 2-6-4T No 80119 calls at Glenluce with the 15.50 Stranraer Town to Dumfries service on 18 July 1964. Note that in addition to the two carriages, the train also has a van for perishables. *W. A. C. Smith*

Left:
Drummond Caledonian 'Standard Goods' 0-6-0 No 57375, the regular Whithorn engine, calls at Glenluce with the SLS 'Wigtownshire Railtour' special on 2 September 1961. Glenluce was the first passing loop on the single line from Challoch Junction and had a signalbox plus a siding to the quarry at Glenjorrie. *Roy Hamilton*

Left:
'Black Five' No 45432 leaves Glenluce with the 8.57am from Castle Douglas to Stranraer Town on 12 July 1963. Again, wagons have been added to the train for goods and mails traffic. The train is just leaving the passing loop — from this side there was access to a small yard, the points leading to which can just be seen. The train will now climb at 1 in 85/1 in 140 before dropping into Kirkcowan.
Michael Mensing

Centre left:
Kirkcowan station is seen on 18 July 1964 with the road set for Newton Stewart. There was a passing loop and sidings here for general goods traffic.
W. A. C. Smith

Lower left:
BR Standard Class 4 Mogul No 76073 approaches Newton Stewart from Stranraer with the lengthy 12.25pm freight from Stranraer to Dumfries Yard on 9 July 1963. This train would have shunted smaller stations en route and carries empty oil tanks from Stranraer in addition to coal empties. All this traffic had to be imported into the area, as there were no natural assets.
Michael Mensing

Right:
No 76073, as seen previously, approaches Newton Stewart at 1.52pm on 9 July 1963 with the 12.25pm freight from Stranraer. To the right can be seen the former engine shed (closed in 1959) and sidings — the turntable was here — and the Whithorn line comes in from the right by Newton Stewart West signalbox, the signals for which can be seen just by the white-painted water tower. *Michael Mensing*

Left:
A view of the layout of Newton Stewart Junction on 2 September 1961, with the signalbox to the right, the line to Whithorn taking the extreme left, the next two roads leading to the former locomotive shed, now used for permanent way traffic.
Bill Rear collection

Right:
The crew of LMS 'Crab' 2-6-0 No 42919 watch the 13.40 passenger train from Stranraer Harbour to Dumfries depart from Newton Stewart at 2.38pm on 24 June 1963. The 'Crab' heads the 12.25pm from Stranraer to Dumfries Yard, where it was booked to arrive at 4.35pm after shunting at stations along the route. *David Holmes*

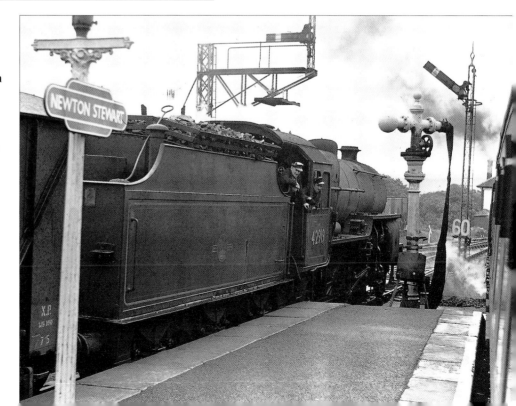

NEWTON STEWART TO GARLIESTON AND WHITHORN

Upper left:

BR Standard Class 2 Mogul No 78026 has worked the branch freight to Whithorn on 27 May 1964 and has arrived back at Newton Stewart where it has run round. The 2-6-0 is now drawing the train forward to shunt into the yard to the left. This is a good view of the yard, with No 1 cabin visible in the distance. No 2 cabin controlled the Whithorn line.
J. Spencer Gilks

Lower left:

The regular Whithorn locomotive for many years was ex-Caledonian 'Standard Goods' No 57375, seen on the turntable at Newton Stewart on 2 September 1961. Newton Stewart shed was closed on 2 February 1959. *The Rev R. T. Hughes*

Right:

Gradient profile — Whithorn to Newton Stewart.

Below:

No 57375 leaves Newton Stewart on the 'Scottish Rambler' railtour on 15 April 1963. The line descended from Newton Stewart through Causewayend Siding before running a relatively level course through Kirkinner to Wigtown. There was originally a station at Causeway End, but this was closed in November 1885. *Derek Cross*

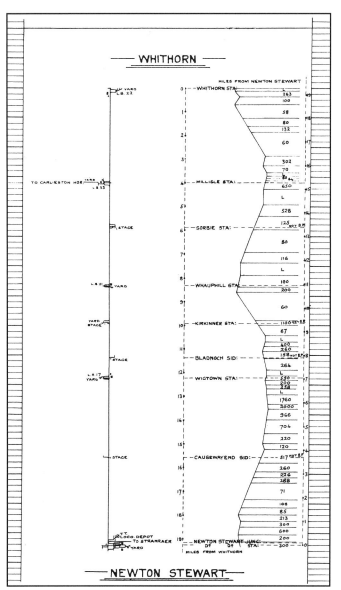

WHITHORN

MILES FROM NEWTON STEWART

WHITHORN STA.
MILLISLE STA.
SORBIE STA.
WHAUPHILL STA.
KIRKINNER STA.
BLADNOCH SID.
WIGTOWN STA.
CAUSEWAYEND SID.
NEWTON STEWART JUNC.

TO CARLIESTON HBR.

MILES FROM WHITHORN

NEWTON STEWART

Above:
Wigtown station is seen with 'Standard Goods' No 57340 posing with the 10am Newton Stewart to Whithorn branch freight on 8 May 1959. Originally, this was the place where the Wigtownshire Railway's maintenance facilities were located. There is a small yard, seen on the right, from where traffic was forwarded by a creamery. *Edwin Wilmshurst*

Left:
No 57375 is seen again, this time passing Kirkinner on 15 April 1963 with the 'Scottish Rambler'. This train originated at Edinburgh Waverley at 9.30am the day before, taking in the lines from Reston to Duns, Tweedmouth to Roxburgh, Jedburgh, St Boswells, Greenlaw, the Waverley Route to Carlisle, Lockerbie to Dumfries, Kirkcudbright, Whithorn, Garlieston, Stranraer, Ayr and Glasgow St Enoch.
W. A. C. Smith

Right:
On 2 September 1961 the SLS 'Wigtownshire Railtour' traversed the line and again, No 57375 was in charge and stopped at Sorbie, where the main traffic from here was to and from the creamery adjacent to the station.
Roy Hamilton

Above:
On the return leg to Newton Stewart with the 'Scottish Rambler No 2' on 15 April 1963 this train also called at Sorbie for No 57375 to take on water.
Derek Cross

Right:
The BR Standard types had replaced the Caledonian 'Standard Goods' by 1964. No 78026 leaves Sorbie with the thrice-weekly freight from Newton Stewart on 11 September that year. *E. J. S. Gadsden*

Upper left:
Later the same day, No 78026 leaves Millisle Junction for Whithorn. Millisle was the junction for the short line to Garlieston Harbour and the thrice-weekly goods shunted there as required. *E. J. S. Gadsden*

Lower left:
Millisle Junction is seen on 8 May 1959. The Garlieston branch is behind the signalbox, and there is shunting in progress. Originally the end of the line, the station was called Garlieston, but when the short branch was opened to the harbour, it was renamed Millisle and had a locomotive shed and goods facilities added. *Edwin Wilmshurst*

Upper right:
The 'Scottish Rambler No 2' of 15 April 1963 traversed the line down to Garlieston using goods wagons and brakevans at either end (would this be allowed today?). No 57375 is seen propelling the train back to Millisle Junction from Garlieston. *Roy Hamilton*

Centre right:
No 57375 has arrived at Garlieston with the special on 15 April 1963 and participants are going to inspect the rail facilities there. This was the only engine allocated to Millisle shed as LMS No 17375 and when the shed closed in the 1930s it remained allocated to Stranraer and continued as regular engine on the Newton Stewart/Whithorn branch into the 1960s. It covered most, if not all, railtours which ran to Whithorn. *W. A. C. Smith*

Lower right:
On 8 May 1959 'Standard Goods' No 57340 shunts at Garlieston. Here the 0-6-0 approaches the former passenger station, having just worked down the line to the granary sidings at the harbour. *John Langford collection*

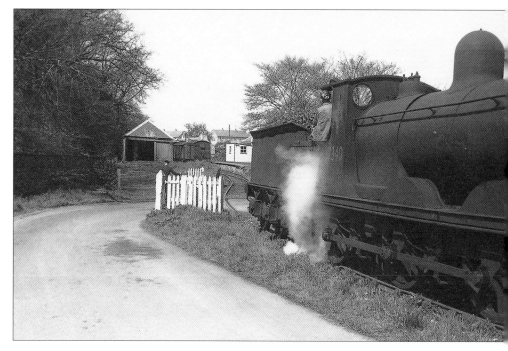

Upper left:
No 57340 is now seen shunting in the granary sidings on the quay at Garlieston on 8 May 1959. Rails can still be found in this area today. *John Langford collection*

Centre left:
Before Whithorn was reached from Millisle, the former station at Broughton Skeog was passed, where a siding remained. The 'Scottish Rambler No 2' with No 57375 in charge arrives at Whithorn on 15 April 1963. Some of the locals have turned out to see a passenger train on the line once more. There is a loading bank immediately in front of the photographer, with a cattle dock and general sidings further to the left. *W. A. C. Smith*

Lower left:
Whithorn was reached after a stiff climb from Millisle in places as steep as 1 in 58. No 57340 is seen at Whithorn with the goods from Newton Stewart on 8 May 1959. Here the 0-6-0 would shunt and then return to Newton Stewart, having already shunted Garlieston in the down direction. Whithorn was just over 19 miles from Newton Stewart. Today the station site is occupied by a fire station. *John Langford*

NEWTON STEWART TO CASTLE DOUGLAS

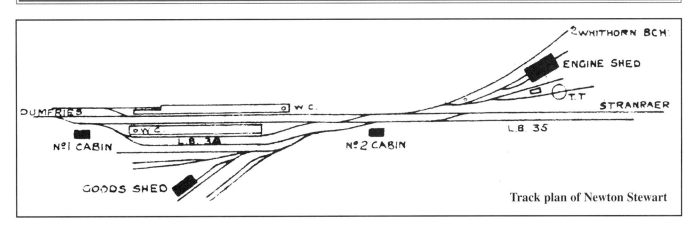

Track plan of Newton Stewart

Above:
'Black Five' No 45485 gets away from Newton Stewart with the 1.40pm from Stranraer Harbour to Dumfries
on 19 July 1963. The train is about to pass Newton Stewart East cabin which controlled that end of the station,
and there was a falling gradient of 1 in 90 after a level section at Palnure, where there was a station with
passing loop (although the down side was subsequently taken out); Carty Siding was also passed between
Newton Stewart and Palnure. A seven-mile climb of 1 in 80 to Gatehouse of Fleet started through the area of
Creetown. *Michael Mensing*

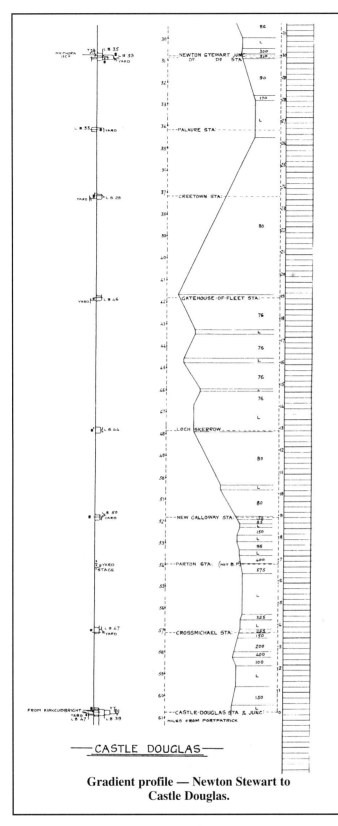

Gradient profile — Newton Stewart to Castle Douglas.

Above:
The crew of No 76074 collect the tablet at Creetown with the 15.35 from Stranraer Town to Dumfries on the last day of services, 14 June 1965. *W. A. C. Smith*

Above:
'Black Five' No 44707 crosses the River Cree with an up freight from Stranraer to Dumfries Yard on 12 June 1965; oil and coal empties can be seen in the train. *W. A. C. Smith*

Right:
'Clan' class No 72006 *Clan Mackenzie* is seen on the 1 in 80 Creetown bank with the 14.10 ten-coach military special from Stranraer Harbour to Woodburn on 16 May 1965, only a month before closure. Based at Kingmoor, five of these locomotives were used on the Euston to Stranraer sleepers from Carlisle to Stranraer, returning later in the day with the up train, after having worked the 11.44am from Stranraer to Glasgow St Enoch and the balancing 5.10pm from there to Stranraer. *W. A. C. Smith*

Above:
'Crab' 2-6-0s were common performers on the 'Port Road' freight services until displaced by the inevitable 'Black Fives'. Here, No 42908 is seen with an up freight to Dumfries Yard, climbing to Gatehouse of Fleet (actually two miles west of the station), on 9 July 1963.
Michael Mensing

Centre left:
Gatehouse of Fleet station looks in very smart condition, both in terms of station buildings and permanent way, on 1 April 1963. Services here were sparse: in 1964 only two down trains called here, at 09.43 FO and at 19.28 on Mondays and Saturdays only. The station was seven miles from the town which did not help generate local passenger business, but as can be seen, it had a loop, signalbox and a yard, although this was much reduced in latter years. *W. A. C. Smith*

Lower left:
At Gatehouse of Fleet there was also a carriage in use as a church, seen on 16 May 1965. This was saloon No SC972002E, a former Great Northern Railway Royal saloon which was withdrawn from service on the Scottish Region. Previously a Caledonian coach stood here. Note too the end portion of another coach, used as a store. *W. A. C. Smith*

Above :
Fairburn Class 4 2-6-4T No 42689 has the 3.50pm from Stranraer Town to Dumfries one mile east of Gatehouse of Fleet on 9 July 1963. This train conveyed mails and has a BG and a PMV in addition to the two passenger coaches. The train is descending from the summit, just west of the station, at 1 in 76 on this section of line.
Michael Mensing

Right:
'Black Five' No 44675 passes through the rugged countryside so typical of this section of the 'Port Road' to the east of Gatehouse of Fleet. The 4-6-0 is climbing the last part of the 1 in 76 on the approach to the station on 16 July 1963. The train is the 8.57am from Castle Douglas to Stranraer Town. Note the very high repeater distant signal that was the warning for the outer home at Gatehouse of Fleet.
Michael Mensing

'Jubilee' class 4-6-0s were rare visitors in the 1960s, but one member of the class hauled the aforementioned 'Scottish Rambler' railtour on 15 April 1963. No 45588 *Kashmir* is seen climbing the 1 in 76 to Gatehouse of Fleet with Big Water of Fleet Viaduct visible in the background, to the right. *W. A. C. Smith*

Right:
Big Water of Fleet Viaduct was the largest and most impressive structure on the 'Port Road'. It has 20 spans and was considerably strengthened, as can be seen from the additions to the supporting piers, as heavy traffic grew on the line. No 76073 crosses the viaduct near Gatehouse of Fleet at 3.22pm with the 12.25pm goods from Stranraer to Dumfries Yard on 9 July 1963 (seen earlier in the book at Newton Stewart). Happily, the structure still stands today, unlike its sister, the nine-span Little Water of Fleet Viaduct, which was demolished by the Army. *Michael Mensing*

Left:
The RCTS/SLS 'Scottish Railtour', which travelled on the line on 23 June 1962, calls at Loch Skerrow. Caledonian Single No 123 piloted GNSR No 49 and departed from Stranraer for Newton Stewart 57 minutes late, as the two locomotives had struggled on the outward run on the Ayr-Stranraer line. The train had been banked out of Girvan by 'Crab' No 42879 as far as the tunnel at Milepost 4, but after this the train brakes had leaked on, bringing the train to a stand. The locomotives recovered to climb over the summit, but at a cost in time. The two locomotives worked the train to Whithorn and returned to Newton Stewart before leaving for Castle Douglas, whereafter they performed much better until at Palnure the tablet was dropped, requiring an emergency stop to pick it up. The train was then hauled from Castle Douglas to Kirkcudbright by Fairburn 2-6-4T No 42699, Nos 123 and 49 having run light to Dumfries, where they took over for the run to Carlisle and the end of the tour. *R. M. Casserley*

Above:
'Black Five' No 45471 calls at Loch Skerrow with the 3.50pm from Stranraer Town to Dumfries on
19 September 1964. This was one of the most isolated crossing points in Scotland, four miles from New
Galloway and six miles from Gatehouse of Fleet. As well as watering facilities, it had a G&SWR timber
signalbox, while short platforms on both running lines were also provided. Trains stopped on request,
passengers often being fishermen visiting the loch; the others were railway staff and their families, the station
being marked as having 'no public access'. After the Grouping, many of the stations on the 'Port Road' were
closed during the night and on Sundays which meant most loops could be switched out. 'Switching out'
apparatus was installed in 1925 by the LMS and this basically released the normal interlocking at the signalbox
that was closed. Loch Skerrow was a terminal point for two of these long sections and thus was kept open at all
times, except for a shift on a Sunday in latter years. *W. A. C. Smith*

Below:
After Loch Skerrow, the four-arch Loch Stroan Viaduct crossed over Black Water of Dee. Then came the neat
station at New Galloway, seen awaiting one of the infrequent passenger services on 17 September 1964. The
station was six miles away from New Galloway itself and was situated at the bottom of the descent from Loch
Skerrow and Gatehouse of Fleet. As well as the passing loop here there were extensive sidings for local traffic.
Originally there was a level crossing here, but a bridge — the one the photograph is being taken from —
replaced it following an accident. *W. A. C. Smith*

Upper left:
Another 'Jubilee', this time No 45718 *Dreadnought*, coupled to a Fowler tender, crosses the three-span bridge over Loch Ken on 2 July 1961 with the 2.20pm from Stranraer Harbour to Newcastle. *W. A. C. Smith*

Centre left:
After the climb through Glenluce and Gatehouse of Fleet the line flattened out for the run to Castle Douglas. Parton was two miles from New Galloway. Here, on 8 July 1961, 'Black Five' No 44885 leaves the station with the 2.50pm Dumfries to Stranraer Town. A wagon can be seen in the yard to the rear of the station, which catered for general traffic and some slate. *W. A. C. Smith*

Lower left:
A second view of Parton station from the Dumfries end. There was no passing loop here. The station has survived as a private residence. *W. A. C. Smith*

Above right:
'Black Five' No 45480 arrives at Crossmichael, where there was some custom for the 3.40pm from Stranraer Town to Dumfries on 8 July 1961. Crossmichael has a loop and sidings and was the last passing loop before Castle Douglas. *W. A. C. Smith*

Lower right:
Ex-LMS 4-4-0 three-cylinder Compound (classified as '4P') No 41132 of 68C (Stranraer and Newton Stewart) calls at Castle Douglas on a Dumfries-Stranraer service in June 1956. These locomotives were common performers in the area until displaced by the more modern 'Black Fives' and Stanier and Fairburn tanks. Parcels and 'sundries' traffic are being unloaded and another barrow awaits loading on to the train. *Ian Allan Library*

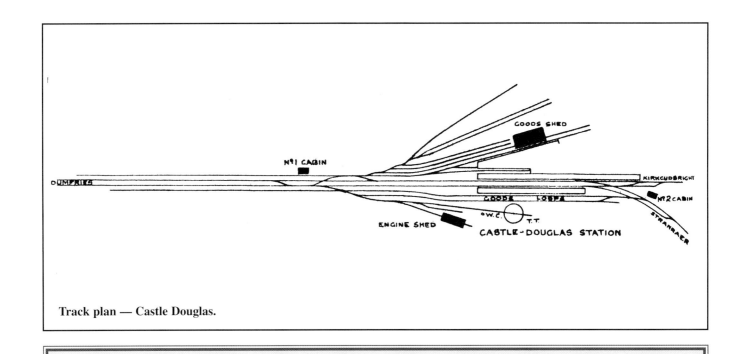

Track plan — Castle Douglas.

CASTLE DOUGLAS TO KIRKCUDBRIGHT

Below:
Castle Douglas was the junction with the Castle Douglas & Dumfries Railway, and services commenced
between here and Stranraer on 11 March 1861. Here too was the line to Kirkcudbright, and on 24 June 1963
BR Standard Class 4 2-6-0 No 76072 has the road at Castle Douglas for the 3.30pm to Kirkcudbright. Note that
the goods loops on the up side have been lifted. The other train, hauled by 'Black Five' No 44957, is the 1.40pm
from Stranraer Harbour to Dumfries. *David Holmes*

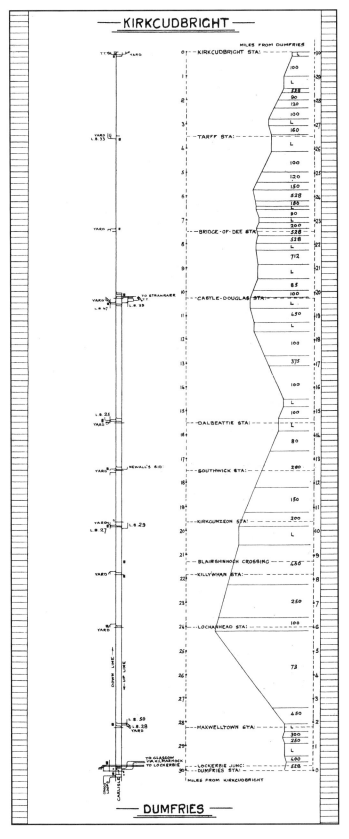

— KIRKCUDBRIGHT —

MILES FROM DUMFRIES

Station	Distance
KIRKCUDBRIGHT STA:	0 · 30
	100
	L · 29
	528
	90
	120
	100
	L
	160 · 27
TARFF STA:	
	L · 26
	100
	120 · 25
	150
	528 · 24
	186
	90
	L · 23
	200
BRIDGE·OF·DEE STA:	528
	528 · 22
	L
	712 · 21
	L
	85
	100 · 20
CASTLE·DOUGLAS STA:	L
	450 · 19
	L
	100 · 18
	375 · 17
	100 · 16
	L
	100 · 15
DALBEATTIE STA:	L
	80 · 14
SOUTHWICK STA:	280 · 13
	150 · 12
KIRKGUNZEON STA:	200 · 11
	L · 10
BLAIRSHINNOCH CROSSING	430 · 9
KILLYWHAN STA:	· 8
	250 · 7
LOCHANHEAD STA:	100 · 6
	73 · 5
	· 4
	450 · 3
MAXWELLTOWN STA:	L · 2
	300
	250
	L · 1
	400
LOCKERBIE JUNC:	528 · 0
DUMFRIES STA:	

MILES FROM KIRKCUDBRIGHT

— DUMFRIES —

Above:
**Gradient profile — Kirkcudbright to
Castle Douglas and Dumfries.**

Right:
**BR Standard 2-6-4 tank No 80023 approaches Castle
Douglas with the 9.30am from Kirkcudbright on
18 July 1963. Two ex-LMS coaches make up the train,
a fairly consistent formation for passenger trains on
this line.** *Michael Mensing*

Above:
**The junction for the Kirkcudbright line can be seen
just under the bridge at the west end of Castle
Douglas station. The line to Newton Stewart,
disappearing to the right, became single at the points.
On the other side of the bridge, by the junction on the
down side stood No 1 cabin. The original track plan
was different here, this being rebuilt before opening to
passengers was allowed.** *Bill Rear collection*

Above:
**No 76072 is impatient to get away from Castle
Douglas with the 12.40pm train from Kirkcudbright
to Dumfries on 19 September 1964. The sidings on the
down side have cattle pens, a bay platform for milk
and other perishables and goods shed. A horsebox
stands in the goods bay platform. No 2 cabin, one of
two at Castle Douglas, can be seen on the down side
in the distance. Only one up side siding survives, this
to serve the water tower, seen to the right.**
W. A. C. Smith

Top:
The 8.7am from Dumfries to Kirkcudbright leaves Tarff with No 76073 in charge on 16 April 1965. Tarff station still survives as a private residence. *W. G. Sumner*

Above:
The same locomotive, No 76073 and stock, return through Tarff with the 9.25am Kirkcudbright-Castle Douglas on 16 April 1965. *W. G. Sumner*

Left:
Tarff station platform and buildings, seen on 29 October 1955. *W. A. C. Smith*

Right:
Another return working for the locomotive that had worked the 6pm Dumfries-Kirkcudbright sees Fairburn Class 4 tank No 42689 1½ miles south of Tarff with an up freight on 11 July 1963. *Michael Mensing*

Below:
Between Tarff and Kirkcudbright was Tongland Bridge, the most impressive structure on the line. BR Standard Class 4MT tank No 80023 crosses over the River Dee with the 9.30am Kirkcudbright to Castle Douglas on 11 July 1963. The bridge has since been demolished, but the stylish road bridge still stands of course. *Michael Mensing*

Upper left:
No 76073 leaves Tongland Bridge with the 6pm Dumfries-Kirkcudbright on 12 July 1963. *Michael Mensing*

Lower left:
No 76073 is now seen arriving at Kirkcudbright with the 3.30pm from Castle Douglas on 15 July 1963. The new petrol storage depot to the left was not rail-connected. *Michael Mensing*

Above:
Before the 'Black Fives', Fairburn tanks and BR Standard types came to dominate services on the line, the older pre-Grouping locomotives were used widely on the 'Port Road' and its branches. Here ex-MR Class 2P 4-4-0 No 40614 spends a quiet hour at Kirkcudbright before departing with the 4.54pm to Dumfries on 30 July 1952. *W. J. Alcock*

Left:
No 76073 pulls up at Kirkcudbright station with the 14.50 from Dumfries on 10 April 1965. The platform canopy once stretched over the lines here, forming a small trainshed.
W. A. C. Smith

Right:
The first of three general views of Kirkcudbright looks towards Castle Douglas, showing the approach to the station and the signalbox on 29 October 1955. The photographer was standing on the former cattle-loading dock.
W. A. C. Smith

Track plan of Kirkcudbright.

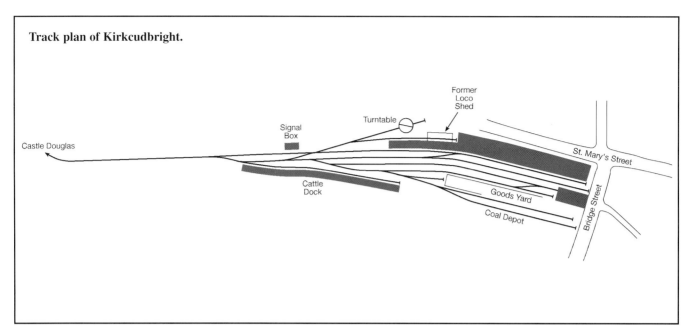

Above:
Ex-LMS 'Crab' 2-6-0 No 42749 prepares to leave Castle Douglas at 12.18pm with the morning freight service from Stranraer to Dumfries Yard on 15 June 1959. Castle Douglas station has been totally demolished since this photograph was taken. A park now occupies the site of the junction of the line to Stranraer, while, ironically, the other part of the area is now a showroom for cars. *David Holmes*

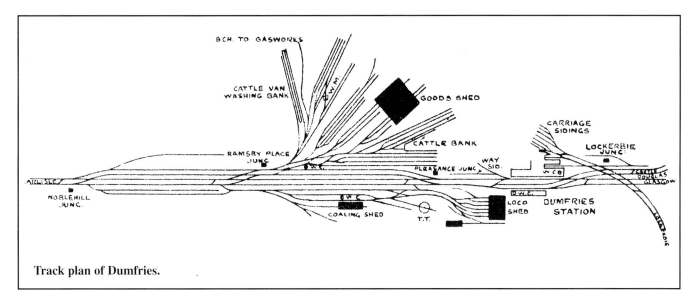

Track plan of Dumfries.

Above:
No 76072 is two miles east of Castle Douglas with the 4.52pm from Kirkcudbright to Dumfries on 10 July 1963. There were falling gradients from here to Dalbeattie, and this section of line to Dumfries was double-track.
Michael Mensing

Below:
'Black Five' No 44996 heads the 8.5am from Stranraer Town to Dumfries, two miles east of Castle Douglas, on 18 July 1963. *Michael Mensing*

Above:
**To the west of Dalbeattie was a fine bridge, later demolished, over Urr Water, over which No 76073 is seen
passing with the 2.50pm from Dumfries to Kirkcudbright on 13 July 1963.** *Michael Mensing*

Above:
**'Black Five' No 44957 approaches Dalbeattie with the 8.5am from Stranraer Town to Dumfries on 8 July 1963.
Before Dalbeattie there was a small halt at Buittle. This survived only until the route was double tracked and
was closed on 1 October 1894, although the associated cottages continued to be occupied by railway staff,
finally being demolished in the 1960s.** *Michael Mensing*

Left:
Another 'Black Five', No 44723, with a small snow plough fitted, calls at Dalbeattie with the 15.50 Stranraer Town-Dumfries on 27 March 1965.
Roy Hamilton

Below:
Ex-CR 'Standard Goods' No 57302 shunts at Dalbeattie at 10.50am on 4 May 1962. These locomotives were common performers on the Dumfries 'Trips' and also worked the branch to and from Kirkcudbright before being displaced by more modern types. Today much of Dalbeattie station and yard is occupied by private houses. *David Holmes*

Left:
From Dalbeattie the line climbed to Lochanhead before descending at 1 in 73 to Dumfries. BR Standard Class 4 tank No 80023 passes Southwick on the 12.40pm from Kirkcudbright to Dumfries on 13 July 1963. The photographer's notes recall: 'The station was open according to the timetable, but deserted. This train sailed through although scheduled to stop. Maybe the train crew knew that no-one wanted to alight and could see no one on the platform?' *Michael Mensing*

Above:

Fairburn Class 4 tank No 42689 heads a freight from Stranraer to Dumfries Yard on 8 July 1963 and is just north of the station at Kirkgunzeon, which was closed on 2 January 1950 and is now a caravan site.

Michael Mensing

Above:

The remains of a wartime poster were evident at Southwick station on 8 July 1963. The poster seeks volunteers for the RAF and depicts a Stirling bomber. The other poster sets out the terms and conditions for the carriage of flowers and plants by rail — what a contrast to war! Southwick's military connection was an armaments factory, with associated railway and sidings, well out of the way of the Luftwaffe. Southwick was closed from 25 September 1939 to 3 February 1941 while various works were carried out. *Michael Mensing*

Below:

BLS 'Scottish Rambler No 2' Joint Easter Railtour, 15 April 1963.

BRANCH LINE SOCIETY

SCOTTISH RAMBLER No 2 JOINT EASTER RAIL TOUR

Monday 15th April 1963

SCHEDULE
(subject to alteration without notice)

		a.m.			p.m.
Carlisle	dep	9.00			
Gretna Jct		(9.11)	Millisle Jct	dep	4.40
Lockerbie	arr	9.32	Wigtown		(4.58)
"	dep	9.34	Newton Stewart	arr	5.27
Shieldhill	arr	10.02	"	dep	5.34
"	dep	10.07	Kirkcowan		(5.44)
Dumfries	arr	10.24	Glenluce		(5.56)
"	dep	11.00	Dunragit		(6.01)
Killywhan		(11.13)	Castle Kennedy		(6.06)
Dalbeattie		(11.26)	Stranraer Town	arr	6.12
Castle Douglas	arr	11.36	"	dep	6.24
Kirkcudbright	dep	11.46	Castle Kennedy		(6.31)
"	arr	12.04p	Dunragit		(6.36)
Castle Douglas	dep	12.14	New Luce		(6.46)
"	arr	12.32	Glenwhilly		(6.54)
Crossmichael	dep	12.38	Barrhill	arr	7.08
New Galloway		(12.44)	"	dep	7.13
Loch Skerrow		(12.52)	Pinwherry		(7.20)
"	arr	1.00	Pinmore		(7.26)
Gatehouse of Fleet	dep	1.05	Girvan	arr	7.33
Creetown		(1.15)	"	dep	7.38
Newton Stewart		(1.21)	Maybole		(7.55)
"	arr	1.32	Ayr	arr	8.07
Wigtown	dep	1.38	"	dep	8.13
Millisle Jct		(2.07)	Troon		(8.23)
Whithorn		(2.38)	Irvine		(8.32)
"	arr	3.04	Kilwinning		8.42
Millisle Jct	dep	3.14	Dalry Jct		(8.45)
"	arr	3.40	Lochside		(8.54)
Garlieston	dep	3.55	Elderslie		(9.02)
"	arr	4.05	Paisley Canal		(9.05)
Millisle Jct	dep	4.15	Shields Road		(9.13)
"	arr	4.25	Glasgow St. Enoch	arr	9.18

Times in brackets are passing times.

The journey from Millisle Jct to Garlieston and back will be in open goods vehicles.

X - Cross 5.10pm Glasgow St. Enoch to Stranraer Harbour.
+ - stops or shunts for following trains to pass.

MOTIVE POWER

Carlisle to Stranraer Town:
(Exclusive of branches)   L.M.S. 6P "Jubilee" 4-6-0.

Castle Douglas to Kirkcudbright: L.M.S. 4MT 2-6-4T.

Newton Stewart to Whithorn
and Garlieston: C.R. 2F 0-6-0 or 2MT 2-6-0 (B.R.

Above:

**'Jubilee' No 45588 *Kashmir* makes a fine site near Killywhan on 15 April 1963 with the SLS/BLS 'Easter Tour',
seen earlier on the Whithorn line. Killywhan had a level crossing and 'box. Today, it is a private residence,
having been closed on 3 August 1959. (This train is seen again later in the book at Locharbriggs on the line
from Lockerbie to Dumfries.) *Roy Hamilton***

Above:

The 8.5am from Stranraer Town to Dumfries has just passed the site of Lochanhead station, which closed on 25 September 1939. 'Black Five' No 45254 heads the train on 20 July 1963, the summit of the climb from Dalbeattie was roughly at this spot. *Michael Mensing*

Upper left:
BR 2-6-4T No 80061 climbs the 1 in 73 to Lochanhead with the 8.20am from Dumfries to Stranraer Town on 29 May 1965. This was one of the last services, the Kirkcudbright trains having already ceased from 1 May while the 'Port Road' was to last until 14 June. *Roy Hamilton*

Lower left:
Ex-Caledonian Pickersgill '3F' 0-6-0 No 57661 heads a lengthy goods into Dumfries at Maxwelltown at 9.46am on 4 May 1962. The locomotive is in splendid condition and makes a fine sight. The Castle Douglas & Dumfries Railway was originally single-track but was doubled in the 1890s with the increase in traffic that was experienced with the development of the 'Port Road'. On closure of the line in 1965, this section, which had been singled again, still saw freight traffic to ICI at Cargenbridge, just further on from Maxwelltown. *David Holmes*

Upper right:
The Old Order, 1: 'Standard Goods' No 57349 gets away from Dumfries with the 6.2pm to Kirkcudbright on 11 August 1956. The train is passing the junction with the line to Glasgow, which is just visible to the left of the train. This must have been one of the last passenger workings by an ex-Caledonian locomotive as they were soon relegated to pilot and freight work with the advent of more modern LMS and BR types.
Roy Hamilton

Centre right:
The Old Order, 2: Ex-LMS three-cylinder Compound (classified '4P') No 40920 leaves Dumfries with the 6.30pm to Stranraer on 11 August 1956. The '4Ps' were common performers in the area, having been displaced from their former routes by the more powerful 'Black Fives'.
Roy Hamilton

Lower right:
The 'Port Road' left Dumfries just north of the station, with the Glasgow & South Western line to the right from where there was a further branch to Moniaive. Coming off the 'Port Road' on 15 August 1964 is 'Black Five' No 45480 with a lengthy all-stations freight from Stranraer.
W. A. C. Smith

Left:
It was fitting that BR Standard Class 4 2-6-0 No 76073 should work the last passenger train from Dumfries to Kirkcudbright. This was the 18.00 on Saturday 1 May 1965, strengthened to four coaches from the usual two. To the left of the train can be seen the track of the branch to Lockerbie, and the Caledonian St Mary's Yard is to the left of that. Closure of the 'Port Road' was to follow on 14 June 1965.
D. A. McNaught

Right:
The last passenger train to Stranraer via the 'Port Road' leaves Dumfries behind 'Black Five' No 45469 on 12 June 1965. The train was the 18.20 to Stranraer Harbour.
W. A. C. Smith

Left:
Former Caledonian locomotives long dominated the motive power on the 'Port Road' together with ex-LMS 4-4-0 Compounds. The advent of LMS 'Crabs', 'Black Fives' and the BR 'Clans' saw the 4-4-0s displaced and withdrawn, but the former 'Standard Goods' and '812' classes lasted longer, until replaced themselves by BR Standard and former LMS 2-6-4 tanks and BR 2-6-0s. 'Standard Goods' No 57302 and Caledonian '812' No 57623 are seen basking in the sunshine at Dumfries shed on 13 June 1959. *W. A. C. Smith*

Dumfries to Lockerbie

Historical perspective

The railway from Dumfries to Lockerbie opened on 1 September 1863, having been authorised originally as the Dumfries, Lochmaben & Lockerbie Railway on 14 June 1860.

The line had been backed by local businessmen who thought that a link between the two main lines that ran between Carlisle and Glasgow (the first being the Glasgow & South Western line via Kirkconnel, the second the Caledonian main line to Glasgow via Carstairs) would make money. The Glasgow & South Western regarded the line as a threat, as it would possibly bring Caledonian traffic into Dumfries and even considered trying to purchase a shareholding in the company. The main reason was that the G&SWR saw the new line as a way of transporting high-quality coal from the Lanarkshire coalfield to South West Scotland — at the expense of the Ayrshire coalfield and its traffic! The G&SWR also realised that the line could carry substantial traffic from the 'Port Road' — at its expense, so this led to the purchase of more shares in the Castle Douglas & Dumfries Railway.

The Caledonian had bid to operate the Dumfries, Lochmaben & Lockerbie Railway for only 30% of the annual income, a very low figure indeed, as it saw the line as a way of getting into Glasgow & South Western territory, with its eyes firmly on the

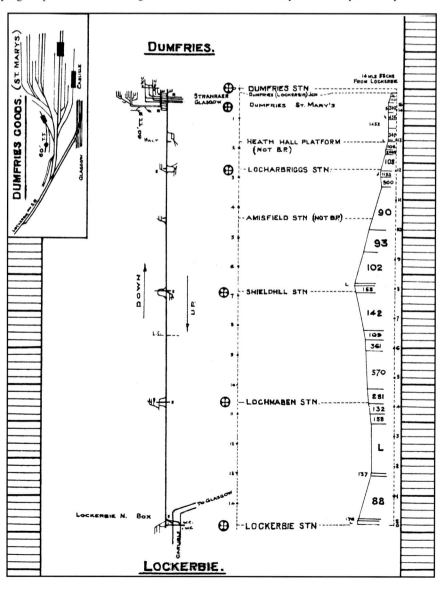

Right:
Gradient profile and track plans, Dumfries to Lockerbie.

'Port Road' line from Stranraer, which was, potentially, very good for business for it. The Portpatrick Railway at Castle Douglas had had a grudging relationship with the G&SWR after the latter had offered an advance of £40,000 in 1859 to assist with the line's finances — to be in return for the G&SWR's securing operating rights on the 'Port Road' at some 72% of income. As previously stated, this offer was turned down in favour of the Caledonian's, and in 1885 the Portpatrick Railway became the Portpatrick & Wigtownshire Joint Railway under a joint working arrangement with the LNWR, G&SWR, CR and MR. The G&SWR retained primacy from Dumfries to Castle Douglas, the Caledonian gaining running rights in exchange for the LNWR's gaining running powers over the former's line from Carlisle to Dumfries and then on to Castle Douglas.

The line was 14 miles 62 chains in length, with stations provided at (from Dumfries) Locharbriggs, Amisfield, Shieldhill and Lochmaben.

From Dumfries, trains to Lockerbie left the main line to Glasgow at Lockerbie Junction. Lockerbie Junction signalbox controlled all movements at the northern end of the station, one of (originally) five cabins at Dumfries. The Caledonian's St Mary's Yard was passed to the right, and after half a mile the line singled as the section to Locharbriggs commenced.

St Mary's Yard once had a locomotive shed for the Caledonian to work the line independently of the G&SWR, but this closed in 1923, as by then the locomotive had moved to the G&SWR shed. This locomotive was also used on an evening trip to Lockerbie, which had the evening milk traffic from the 'Port Road'.

After just under two miles there was a halt that served the Arrol-Johnston motor works at Heath Hall (special trains originally ran to and from here for workers), together with a private siding that had a run-round loop. Locharbriggs was reached just under three miles from Lockerbie Junction. At Locharbriggs there were quarries for red sandstone — many of the area's buildings are examples of this — and as well as a

passing loop there were sidings here for that traffic as well as general goods.

From Locharbriggs the line started to climb at 1 in 90 to the next station at Amisfield. Here were two sidings but no loop, and the climb continued for a further 2¾ miles to Shieldhill, where there was another passing loop and sidings. Just under seven miles from Lockerbie Junction, Shieldhill was the summit of the line, the trip from there to Lockerbie being nearly all downgrade.

After falling gradients, the line reached Lochmaben, with a loop and sidings, at just over 10½ miles. This was the last block post before Lockerbie, where there was a short bank of 1 in 80 for 1¾ miles before Lockerbie North signalbox was passed and the station was reached. At the station there was a run-round loop and a number of sidings for traffic off the line to be shunted across on to main line services — in the main, wagons were attached and detached for the Edinburgh area.

Passenger services
The initial service was five trains in either direction on weekdays, some running as mixed, although one train had been lost after the end of World War 2 when there were only four — all worked as motor train services. The working timetable for 1927 shows workmen's trains that ran out to Heath Hall and Locharbriggs at 6.55am and 1.30pm SX. The trains went on to Locharbriggs so that they could be run round, and then returned as empty coaching stock. The down service ran back from Locharbriggs at 12.10pm SX, 11.53am SO, with an evening service at 5.17pm SX. By 1947, there were still four motor trains from Dumfries to Lockerbie, leaving at 6.38am, 12.20 SX, 12.40 SO, 4.25 and 7.28pm. From Lockerbie, the same train set departed at 7.37am, 1.20 SX, 1.26 SO, 6.22 and 8.20pm.

In the summer of 1948 there were four trains per day in either direction. These left Lockerbie at 7.35am, 1.20, 6.23 and 8.20pm and called at all stations to Dumfries. In the opposite direction there were four more trains, the first leaving Dumfries at 6.38am

Left:
LMS working timetable, Dumfries to Lockerbie, 16 June to 5 October 1947.

Upper right:
BR ScR passenger timetable, 31 May to 26 September 1948 — Lockerbie-Dumfries.

Lower right:
BR ScR passenger timetable, 15 June to 6 September 1964 — Lockerbie-Dumfries bus service.

Table 12   Lockerbie and Dumfries

Table 12 — Lockerbie and Dumfries

	a.m		a.m		p.m		p.m		
Glasgow (Central) lev.	—	—	1046	—	4 0	—	5 40	—	
Edinburgh (Pr. St.) ,,	—	—	1040	—	4 5	—	5 35	—	
Carlisle ,,	5 14	—	1140*	—	4 30	—	6 10	—	
Lockerbie . . . lev	7 35	—	1 20	—	6 23	—	8 20	—	
Lochmaben . . .	7 43	—	1 28	—	6 31	—	8 28	—	
Shieldhill . . .	7 49	—	1 34	—	6 37	—	8 34	—	
Amisfield . . .	7 57	—	1 42	—	6 45	—	8 42	—	
Locharbriggs . . .	8 2	—	1 47	—	6 50	—	8 47	—	
Dumfries — — arr.	8 9	—	1 54	—	6 57	—	8 54	—	

	a.m		p.m		p.m		p.m		
Dumfries — — lev.	6 38	—	1220	—	4 25	—	7 30	—	
Locharbriggs			1227		4 32		7 37		
Amisfield	6 47		1233		4 38		7 43		
Shieldhill			1238		4 43		7 48		
Lochmaben	7 0		1245		4 51		7 56		
Lockerbie — — arr.	7 7		1253		4 58		8 3		
Carlisle arr.	1026		1 52		6 50				
Edinburgh (Pr. St.) ,,	9 27		3 51		7 40		1050		
Glasgow (Central) ,,	9 30		3 45		7 30		1045		

Table 13 — Beattock and Moffat

	a.m		a.m		a.m		a.m		a.m		a.m		p.m		p.m		p.m		p.m		p.m	
Glasgow Central Stn. lev.			7 0				9*15		1030		1046						4 10		4 45		5 40	
Edin. (Pr. St.)			6 47		8 50		1010		1040		1140*		2 2		4 5		4 50		5 35			
Carlisle lev.	5 14														4 34				5 20			
Beattock lev.	6 45		8 30	9 15	1015		12 0	1220	1250	1 55			3 10		4 15		5 35		6 5		6 49	7 35
Moffat arr.	6 50		8 35	9 20	1020		12 5	1225	1255	2 0			3 35		4 25		5 40		6 10		6 53	7 40

	a.m		a.m		a.m		a.m	p.m		p.m	p.m		p.m		p.m		p.m		p.m		p.m	p.m		p.m	
Moffat — lev.	7 20		9 0		9 50		1145	1210		1230	1 15		2 10		3 5		4 0		5 15	5 50		6 25		7 20	7 45
Beattock arr.	7 25		9 5		9 55		1150	1215		1235	1 20		2 15		3 10		4 5		5 20	5 55		6 30		7 25	7 50
Carlisle arr.			1026		1147*				1245	1 18		1 52					5 20			6 50		7 47		8 25	
Edin. (Pr. St.)	9 27		1222							3 31					5 20		7 40	7 47						1050	
Glasgow Cen	9 30		1215				2*25		3 20			4*35		5*54			7 30	7 55						1045	

Table 14 — Symington, Biggar, and Peebles

	a.m	a.m	Sats only p.m	Ex Sats p.m	Ex Sats p.m	Sats only p.m	p.m	p.m	
Glasgow (Central) lev.	7 0	1046	1225	2 0	4 45	5 40	—		
Edinburgh (Pr. St.) ,,	6 47	1040	1223	1 0	4 50	5 47	.		
Carlisle ,,	5 14	8 50		1252	3 50	3 50			
Symington . . . lev.	8 34	12 4	1 45	3 30	6 5	7 7			
Coulter — — . .	8 38	12 8	1 49	3 34	6 7	7 11			
Biggar — — . .	8 42	1211	1 52	3 37	6 10	7 14			
Broughton — — . .	8 51	1219	2 0	3 45	6 18	7 22			
Stobo — — . .	8 59	1227	2 8	3 53	6 26	7 30			
Lyne (Halt) — — . .	9 6	1234	2 15	4 0	6 33	7 37			
Peebles . . . arr.	9 11	1239	2 20	4 5	6 38	7 42			

	a.m	a.m	a.m	Sats only p.m	Ex Sats p.m	Sats only p.m	Ex Sats p.m	Ex Sats p.m	Sats only p.m	
Peebles . . . lev.	7 40	9 55	1255	5 5	5 30	—	4 19	7 5	8 5	
Lyne (Halt) . . .	7 46	10 1	1 11	5 6	5 35	R	4 24	7 11	8 11	
Stobo . . .	7 53	10 8	1 18	3 33	43		4 32	7 18	8 18	
Broughton . . .	8 0	1014	1 14	9	3 49		4 38	7 24	8 24	
Biggar . . .	8 8	1022	2 22	1 13	5 7	4 3	4 46	7 40	8 32	
Coulter . . .	8 13	1027	2 27	2 24	2 4	7	4 51	7 45	8 37	
Symington arr.	8 17	1031	1 31	2 26	4	4 11	4 55	7 51	8 41	
Carlisle arr.	1026		1225	2 15	5 20	6 50	6 50	10 0	10 0	
Edinburgh (Pr. St.) ,,	9 27		1222	3 31	3 15	5 20	6 15	10 0	10 0	
Glasgow (Central) ,,	9 30		1215	3 45	4 55	4 55	6 25	9 47	10 5	

Table 15 — Dumfries and Moniaive

The Passenger Train Service between Dumfries and Moniaive has been discontinued.
The Caledonian Omnibus Company operate an Omnibus Service over the route.

* Saturdays only   † Except Saturdays   Except Mondays   Mondays only   L Via Lanark
R Saturdays 10-30 a.m   J Calls to take up, on notice to Station Master the previous day
R Does not run during Local School Holidays .   s Via Carstairs   TC Through Carriages   V Sats. 5-45 p.m.   Z Change Motherwell

---

Table 62   DUMFRIES and LOCKERBIE

WESTERN S.M.T. CO., LTD., PORTLAND STREET, KILMARNOCK

Week Days

Outward from Dumfries	am		pm		pm		pm		pm		GW pm		GS pm		GS pm														
Dumfries Whitesands dep	6 25	..	1215	..	2 30	..	4 15	..	5 0	..	7 15	..	9 0	..	..	..	..	..	..	..	..	..	..	..	..			
Locharbriggs	..	..	..	..	..	..	..	..																				
Amisfield	..	..	..	..	2 40	..			5 10	..			9 10	..														
Shieldhill	..	..	..	..	2 50	..			5 20	..			9 20	..														
Lochmaben	6 53	..	1243	..			4 43	..			7 43	..																
Lockerbie Bridge St... arr	7 5	..	1255	..			4 55	..			7 55	..																

Inward to Dumfries	am		am		am		GW am		pm		GS pm		WS pm		GS pm		S pm		S pm		S pm	
Lockerbie Bridge St. dep	7 10	..	7 30	..	8 0	..	..	..	1 0	..	1 30	..	6 0	..	..	..	6 30	..	8 30	..	9 30	
Lochmaben	7 22	..	8 0	..	8 12	..	..	..	12	..	1 42	..	6 12	..	..	..	6 42	..	8 42	..	9 42	
Shieldhill	..	..	8 18	..	..	..	1010	..	1 40	..			6 40	..			..	..	..	..	..	
Amisfield	..	..	8 25	..	..	..	1020	..	1 45	..			6 50	..			..	..	..	..	..	
Locharbriggs	..	..	8 30	..	..	..	1023	..	1 53	..							..	..	..	..	..	
Dumfries Whitesands arr	7 50	..	8 40	..	8 40	..	1030	..	1 40	..	2 0	..	2 10	..	6 40	..	7 0	..	7 10	..	9 10	.. 1010

G Operated by Messrs. James Gibson & Sons, Moffat.   S Saturdays only
W Wednesdays only.   WS Wednesdays and Saturdays only

(not calling at Locharbriggs, Amisfield being on request to the stationmaster the previous day, not Shieldhill, but calling at Lochmaben) before terminating in Lockerbie at 7.7am. This train then formed the return 7.35am to Dumfries. Other services left Dumfries at 12.20, 4.25 and 7.30pm, all working out from Dumfries and returning there at the end of the day's work.

By the early 1950s the line's local passenger receipts had fallen, and the cost of providing the local services was seen to be cheaper by bus. An alternative arrangement was made by British Railways to advertise the replacement road service, thus withdrawing the trains, and the line was closed to regular passenger traffic from 19 May 1952. This was not quite the end in terms of passenger services, however, as a number of excursions ran on the line in its latter days. These included the SLS 'Golden Jubilee' special with GNSR No 49 on 13 June 1959 and the SLS/BLS 'Easter Tour' on 15 April 1963 with 'Jubilee' No 45588 *Kashmir*. On 15 May 1965 a special from Lincoln to Castle Douglas, hauled as far as Dumfries by preserved Gresley 'A3' No 4472 *Flying Scotsman*,

returned via the line, as the Pacific could not be turned on the Dumfries turntable for the return run to Carlisle.

The replacement bus services were operated in the main by Western SMT, with some other services being offered by James Gibson & Sons of Moffat. Although providing a direct link between Lockerbie and Dumfries, they did not offer a similar link for the local stops in between; only one service from Lockerbie, the 07.30, called at 'all stations', and the route did not include the railway stations. This may have been justified, as intermediate use was light, but it was another example of the loss of a railway passenger service that was not replicated by the alternative buses.

Freight services

Internally, freight traffic had been generated from the quarries at Locharbriggs; there was a daily freight from Dumfries to and from here and the engine factory at Heath Hall. The other stations received coal and general merchandise traffic, and there was a daily pick-up from the other stations, but the larger volumes of traffic passed from Lockerbie to and from St Mary's Yard for exchange with the 'Port Road'. This included coal, dairy traffic, some livestock, and latterly, some parcels traffic, but virtually all at night.

The LMS working timetable for 1947 shows two 'milk empties' services, one being a train from the Edinburgh area. In the up direction, there was a 9.40pm 'milk' from Carnation at Maxwelltown to Perth. As can be seen, these trains also ran on Sunday mornings and evenings.

From the end of World War 2 there was a daily freight trip that called at all local stations in both directions, together with a Saturday service. In addition, in 1952, milk services still used the route, but much reduced, and only in the down direction at 8.15am MO (empties), from Lockerbie to Dumfries, with more empties daily from Edinburgh at 7.30pm. This train left Lockerbie at 7.30pm for St Mary's Yard only. It ran two hours later, at 9.33pm on Sundays. There was one more service that ran MX, from Lockerbie, at 2.5am — this being a parcels service to Dumfries.

Above:
BR freight working timetable, Lockerbie-Dumfries, Summer 1955.

Left:
BR freight working timetable, Lockerbie-Dumfries, 11 September 1961 to 17 June 1962.

The Summer 1955 freight working timetable illustrates the basic one trip working per day that ran on the line. This worked out from Dumfries, as Trip K92, at 10.20am SX and called at all local stations to Lockerbie where it arrived at 12.35pm. It then worked back to Dumfries at 1.40pm, calling at all stations and arriving back at Dumfries for 3.55pm. On Saturdays, the trip left at 7.20am calling additionally at Heath Hall Works where it shunted coal wagons.

It arrived in Lockerbie at 9.45 and by 10.30am it was on its way back home to Carlisle, arriving at 12.55pm. The trip — K93 — that shunted St Mary's Yard is also shown leaving Dumfries at 7.25, returning from St Mary's 11.45am as well as Trip K96 which left Dumfries as light engine at 2.55am having run to Lockerbie and arriving at 3.25am and then picked up wagons from Edinburgh. This trip then arrived back at Dumfries at 5am, 4.15am off Dumfries. On Saturdays only, Trip K94 worked out from St Mary's Yard at 3.45pm with traffic that was to be attached for an Edinburgh goods at Lockerbie. This trip then returned from Lockerbie at 6.40pm, running nonstop to Dumfries, arriving at 7.25pm.

By the period 15 June to 13 September 1959 the line saw just one trip in the working timetable, all the milk traffic having gone; the 2.5am parcels from Lockerbie to Dumfries ran on weekdays.

The Trip Book for 5 January 1959 shows a night turn (K64) which took Edinburgh traffic out from Dumfries at 11.40. The engine then worked the 2.5am parcels back to Dumfries, where it then shunted St Mary's Yard, returning at 3.13am, arriving back at Lockerbie at 3.48am. It then finished its work, leaving at 4.15am with traffic for Dumfries. A second trip (K68) worked out from Dumfries at 2.15pm with a Class K pick-up service to Lockerbie, arriving at 3.55pm. It left Lockerbie at 4.10pm and then returned to St Mary's at 5.20pm.

From 11 September 1961 to 17 June 1962 services consisted of the 2.5am MX parcels from Lockerbie to Dumfries, the 8.20am MO milk empties and more milk empties from Edinburgh, which ran forward to Shieldhill and Dumfries St Mary's Yard at 7.30pm (but is shown as 'Suspended'). On Sundays, this latter milk train departed at 9.33pm, having left Edinburgh at 7.15pm. There were no timetabled services in the up direction.

Freight traffic was finally withdrawn from 18 April 1966 as the demise of the 'Port Road' a year earlier and the loss of dairy, parcels and other through traffic, the main reason the line had come into being in the first place, had been removed.

Dismantling of the line began in September 1966, the train working from the Dumfries end. The junction with the G&SWR was taken out in July of that year, with the train gradually working back to Lockerbie.

Above:
Shieldhill station, with No 49 and its train on 13 June 1959. Just after this point the line descended to Amisfield and Locharbriggs. *Stuart Sellar*

Below:
Locharbriggs station plays host No 49 on the special train. The passing loop is on the up side, unlike at Shieldhill and Lochmaben, where it was on the down. *Stuart Sellar*

Beattock to Moffat

Historical perspective

The Moffat Railway was authorised in 1881, opening on 2 April 1883, two years being taken to construct a line of just 1 mile 71 chains in length. As with many lines, it was taken over, in 1902, by the Caledonian, who had previously operated it, and at the Grouping it became part of the London Midland & Scottish Railway.

A classic small branch line, built mainly in the hope that the spa in Moffat would generate significant traffic, it once boasted a through service to Glasgow and was the home of a steam railcar, No 10657, for many years. There was also a daily mixed train to and from Beattock, and after the railcar had gone the passenger service was converted to a railmotor push-pull type operation. The line always had a good service of passenger trains, which may have had something to do with the number of railway staff that lived in Moffat who worked at Beattock, with as many as 13 services on weekdays before World War 1.

Despite what must have been small operating costs, the line was never destined to be a survivor, even pre-Beeching. Passenger services were withdrawn from 4 December 1954, the last train being seen off from Moffat by the town's Provost and the local beauty queen. Freight services continued until 6 April 1964, operated as a trip working from Beattock.

Train services

In the Caledonian period, passenger services were normally provided by a train that comprised two four-wheel coaches plus an eight-wheeler, normally worked by Drummond 0-4-4 tank No 194, plus other locomotives that may not have been required on banking duties. Drummond 4-4-0 mixed traffic locomotives were also used on the line, the most common being Nos 84 and 198, but sometimes a 'Dunalastair' 4-4-0 was used — a rare treat.

The timetable allowed six minutes for the journey, with the exception of the through 'express' working that left for Glasgow — known locally as the 'Tinto', as was the Caledonian's train from Peebles and Symington to Glasgow, which allowed only four! Named after a mountain near Symington, this train left Moffat at 7.28am, Beattock arrival was 7.32am, with a departure at 7.35am, calling at all stations to Carstairs and then fast to Motherwell and Glasgow.

The branch engine would haul the train to Beattock and then a larger locomotive would take the train forward to Glasgow. This was, for many years, 'Dunalastair' 4-4-0 No 778. The train consisted of three 12-wheeled corridor coaches, complete with destination boards.

In the mid-1920s the line was operated by an ex-LNWR steam railcar, No 10657, in conjunction with a more conventional tank locomotive and a single coach. The railcar survived at Beattock until after World War 2, before services reverted completely to locomotive and coach on a push-pull railmotor system.

The LMS working timetable dated 16 June to 5 October 1947 shows 15 trains per day — one fewer on Saturdays — all worked by railmotor with the exception of some services which ran as mixed trains. The first of these was the 6.45am from Beattock, which tripped loaded wagons inwards (and any empty requirements for loading) to Moffat. The 10.25am ran out as locomotive and coach, working a return from Moffat at 10.40, before leaving Beattock again at 11.5am. After allowing some time for shunting, it worked the 11.45am mixed train back to Beattock. The 12.50 and the 2.40pm would also work back as mixed with customers' loaded wagons as required. There were certainly enough locomotives due to the large amount of activity at Beattock shed, the banking engines, usually Caley '431' class 0-4-4 tanks, providing the power.

MOFFAT BRANCH (Worked by Steam Rail Motor)—WEEK DAYS ONLY

Miles		1	2	3	4	5	6	7	8	9	10	11	12	13	14	15	16
						A	**AB**										
		a.m.		a.m.	a.m.	a.m.	a.m.		p.m.		p.m.	p.m.	p.m.				
0	MOFFAT .. .. dep.	7 20	..	9 0	10 0	10 40	11 45	..	12 35	..	1 30	2 20	3 0	..	..	..	..
2	BEATTOCK ...... ♀ .... arr.	7 25	....	9 5	10 5	10 45	11 50	....	12 40	....	1 35	2 25	3 5	....	....	....	....

		17	18	19	20	21	22	23	24	25	26	27	28	29	30	31	32	33
				SX														
				p.m.		p.m.		p.m.		p.m.		p.m.		p.m.				
	MOFFAT .. .. '' .. dep.	..	...	4 5	..	5 10	..	5 50	...	6 25	..	7 20	....	7 45	..	..	..	..
	BEATTOCK .... ♀ .... arr.	....	...	4 10	...	5 15	....	5 55	...	6 30	...	7 25	....	7 50	....	....	....	...

Miles		1	2	3	4	5	6	7	8	9	10	11	12	13	14	15	16
		B					**A**	**A**			**D**			**D**			
		a.m.		a.m.		a.m.	a.m.	a.m.		p.m.	p.m.		p.m.	p.m.		p.m.	
0	BEATTOCK .. ♀ .. dep.	6 45	..	8 30	..	9 15	10 25	11 5	..	12 20	12 50	..	2 0	2 45	....	3 25	..
2	MOFFAT .... arr.	6 50	....	8 35	....	9 20	10 30	11 10	...	12 25	12 55	....	2 0	2 45	....	3 30	....	....

		17	18	19	20	21	22	23	24	25	26	27	28	29	30	31	32	33
				SX														
				p.m.		p.m.		p.m.		p.m.		p.m.		p.m.				
	BEATTOCK .. ♀ .. dep.	..	4 20	..	5 35	..	6 7	..	6 45	..	7 35	..	..	..	..	..	...
	MOFFAT ....arr.	....	4 25	....	5 40	....	6 12	....	6 50	....	7 40	....	....	....	....	....	...

A—Worked by Engine.
B—Mixed Trains.
C—Mixed Train
D—Mixed Train SX.

Left:
LMS working timetable, Moffat branch, 16 June to 5 October 1947.

Right:
BR working timetable, Moffat branch, 30 June 1952.

MOFFAT BRANCH (Worked by Motor Train)

WEEK DAYS ONLY   THIRD CLASS ONLY

Miles		1	2	3	4	5	6	7	8	9	10	11	12	13	14	15	16
	Class	B				B	B		B(SO)		B	B(SO)	B				
0	MOFFAT .. dep.	a.m. 7 25				a.m. 10 0	a.m. 11†43		p.m. 12 20		p.m. 1 35	p.m. 2 10	p.m. 3 5				
2	BEATTOCK arr.	7 30				10 5	11†48		12 25		1 40	2 15	3 10				

		17	18	19	20	21	22	23	24	25	26	27	28	29	30	31	32	33
	Class		B		B	B	B					B		B				
	MOFFAT .. dep.		p.m. 3 53 (SX)		5 25	5 45	6 5					7 20		7 45				
	BEATTOCK arr.		3 58		5 30	5 50	6 10					7 25		7 50				

Miles		1	2	3	4	5	6	7	8	9	10	11	12	13	14	15	16
	Class	B				B	B	B(SO)			B		B	B(SO)			B
0	BEATTOCK .. dep.	a.m. 6 45				9 10	10 20	Noon 12 0			p.m. 12♯40		2 0	2 25			p.m. 3 30
2	MOFFAT arr.	6 50				9 15	10 25	12p 5			12♯45		2 5	2 30			3 35

		17	18	19	20	21	22	23	24	25	26	27	28	29	30	31	32	33
	Class		B	B	B						B		B					
	BEATTOCK .. dep.		p.m. 4 10 (SX)	5 35	5 55						6 42		7 35					
	MOFFAT arr.		4 15	5 40	6 0						6 47		7 40					

†—Mixed Trains.
D—P.B. 6.11 p.m.
§—Mixed Train SX.

Above:
BR Train, Trip & Shunting Engine Notice S.7. Beattock No 6 Shunt, 5 January 1959.

S.7.
Beattock No.6 Shunt.
Class 4 MT. Engine.

6.15am to 2.15pm SX.
6.30am to 2.30pm SO.

Beattock Guard.

6.15am to 2.15pm SX.
6.30am to 2.30pm SO.

	SX. Arr. a.m.	S.X. Dep. a.m.	Class
Beattock E.S.	-	7.30	LE.
	S.O. Arr. a.m.	S.O. Dep. a.m.	
Beattock E.S.	-	7.15	LE.

Shunts Motive Power Coal Bench Repair Siding and Beattock Yd. Makes trip at 9.30am dly. to Moffat arriving 9.35am. Works return trip from Moffat at 10.25am due Beattock 10.30am. Works 12.10pm SO. 'B' Beattock to Summit and 1.12pm 'B' Summit to Beattock.

Assist as required between 1.0pm and 2.0pm SX.

Right:
BR working timetable, Beattock to Moffat, 8 June to 20 September 1953

BEATTOCK AND MOFFAT   WEEKDAYS

DOWN

	B	B	B	B	B	B	B	B	B	B	B	B	B	B
	Rail Motor	Rail Motor	Rail Motor	Rail Motor	Mixed	Rail Motor	Rail Motor	Rail Motor	Rail Motor	Rail Motor	Rail Motor	Rail Motor	Rail Motor	Rail Motor
				SO	SX	SO		SO		SX				
BEATTOCK dep	am 6 45	am 9 10	am 10 20	PM 12 10	PM 12 40	PM 12 40	PM 2 0	PM 2 30	PM 3 30	PM 4 10	PM 5 35	PM 5 55	PM 6 42	PM 7 35
MOFFAT arr	6 50	9 15	10 25	12 15	12 45	12 45	2 5	2 35	3 35	4 15	5 40	6 0	6 47	7 40

UP

	B	B	B	B	B	B	B	B	B	B	B	B	B	B
	Rail Motor	Rail Motor	Mixed	Rail Motor	Rail Motor	Rail Motor	Rail Motor	Rail Motor	Rail Motor	Rail Motor	Rail Motor	Rail Motor	Rail Motor	Rail Motor
				SO		SO		SX			‡6.11 pm			
MOFFAT dep	am 7 22	am 10 0	am 11 50	PM 12 20	PM 1 35	PM 2 10	PM 3 5	PM 3 53	PM 5 25	PM 5 45	PM 6 5	PM 7 20	PM 7 45	
BEATTOCK arr	7 27	10 5	11 55	12 25	1 40	2 15	3 10	3 58	5 30	5 50	6‡10	7 25	7 50	

By 1952 the number of services had been reduced to 11 on weekdays, with 12 on Saturdays from Moffat, and similar in the opposite direction. Mixed trains still featured, with the passenger services operated on the push-pull principle. However, the exception was the mixed trains when the locomotive would marshal the train with the wagons behind the coach and then pull the train back to Beattock. Only one mixed service a day back to Beattock was now officially timetabled, this being the 12.40pm from Moffat, the train having left Beattock at 11.43am. It was allowed just under an hour to shunt the sidings at Moffat and prepare the train for the return journey.

As the 1953 working timetable shows, this pattern of continued roughly into BR days, with one mixed service, the rest being railmotors. Passenger services were withdrawn from 6 December 1954, replacement buses in the area being operated by James Gibson & Sons of Moffat and Blue Band Motors of Lockerbie.

After the line had closed to passengers on 6 December 1954, a daily freight trip continued. These workings were shown in the 'Trip Book' as turn S7, for Beattock No 6 Shunt, rostered for a Class 4MT locomotive which was one of the bankers. This turn worked to Moffat at 9.30am on Mondays to Saturdays, arriving at 9.35am. After dropping off wagons, shunting and delivering operational supplies, it left for Beattock at 10.25am, arriving there at 10.30am, from where it went on to 'Assist as required' with banking duties. Another train also ran, semi unofficially, for railway staff on Saturdays which connected at Beattock for Glasgow or Carlisle. Freight services were finally withdrawn on 6 April 1964.

A journey on the branch to Moffat started from the bay platform at Beattock station on the Caledonian main line. It diverged from the main line at Milepost 40. Beattock is more renowned for its location at the bottom of a 10-mile climb to Beattock Summit at 1,015ft above sea level on the West Coast main line. The station consisted of up and down platforms, with two loops on the down side for recessing trains that were awaiting banking engines. As well as this important activity, passenger services called at Beattock in the form of stopping services from Carlisle to Motherwell and Glasgow.

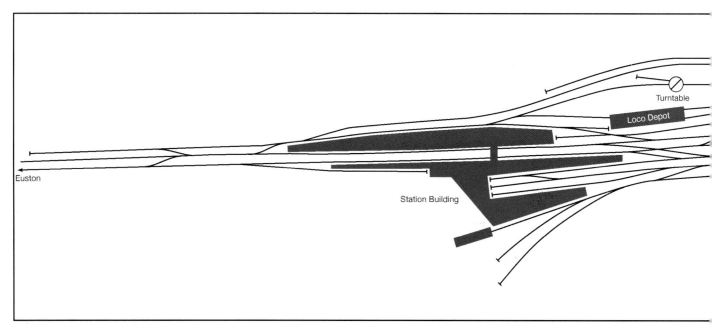

Above:
Track plan of Beattock.

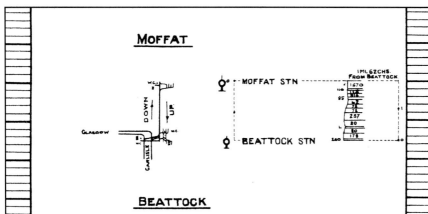

Left:
**Gradient profile and track plan,
Beattock to Moffat.**

Below:
Track plan of Moffat.

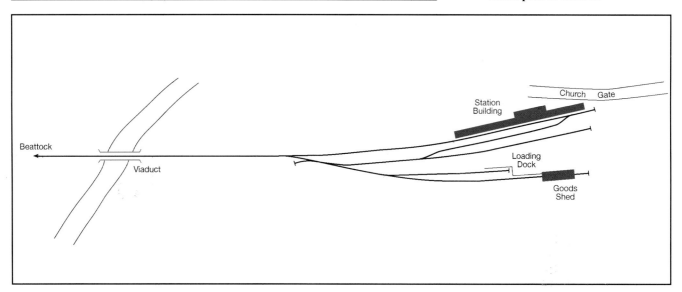

On the down side was the stabling point and turntable for the bankers as well as the Moffat engines — shed coded 68D. The main station buildings were on the up side and the approach road led to a number of railway cottages known as Craigielands.

Moffat trains left from a bay platform situated on the up side and ran alongside the up main line in a northerly direction, passing under a road bridge before turning east and away from the main line into a cutting on a falling gradient of 1 in 80, then over Dragons Pool on the Elvan Water (bridge No 3) and under the main road bridge out of Beattock (bridge No 5) before emerging

from the cutting. The line straightened out for the run to Moffat, running roughly parallel to the road linking Beattock to Moffat.

After underbridge No 7, the line ran through a small cutting and then crossed the aforementioned road (bridge No 8) as it traversed the flood plain of the River Annan, an area where no fewer than 10 culverts were crossed in less than a quarter of a mile. To the south of the cutting is the site of Three Standing Stones, which marks the scene of a 13th-century battle. Immediately before Moffat station the

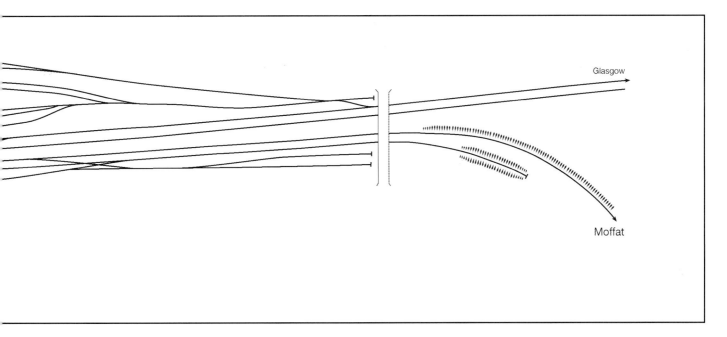

line was carried over a small viaduct (bridge No 21) across the River Annan. Still on an embankment, a set of points signified the start of the station area. Carrying straight on, the line reached the platform, where there was a run-round loop and a siding. Further to the right of these were two more sidings, one with an unloading dock and the other which ran into a small goods shed. All of these sidings and the run-round loop were protected from the main line by a set of catch points. Immediately to the front of the station was a small gasworks, the recipient of coal traffic, while to the south was a slaughterhouse. Small station buildings were provided on the platform — these were attractive in style, as can be seen from the accompanying photographs. The entrance into Moffat was by Church Gate, the church being situated to the north of the station and clearly visible in many of the illustrations.

Below:
A pair of Clayton diesels, Nos D8543 and D8572, approach Beattock station with a freight for Carlisle Kingmoor in the early 1960s. The Moffat line can be seen running off to the right, above the cab of the leading locomotive, as can the headshunt of the sidings on the Moffat bay side of the main line. The line fell away at 1 in 80 before a relatively level run of 1 mile 71 chains. *T. G. Hepburn/Rail Archive Stephenson*

Right:
A general view of Moffat station and yard, showing the platform with the attractive station canopy that befitted a spa town. On 4 December 1954 No 55232 and its motor train occupy the platform road and coal wagons can be seen in the sidings and yard to the right, where there is a goods shed and a small crane. *W. A. C. Smith*

Below:
After the withdrawal of passenger services, Fairburn 2-6-4T No 42192, one of the banking engines from Beattock, works the daily branch freight, being seen at Moffat on Trip S7 on 3 April 1961. This train arrived at Moffat at 9.35am, before shunting and departing for Beattock at 10.25am. *A. Tyson*

Peebles West to Symington

Historical perspective

In 1846 a proposal to build a line from the main Caledonian route at Symington to Peebles — the 'Caledonian Extension Railway' — was put before Parliament. It was rejected, not least because of opposition from the North British Railway, which had planned its line to Peebles from Edinburgh in July 1855, with an extension to Galashiels planned to open in October 1864. Thus the Caledonian's scheme progressed in the form of the Symington, Biggar & Broughton Railway, incorporated on 21 May 1858 and opened on 5 November 1860; it was extended to the Caledonian station at Peebles on 1 October 1864, the same day the NBR's Peebles-Galashiels line opened, together with a spur connecting the two. However, this connection was used only for freight traffic and latterly for wagon storage at Peebles West, the Caledonian station.

The Caledonian station at Peebles was situated on the south bank of the River Tweed, and, although trains from Symington terminated there, services were not extended to connect with the North British station at Peebles New (later Peebles East), even in BR days! In pre-Grouping days travellers from Galashiels hoping to travel via the Caledonian route from Peebles to Glasgow were frustrated by the timing of the NBR's trains, which were timed to arrive ten minutes after the Caledonian's train had departed. This meant that NBR passengers had to travel via Edinburgh Waverley to Glasgow Queen Street, a longer route!

Leaving Peebles, the line passed along the south bank of the River Tweed before entering Neidpath Tunnel (where, in World War 2, the Royal Train was stabled overnight when the King and Queen visited the Clyde shipyards to view bomb damage). Following the tunnel under Cademuir Hill came a viaduct over the river from where Neidpath Castle could be seen, which was once attacked by Oliver Cromwell in 1650. The first station was Lyne Halt, and 3½ miles further on Stobo station was reached, named after the castle, as there was no village, the station being built to serve the castle and surrounding farms. A further 4½ miles from Stobo came Broughton, the original terminus of the line from Symington. Here was the first block post and passing loop with two platforms, one of which was built as an island with a further face for projected additional traffic associated with the Talla Reservoir.

From Broughton, which forwarded meat and agricultural traffic as well as receiving livestock and coal, came the Talla Railway, as detailed earlier, which left the Caledonian line ¾ mile before Broughton was reached from Peebles. From Broughton, a further 4½ miles saw the line reach Biggar, where there was another loop, signalbox and sidings mainly for agricultural and meat traffic, and the town itself saw much commuter travel to and from Glasgow.

Between Biggar and Symington was Coulter which had a single platform face and sidings for freight and livestock which were controlled from a small ground frame situated on the platform. After the station the line crossed the River Clyde on a girder viaduct before arriving at Symington, passenger trains terminating at an island platform on the up side of the West Coast main line.

Passenger traffic

Not surprisingly, the relationship with the NBR at Peebles was not good. Peebles was almost a commuting area for Glasgow as well as Edinburgh and was a town that attracted a number of weekend visitors and holidaymakers. As a result, the Caledonian and NBR services were competing with each other. Peebles saw two trains that ran to Edinburgh, one via the North British route, 'The

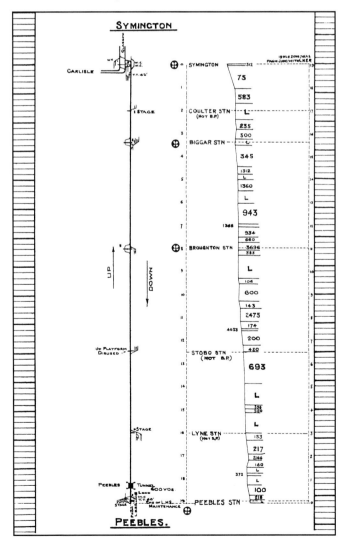

Side plan and gradient profile — Peebles to Symington.

97

WEEK DAYS (columns 1–16)

Miles	Station	1 PARCELS 6.10 a.m. from Carstairs	2	3	4 MIXED	5	6	7 PASSENGER	8	9	10 PASSENGER	11	12	13 PASSENGER	14	15	16 EMPTY STOCK 3.0 p.m. from Carstairs
					SX									SO			SX
		a.m.			a.m.			a.m.			p.m.			p.m.			p.m.
0	SYMINGTON .. ⊕ ..dep.	6 24	..	...	...	..	..	8 34	...	...	12 6	..	...	1 45	...	...	3 22
2	Coulter							8 38			12 10			1 49			
3¼	Biggar ....⊕..{ arr.	6 30						8 42			12 13			1 53			3 30
	Biggar ....⊕..{ dep.	6 31						8 44			12 14			1 54			
8	Broughton ....⊕..{ arr.	6 40						8 52			12 21			2 2			
	Broughton ....⊕..{ dep.	6 41			8 8			8 54			12 22			2 3			
12½	Stobo	6 49			8 30			9 1			12 28			2 10			
16	Lyne							9 7			12 35			2 16			
19	PEEBLES ....⊕.... arr.	7 2			8 45			9 13			12 41			2 22			

(Column 2 note: Does not run on local School holidays. Column 4 note: Not advertised. Column 15 note: Terminates at Symington on local School holidays.)

WEEK DAYS (columns 17–26) / **SUNDAYS** (columns 1–6)

Station	17	18 PASSENGER	19	20	21 PASSENGER	22	23	24 PASSENGER	25	26	1	2	3	4	5	6
		SX			SX			SO								
		p.m.			p.m.			p.m.								
SYMINGTON .. ⊕ ..dep.		3 37	..		6 0	..		7 10	..							
Coulter		3 41			6 4			7 14								
Biggar ....⊕..{ arr.		3 45			6 8			7 19								
Biggar ....⊕..{ dep.		3 46			6 10			7 20								
Broughton ....⊕..{ arr.		3 53			6 18			7 28								
Broughton ....⊕..{ dep.		3 54			6 19			7 29								
Stobo		4 1			6 27			7 36								
Lyne		4 7			6 33			7 42								
PEEBLES ....⊕.... arr.		4 13			6 39			7 48								

(Columns 25–26: COMMENCES SUNDAY SERVICES)

WEEK DAYS (columns 1–16)

Miles	Station	1 PASSENGER	2	3	4 PASSENGER to Carstairs	5	6	7 PASSENGER	8	9	10 PASSENGER	11	12	13 PASSENGER	14	15	16 PASSENGER
								SO			SX			SO			SX
		a.m.			a.m.			p.m.			p.m.			p.m.			p.m.
0	PEEBLES.. .. ⊕ ..dep.	7 40			9 55	..		12 55	..		1 40	..		3 20	..		
3	Lyne	7 46			10 1			1 1			1 46			3 26			
6½	Stobo	7 54			10 8			1 8			1 53			3 33			
11	Broughton ....⊕..{ arr.	8 1			10 15			1 15			2 0			3 40			
	Broughton ....⊕..{ dep.	8 2			10 16			1 16			2 1			3 41			
15½	Biggar ....⊕..{ arr.	8 9			10 23			1 23			2 8			3 48			
	Biggar ....⊕..{ dep.	8 10			10 24			1 24			2 9			3 49			3 55
17	Coulter	8 14			10 28			1 28			2 13			3 53			3 59
19	SYMINGTON .. ⊕ .. arr.	8 18			10 32			1 32			2 17			3 57			4 3

(Column 1 note: Arr. 7.52 a.m. Column 15 note: Does not run on local School holidays.)

WEEK DAYS (columns 17–26) / **SUNDAYS** (columns 1–6)

Station	17	18 PASSENGER	19	20	21 PASSENGER to Lanark	22	23	24 PASSENGER to Carstairs	25	26	1	2	3	4	5	6
		SX			SX			SO								
		p.m.			p.m.			p.m.								
PEEBLES.. .. ⊕ ..dep.		4 25	..		7 5	..		8 12	..							
Lyne		4 31			7 11			8 18								
Stobo		4 38			7 18			8 25								
Broughton ....⊕..{ arr.		4 45			7 25			8 32								
Broughton ....⊕..{ dep.		4 46			7 26			8 33								
Biggar ....⊕..{ arr.		4 53			7 33			8 40								
Biggar ....⊕..{ dep.		4 54			7 40			8 41								
Coulter		4 58			7 45			8 45								
SYMINGTON .. ⊕ .. arr.		5 2			7 51			8 49								

(Column 20 note: Mixed from Biggar, when required. Columns 25–26: COMMENCES SUNDAY SERVICES)

Left:
LMS working timetable, Peebles branch, 1947.

Upper right:
BR ScR timetable, 31 May to 26 September 1948 — Symington, Biggar and Peebles.

Lower right:
BR ScR Train Trip & Shunting Engine Notice, 5 January 1959 — 'Until Further Notice' trip No S13.

Far right:
BR ScR timetable, 15 June to 6 September 1964 — Symington-Peebles bus service.

Peeblesshire', the other via the Caledonian route, the 'Tinto', which divided at Symington for Glasgow, while NBR passengers had to change at Edinburgh for Glasgow. The 'Tinto' left Peebles West at 7.45am and called all stations to Symington, where it split into portions for Glasgow and Edinburgh, giving arrival times of 9.30am and 9.32am respectively.

In the year before Nationalisation there were four weekday passenger services, two others running Saturdays excepted, one for early morning schools traffic, the other an afternoon school train that ran through to Carstairs in term times. There was also passenger traffic to and from local towns to the high school in Biggar. On Saturdays there were additional services, while a daily parcels service also ran from Symington to Peebles.

In 1948 there were still four trains per day, Mondays to Saturdays, giving good connections at Symington for Glasgow Central and Edinburgh Princes Street. But it was unlikely, even pre-Beeching, that a town like Peebles would retain two passenger stations and routes to Edinburgh or Glasgow.

There was already a good local bus service that ran with no fewer than 11 services a day, plus extras to and from Biggar, so it came as no surprise that passenger services were withdrawn from 5 June 1950 (although a local schools service remained to and from Biggar until arrangements were made with the bus company) and that BR chose to advertise the bus service in future timetables.

Freight traffic
The line ran through a prime agricultural area so it was not surprising that the main type of forwarded traffic was associated with that industry, this being livestock, grain, beet and root crops. Coal, farm machinery and fertilisers were the main inward traffic. The chief source of income was from meat traffic from Broughton and Biggar, and

Table 14   Symington, Biggar, and Peebles

	a.m	a.m		Sats only	Ex Sats		Ex Sats	Sats only				(Central)	a.m		Sats only	Ex Sats	Sats only	Ex Sats		Ex Sats		Ex Sats		Sats only	
					p.m		p.m	p.m					a.m	a.m	p.m	p.m	p.m	p.m	p.m	p.m	p.m	p.m	p.m	p.m	
GLASGOW (Central) lev.	7 0	1046	—	1225	2 0	—	4 45	5 40	—	Peebles — — — lev.		7 40	9 55	1255	1 50	3 30	—	4 19	—	7 5	—	8 5	—
EDINBURGH (Pr. St.) ,,	6 47	1040	.	1223	1 0	.	4 50	5 47	.	Lyne (Halt) . . .		7 46	10 1	1 1	1 56	3 35		4 25		7 11	—	8 11	.
CARLISLE __ __ ,,	5 14	8 50	.	—	1252	.	3 50	3 50	.	Stobo		7 51	9 56	1 8	2 3	3 43	R	4 32		7 18	—	8 18	.
Symington . . lev.	8 34	12 4	.	1 45	3 30	—	6 3	7 7	.	Broughton . . .		7 53	3 0	1014	2 9	3 49	.	4 38		7 24	—	8 24	.
Coulter _ _ _ _	8 38	12 8	.	1 49	3 34	.	6 7	7 11	.	Biggar		8 8	1022	1 22	2 17	3 57	4 3	4 46		7 40	—	8 37	.
Biggar	8 42	1211	.	1 52	3 37	.	6 10	7 14	.	Coulter		8 13	1027	1 27	2 22	4	4 7	4 51		7 45	—	8 37	.
Broughton _ _ _ .	8 51	1219	.	2 0	3 45	.	6 18	7 22	.	Symington __ arr.		8 17	1031	1 31	2 26	4	4 11	4 55		7 51	—	8 41	.
Stobo	8 59	1227	.	2 8	3 53	.	6 26	7 30	.	CARLISLE . . arr.	1026H	9 27	1228	3 21	5 20	6 50		6 50		1234s	a	1234s	a
Lyne (Halt) _ _ _	9 6	1234	.	2 15	4 0	.	6 33	7 37	.	EDINBURGH (Pr. St.) ,,	9 27	1222	3 31	3 31	5 20	5 20		6 15		10 0	—	10 0	.
Peebles . . . arr.	9 11	1239	.	2 20	4 5	.	6 38	7 42	.	GLASGOW (Central) ,,	9 30	1215	3 45	3 45	5 45	5 55		6 25		9L47	.	10 5	.

Table 64	**SYMINGTON and PEEBLES**																									
	CENTRAL S.M.T. CO., LTD., HAMILTON ROAD, MOTHERWELL																									

Week Days

Outward from Symington	am	am	am	am	E am	S am	E am	S am	pm	pm	pm	pm	S pm	pm	pm	pm	pm	pm	pm	pm	pm	pm	pm	pm	S pm
Symington Police Stn. dep	6 40	7 35	8 40	9 40	1040	1040	1140	1240	1240	402	403	40	..	4 40	..	5 40	6 40	7 40	..	8 40	9 40	1040	..
Biggar	6 50	7 45	8 50	9 50	1050	1050	1150	1253	1253	532	533	50	..	4 50	..	5 53	6 50	7 50	..	8 53	9 50	1053	..
Skirling School	..	7 51	..	9 56	..	1056	1156	..	1259	592	593	56	..	4 56	..	5 59	6 56	7 56	..	8 59	9 56	..	..
Broughton Hall	..	8 4	..	10 9	..	..	12 9	..	..	2 12	..	4	9	4 59	..	6 12	7 9	8 9	..	..	10 9	..	1129
Rachan	..	8 9	..	1014	..	..	1214	..	..	2 17	..	4	14	..	..	6 17	7 14	8 14	..	..	1014	..	1134
Drumelzier Post Office	..	8 14	..	1019	..	..	1219	..	..	2 22	..	4	19	..	..	6 22	7 19	8 19	..	..	1019	..	1139
Stobo Hall	..	8 24	..	1029	..	..	1229	..	..	2 32	..	4	29	5 19	..	6 32	7 29	8 29	..	..	1029	..	1149
Blyth Bridge	..	..	..	1111	..	..	..	..	1 11	..	..	4	..	..	..	..	..	9 11	..	..	..	..	..
Lyne Railway Station	..	8 33	..	1038	..	1133	1238	..	1 362	413	364	385	285	33	..	6 41	7 38	8 38	..	9 36	1038	..	1158
Peebles High Street . . arr	..	8 41	..	1046	..	1141	1246	..	1 442	493	444	465	365	41	..	6 49	7 46	8 46	..	9 44	1046	..	12 6

Inward to Symington	am	E am	S am	am	am	am	am	am	E am	S am	am	pm	pm	pm	pm	E pm	S pm	pm	pm	pm	pm	pm	pm	pm	pm	S pm
Peebles High Street . . dep	..	6 55	7 5	..	9 5	..	1010	1 5	..	..	1210	..	52	10	..	3 54	5 5	5 6	10 7	..	5 8	10 9	5 ..	1050
Lyne Railway Station	..	7 3	7 13	..	9 13	..	1018	1113	..	..	1218	1 32	18	..	3 13	4 13	5 13	5 6	13 ..	..	5 ..	..	..	1058
Blyth Bridge	..	..	..	..	..	..	1040	..	..	..	1240	2 40	..	..	..	6 40	..	8 40	..	..	..	..	..	..
Stobo Hall	..	7 12	7 22	..	9 22	..	1122	..	..	..	..	22	..	3 22	4 22	5 22	5 22	..	7 22	..	9 22	..	11 7
Drumelzier Post Office	..	7 22	7 32	..	9 32	..	1132	..	..	..	..	32	..	3 32	4 32	5 32	5 32	..	7 32	..	9 32	..	1117
Rachan	..	7 27	7 37	..	9 37	..	1137	..	..	..	..	37	..	3 37	4 37	5 37	5 37	..	7 37	..	9 37	..	1122
Broughton Hall	..	7 32	7 42	..	9 42	..	1142	..	..	..	..	42	..	3 42	4 42	5 42	5 42	..	7 42	..	9 42	..	1127
Skirling School	..	7 36	7 46	..	9 46	..	..	1055	1155	..	..	1255	5 52	55	..	3 55	4 55	5 55	5 56	55 7	55 8	55 9	55 ..	..
Biggar	..	7 17	5 18	8 19	6 10	1 11	11 12	1 ..	..	1 12	13 1	..	4 15	16	17	18	19	1 10	11 1	..	11 14	..	..
Symington Police Stn. arr	7 14	8 4	8 14	9 19	1011	11 11	11 11	1211	..	..	1 41	1 42	11 3	11 ..	4 14	5 14	6 14	11 7	11 8	11 9	11 10	11 14	..

E Saturdays excepted.   S Saturdays only

this was handled by a daily freight service; on occasions a further train was run 'as required'. In Caledonian days these trains were run as mixed services. During the construction of the Talla Reservoir a number of stone trains ran on the line, leaving it at Broughton.

In LMS days the daily freight service was also supplemented by a morning parcels train that ran between Symington and Peebles, this service being withdrawn in the BR era when all such traffic from Peebles was transferred to the NBR route. With little freight business generated between Broughton and Peebles, this was withdrawn upon closure of the passenger service in June 1950, but the meat traffic and other merchandise survived the closure, the line between Broughton and Symington remaining open. This saw daily operation, including Sundays, retained on the line. As well as coal and other general agricultural goods, meat was hauled back to Symington, from where it was then sent forward on a Class C service for Carlisle Upperby and London Broad Street (for Smithfield Market). Timber was also forwarded to the wagon works at Faverdale.

The January 1959 *The Railway Magazine* carried a piece on the current status of the line at that time. 'More than half the branch of the former Caledonian Railway from Symington on the main line from Carlisle to Edinburgh, to Peebles has been dismantled. Mr Ivor J. Smith writes that, when he visited the line recently, he found that the track had been lifted from Broughton (eight miles east of Symington), to a point near Peebles, about midway between the tunnel and the Caledonian station, a distance of about 10½ miles. The signalbox at the station is in use for the daily goods train over the connecting line from Peebles East (the former North British station). The engine of this train is turned at the Caledonian station.'

Traffic to Peebles West continued but only via Peebles East and the NBR connection. This centred mainly around wagon storage, and by 1 August 1959 this part of the route was finally closed. The connection from Peebles Junction to Peebles West was lifted by November 1961.

Broughton to Symington finally closed on 4 April 1966, the meat traffic being converted to road haulage in new refrigerated trucks. The line was lifted in December 1966, and by 1967 Symington station had been demolished, although a small area of platform and a water column were still extant.

Above:

'J37' 0-6-0 No 64614 of St Margarets shed arrives at Peebles East Junction with the track-lifting train off the line to the Caledonian station at Peebles West on 14 November 1961. By this time the line was severed from Peebles West to Broughton, the former link to West station having been retained for wagon storage at the station. The lines in the foreground are those of the North British 'Peebles Loop' from Galashiels to Hardengreen Junction, near Edinburgh. *Stuart Sellar*

Track plan of Peebles (Caledonian).

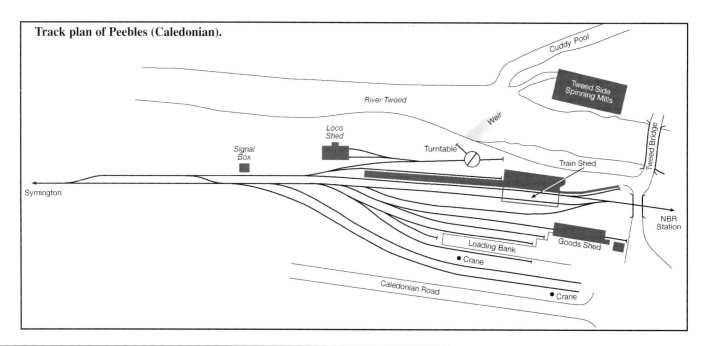

Right:
Another pre-Nationalisation view of the immaculate station at Peebles West, with a number of enamel signs in view. The line through bridge No 6 in the distance disappears to Peebles East. *John Langford collection/Stations UK*

Left:
Contrasting with the earlier photographs, things now look in a very run-down condition as Class J37 No 64614 leaves Peebles West for Peebles East with the track-lifting train on 14 November 1961. *Stuart Sellar*

Right:
Ex-Caledonian McIntosh '19' class 0-4-4T No 55124, built in 1895, stands at Broughton on 30 September 1961. Although passenger services had been withdrawn on 5 June 1950, the line later saw a handful of specials. This one was organised by the Branch Line Society and was grandly titled the 'Pentlands-Tinto Express', echoing the former Caledonian service to Glasgow and Edinburgh. At the time this locomotive was the last member of the class in operation. The train is in the sidings at the station, the locomotive running round for the trip back to Symington. *Roy Hamilton*

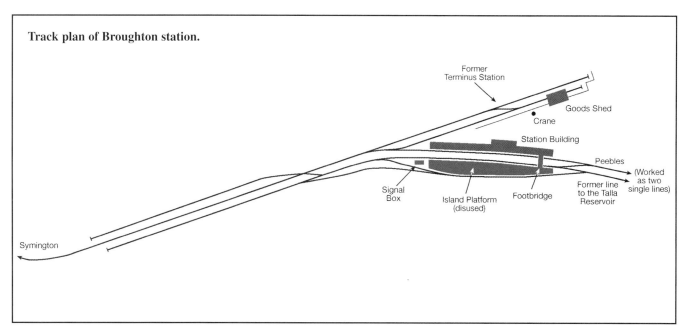

Track plan of Broughton station.

Former Terminus Station

Goods Shed

Crane

Station Building

Peebles

(Worked as two single lines)

Former line to the Talla Reservoir

Signal Box

Island Platform (disused)

Footbridge

Symington

Centre left:
Broughton station, seen on 27 February 1960. The goods sidings and shed are to the left behind the main platform and the platform to the right is an island, although now devoid of track. At this time, there was still significant meat traffic forwarded from both here and Biggar. The formation off to Peebles in the distance was originally double track, for it was from here that the line to the Talla Reservoir ran. This was a single line parallel with the Peebles route before it diverged to the south from the 'main' line. There was once a footbridge just beyond the station buildings which linked the two platforms. *Stuart Sellar*

Lower left:
'Crab' 2-6-0 No 42737 of Ayr shed on a special at Broughton on 29 March 1964. This was the BLS/SLS 'Scottish Rambler No 3' tour. Broughton originally had a locomotive shed when it was the terminus of the line, (this becoming the goods yard), until the line was extended to Peebles, at which point the shed was closed shortly afterwards. The island platform for the Talla Railway can be seen to the left. *Stuart Sellar*

Upper right:
**No 42737 again, this time
approaching Broughton with the
'Scottish Rambler No 3'. This
train also visited the Moffat
branch on the same day. The
freight service had been
withdrawn between Peebles and
Broughton on 7 June 1954.**
Roy Hamilton

Centre right:
**The next station towards
Symington was Biggar, where No
55124 is seen on 30 September
1961 with the 'Pentlands-Tinto
Express', recorded earlier at
Broughton. In the background
are a number of wagons used for
meat traffic, the main reason the
line from Symington had been
retained; there was a
slaughterhouse at Biggar, and this
traffic ran to Symington and
thence to London for Smithfield
Market.** *Roy Hamilton*

Lower right:
**No 42737 at Biggar on 29 March
1964 with the 'Scottish Rambler
No 3' tour. The centre of an
agricultural area, Biggar
generated considerable traffic, the
sidings being to the right of the
signalbox, mainly for meat traffic
from here and Broughton. Freight
services between Biggar and
Broughton were finally
withdrawn on 4 April 1966.**
R. B. Parr

Left:

Seen at Biggar on 2 May 1962, 'Black Five' No 45161 heads back to Carstairs Junction with the branch freight trip (S13). This worked the general merchandise and coal deliveries to the branch and conveyed meat traffic off it, as required; more meat wagons can be seen in the area of the station. Even as late as this, the *Railway Observer* **reported that '[Biggar signalbox] is nicely painted up and still sports a nameboard; however, there is absolutely nothing in the way of instruments, frame, etc inside. An LNWR crane endorsed "Loco Department — Huddersfield" is scotched onto some rails on a pedestal stranded on the goods loading bank and is used for loading containers on to the motor lorry's trailer.'** *Stuart Sellar*

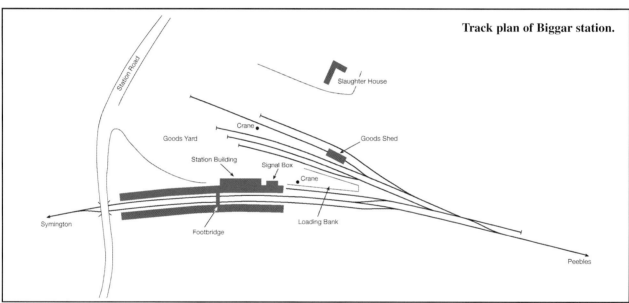

Track plan of Biggar station.

Left:

Coulter station, where there were two sidings, was also visited by No 45161 on Trip S13 on 2 May 1962. The train is pausing on its way to Broughton. The station here has now been converted into a residential dwelling. Just beyond the station was the bridge over the River Clyde. *Stuart Sellar*

Above:
No 45161 seen again later the same day, crossing the River Clyde at Coulter by means of the 339ft, seven-span bridge and heading for Broughton.
Stuart Sellar

Centre right:
Symington station on 9 June 1949. Class 4P No 40903 is seen with the 12.08pm Symington–Peebles.
SLS collection

Lower right:
'Crab' 2-6-0 No 42832 pauses at the Peebles platform at Symington with the empty stock from a special on 16 July 1960.
Stuart Sellar

Riddings Junction — Langholm

Historical perspective

The coming of a railway to Langholm was not without a degree of fighting between the two great rivals — the North British and the Caledonian. The North British Railway wanted to extend its line from Edinburgh to Hawick which had opened on 1 November 1849, as it was keen to reach Carlisle and gain its own route between England and Scotland, removing its dependency on the North Eastern Railway. The North British had already applied to extend the line from Hawick to Langholm and Carlisle in 1845 — putting it on the Waverley Route — but this was objected to by the Caledonian who, with its partner, the London & North Western, wanted at all costs to stop the NBR reaching Carlisle. The objection was successful, but this did not stop things and alternative plans were put forward that missed Langholm altogether, the railway passing through Liddelsdale instead. The Caledonian's spoiling tactic was to apply for its own route to Hawick (not using the NBR station in Hawick, but a new terminus!) via Langholm, which was approved, the NBR's plans again being rejected. The town of Hawick was outraged, a public meeting was held and a petition drawn up, which was followed by an appeal to the House of Lords. As a result, the Caledonian's route was vetoed, and the plans for the NBR's direct route were reinstated.

The implications for Langholm were that it would not now be on the direct line from Carlisle to Edinburgh (the NBR scheme ran through Liddelsdale) and thus a seven-mile branch would be necessary from the new Riddings Junction — known as 'The Moat' locally — to allow a connection to Edinburgh or Carlisle.

Because they had been denied a shorter, through route to Edinburgh, passenger fares from Langholm were set on a mileage 'as the crow flies' basis, but interestingly, this applied only to Langholm, it being more expensive to travel to Edinburgh from Gilnockie or Canonbie.

The route described

The line to Langholm was extended from the railway that ran from Riddings to Canonbie where there was a coal mine at Rowanburn, which had been opened in 1862. From Canonbie, the line was opened on 11 April 1864 to both passenger and freight traffic, running through the Esk Valley. Intermediate stations were provided at Canonbie, which had been open since May 1862, and at Gilnockie, which followed the opening of the whole line, in December 1864.

Almost immediately, a crisis arose that stopped passenger services: Byreburn Viaduct, situated between Canonbie and Gilnockie, suffered a structural collapse leading to train services being withdrawn and passengers having to walk across the viaduct to a replacement service that ran to and from Langholm! Repairs were completed by 2 November.

The branch ran from an island platform at Riddings Junction parallel to the Waverley Route before turning away to the north west and climbing at 1 in 60 to Canonbie, which was 1½ miles

from the junction. The first major feature was the viaduct over Liddel Water, a magnificent nine-arch structure that still stands today.

Before Canonbie station was reached, to the right of the line were sidings associated with the colliery at Rowanburn. The station was originally named Canobie, incorrectly, by the NBR but was later (from 1902) amended to the correct spelling of Canonbie. There was originally a signalbox here, but this was closed as early as 1924 as the colliery workings reduced significantly.

Following Canonbie station, the climb continued to the aforementioned viaduct at Byreburn. This structure was also of nine arches and was on a level grade; thereafter there was a dip to the next station, Gilnockie, some 2¾ miles from Riddings.

Gilnockie was opened in 1864 and had a loop and siding for the small amount of freight it received, usually a wagon of coal, but some timber was also forwarded from here. A small lever frame, situated on the platform, controlled the level crossing at the Riddings end of the station. Despite having a stationmaster in NBR and LNER days, the station became unstaffed in 1953. However, the crossing keeper remained.

Shortly after Gilnockie came the third viaduct, at Tarras — 13 arches — before Glentarras Siding was reached. Glentarras Siding was just that, a siding that had been put in to serve the distillery and also a tile works. Traffic was never heavy and the siding became the first casualty on the branch, being closed and lifted in 1955.

The approach to Langholm station, seven miles from Riddings Junction, was reached on a falling gradient of 1 in 90. The station was situated on the level and had a signalbox, a small locomotive shed, turntable, platform with overall roof (later demolished), and a number of goods sidings to serve local industry, farmers and merchants. When the LNER introduced the steam railcar services the shed closed in May 1932; the turntable had also been removed some years earlier to provide much needed metal for use in World War 1. The war also saw an increase in passenger traffic generated from the ammunition factory at Gretna — trains made a special stop at Glentarras, where workers were billeted in the distillery. Other military specials also used the line, transporting troops and equipment for training exercises.

Following the war, even in the 1930s, as with other branch lines, passenger use was not great, so to effect economies the line was operated by steam railcars *Protector* and *Nettle*. These found some of the gradients, especially the two miles at 1 in 60 from Riddings Junction to the viaduct at Byreburn, difficult to handle, but nevertheless, they remained in traffic until World War 2, supplemented by the daily branch freight and a number of excursions, primarily Sunday outings from Langholm to various destinations. There were also specials run for Boy Scouts who alighted at Glentarras where there was a camp.

With hostilities returning in 1939, as with all lines, traffic

increased in the war years and the town's proximity to munitions depots at Longtown as well as Army training areas saw significant growth in all commodities as well as an increase in inbound coal traffic for various mills and the forwarding of finished cloth. Again, special locomotive-hauled trains took workers to the factories, and there were trains of military vehicles such as tanks that were unloaded at the station for despatch to units. Wagons were forwarded from Gilnockie loaded with wood cut from local forests.

When all this extra war business came to an end in 1945, the line reverted to carrying on average only 400 passengers a week. Freight was also in decline, the sidings at Glentarras closing in 1955. (It could be argued that this rationalisation had started with the demolition of Langholm turntable in World War 1, the closure of the block post at Canonbie in 1921, the closure of Langholm engine shed in 1932, and the demolition of its train shed during World War 2.)

With the eagle eye of the accountants firmly on many lines of this type it is perhaps a little surprising that Langholm was not closed to passengers until 1964. Further economies had been made from 21 August 1960, when the electronic token working on the line was discontinued and the signalbox at Langholm closed. The line was then operated on the one-engine-in-steam principle, but this was not enough.

Notices for closure were posted following Scottish TUCC approval which was given on 9 September 1963. BR announced that passenger services would end on 15 June 1964. This announcement was made rather late, and was carried in newspapers only a week before the last train was to run on 13 June.

Train services
The original passenger service offered five return workings per day. These left Riddings Junction at 8.55, 10.39am, 2.40, 4pm and 7pm. In the opposite direction trains left Langholm at 8am, 10.8am, 2.3, 3.28 and 6.20pm. Connections were made at Riddings Junction for Waverley Route destinations and all trains called at Gilnockie and Canonbie. The NBR used an 0-6-0 tank locomotive, No 22 *Langholm* on most services, these being formed of four and six-wheeled coaches that ran to and from Riddings Junction.

Originally there were two passenger trains that ran on Sundays. These fell foul of local religious opinion and were also poorly patronised so they were withdrawn in early 1865, never to return, the only Sunday trains being excursions and specials.

By 1922 there were six departures starting from Langholm, at 7.5, 8.7, 9.34am, 12.55, 3.10 and 6.30pm, the last two running to Carlisle. From Riddings, trains left at 7.40, 8.45, 10.11am and 1.34pm. Two other departures came back from Carlisle, at 4.50 and 7.53pm, departing Riddings at 5.28 and 8.29pm.

With weekday traffic never substantial, the LNER introduced steam railcars in the 1930s to operate the service. These had gone by World War 2 and the service in 1944 consisted of seven departures from Langholm. The 7.12 and 8.51am both ran as far as Riddings Junction; the 10.54am, 1.20, 3.26 SX, 3.33 SO, 6.24 and 9.32pm all worked through to Carlisle.

In the down direction there were departures from Riddings at 7.47 (the balancing working of the 7.12am ex Langholm), the rest of the trains being through services from Carlisle that left Riddings at 9.55am, 1.58 SX, 2pm SO, 5.24 and 8.54pm.

As the shed at Langholm was closed in 1932, the coaches for the first train ran out ECS from Canal Yard with any wagons. They returned later that day on a through service. In the middle of the day, the branch freight had visited the line and shunted Langholm and the other local stations as required. Passenger trains carried the perishables out, such as milk in churns, and brought in newspapers, parcels and foodstuffs, including fish.

Postwar, the Summer 1948 timetable shows a similar pattern to the LNER wartime one. Trains left Langholm at 7.12, 9am, 11am SX, 11.15am SO, 1.25, 3.20, 6.24 and 9.40pm. These were balanced from Riddings by the 7.47, 10.2am, 2.10, 5.33, 9.1pm, the afternoon trains running to and from Carlisle. Gilnockie is also mentioned in the timetables as Claygate; this had started in NBR days and it just lived on until closure. The branch freight ran in between the 10.2am and 2.10pm departures from Riddings.

The BR working timetable for the Langholm branch from September 1953 shows the first train on the branch as the 5.25am from Carlisle Canal Yard, which conveyed wagons and the ECS

Above:
LNER passenger timetable, 22 May 1944 — Riddings and Langholm.

Right:
BR ScR passenger timetable, 1 May to 26 September 1948 — Riddings and Langholm.

LANGHOLM BRANCH

UP TRAINS — **WEEKDAYS**

	No.	58	60	228	442	62	444	446	446	448
	Description	Mxd.								
	Class	B	B	B	B	K	B	B	B	B
M. C.										
			am	am	am	SO PM	SX PM	PM	SX PM	SO PM	SO PM
	Langholm ....⑤..	7 5	9 2	10 42	....	1 2	12 45	3 28	6 22	6 25	9 33
4 26	Gilnockie (for Claygate)	7 18	..	......	..	1 13	..	1 15	3 39	6 33	6 36	9 44
5 59	Canonbie	7 24	..	10 54	....	1 18	..	1 25	3 44	6 38	6 41	9 48
7 8	Riddings Junction ⑤..	7 28	9 17	10 58	..	1 22	..	1 35	3 48	6 42	6 45	9†53
	Arrives at	Carlisle 11.24 a.m.						Carlisle 4.16 p.m.	Carlisle 7.23 p.m.	Carlisle 7.13 p.m.	Canal Yard 10†12 p.m.
	Forward Times on Page	W27						W29	W31	W 31	W 32

No. 58—Three additional minutes to be allowed
when an attachment is made at Gilnockie, and five
minutes when an attachment is made at Canonbie.
Nos. 58, 442, 444, 446 and 448—Time allowed at Gilnockie for guard doing station duties.

No. 448—Departs Canonbie 9†49 p.m.

LANGHOLM BRANCH

DOWN TRAINS — **WEEKDAYS**

	No.	555‡	99	229	295	218	103	259	259	277	
	Description				§	ECS					
	Class	K	B	B	G	C	B	B	B	B	
	Departs from	Carlisle 5.25 a.m.			Canal Shed 11.20 a.m.	Canal Yard 12.0 noon		Carlisle 5.8 p.m.	Carlisle 5.8 p.m.	Carlisle 8.26 p.m.	
	Previous Times on Page	W37			W40	W 40		W42	W42	W43	
M. C.											
			am	am	am	SX am	SO PM	PM	SO PM	SX PM	SO PM	
	Riddings Junction ⑤ ..	6 7	7 45	10 4	....	11 40	12 20	....	2 0	5 34	5 38	8 54	....
1 29	Canonbie ..		7 50	10 9	....				2 5	5 39	5 43	8 59	....
2 62	Gilnockie (for Claygate) ..		7 57	10 16	....				2 12	5 46	5 50	....	
7 8	Langholm ....⑤..	6 35	8 6	10 25	..	12 0	..	12 40	..	2 21	5 55	5 59	9 12	..

Nos. 99, 229, 103 and 259—Time allowed at Gilnockie
for guard doing station duties.

Above:
**BR working timetable, Langholm branch,
21 September 1953.**

for the first train back to Riddings which left at 7.28am. This train then returned to Langholm at 7.45am and worked back to Riddings at 9.2am. It ran fast to Riddings and returned at 10.4am; it then worked back at 10.42 to Carlisle, where it arrived at 11.24am. The intervening period allowed time for the branch freight, and on Saturdays only a 12.20pm ECS ran out to Langholm from Carlisle to form the 1.2pm SO back to Riddings, where it arrived at 1.22pm.

On weekdays, a light engine left Carlisle Canal at 11.20am to travel to Langholm where it arrived at 12 noon — it worked the 12.45pm SX goods back to Carlisle. Then there was a 2pm train from Riddings Junction, arriving at Langholm at 2.21pm; this then formed the 3.28pm to Carlisle. Back from Carlisle came the 5.38pm SX (5.43pm SO) to Langholm, this service returning to Carlisle at 6.22pm SX and 6.25pm SO. This left one more service that ran SO which was the 8.26pm from Carlisle, arriving at Langholm at 9.12pm, before returning as far as Canonbie only at 9.33, the rest of the journey to Canal Yard was ECS.

On the motive power side, common performers were 'J35' and 'J39' class 0-6-0s, but Ivatt Class 4MT 2-6-0 tender locomotives of the 43000 series from Carlisle Canal shed

eventually replaced them, Nos 43000, 43011 and 43139 being the most common performers on the Langholm services. In the spring of 1961 some ex-LMS Fowler, Fairburn and Stanier 2-6-4 tank locomotives arrived at Carlisle Canal and started appearing on the Langholm trains. On 1 July the 5.18pm from Carlisle to Langholm and its return working at 6.23pm were hauled by No 42210. This general pattern of operation remained until the end of passenger services. On 2 May 1964 BRCW Type 2 diesel No D5236 worked the 17.18 to Langholm from Carlisle. It also then headed the 20.33 service, having probably substituted for a failed Ivatt 2-6-0.

The general closure frenzy that followed the Beeching Report saw the final services running on the line (despite objections made to the Scottish TUCC) on 13 June 1964, the last train being hauled by one of the line's regular performers, No 43139. This locomotive had been allocated as new to Carlisle Canal shed in 1951.

The train was the 20.33 from Carlisle strengthened to five coaches, which required a stop at Riddings Junction to raise steam for the run to Canonbie. Local people turned out in force along the line to witness the passing of one hundred years of service. Three pipers played a lament and another band, this time fife and drums, played 'Auld Lang Syne' as the 21.33 return working from Langholm pulled out for the last time. This train usually ran on passenger service to Canonbie only, and from there it continued as empty stock to Carlisle Upperby, but on this final run it carried passengers to Carlisle Citadel station, and another 'Borders' rail service ceased that could have been extremely useful today.

Passenger services were advertised in the BR Scottish Region Summer 1964 timetable as being operated by Scottish Omnibuses, which ran to and from Hawick (where there would be Waverley Route services for a few more years), and Western SMT, which operated a service in the opposite direction, to and from Carlisle.

But that was not quite the end for passenger services. On Sunday 26 March 1967 Ivatt Class 4MT No 43121 hauled a railtour on the line, that had originated from Glasgow Central with 'Britannia' No 70032 *Tennyson* in charge. The 2-6-0 took over the train at Carlisle and worked it to Alston as well as Langholm. Problems were experienced at Langholm as the five-coach train was extremely tight for the loop there. As a result, the tender of No 43121 scraped the side of the rear coach! The train returned to Glasgow via the G&SWR route, hauled by '9F' 2-10-0 No 92009.

Freight services

From originally being a colliery railway from Riddings to Canonbie, on the opening of the line through to Langholm, a daily branch freight served the line, and the general pattern saw the following traffic:

Canonbie

Forwarded: coal (until *c*1926)
Received: general merchandise, newspapers and parcels

Gilnockie

Forwarded: timber
Received: coal, general merchandise, newspapers and parcels

Glentarras (closed 1955)

Forwarded: whisky
Received: coal

Langholm

Forwarded: cattle, textile products, whisky, general merchandise, parcels
Received: coal, general merchandise, newspapers, parcels and agricultural supplies

In addition to this day-to-day traffic, other goods were brought into the area as required. In 1910 the Eskdalemuir observatory was constructed, and the majority of building materials for this were brought in by rail.

World War 1 saw military specials to Longtown near Carlisle in connection with the construction of the military depot at Gretna; this period also saw a large number of military specials on the line for training purposes, and these were often double-headed.

World War 2 also saw an increase in military traffic, most notably armoured vehicles being brought in for delivery to and from training areas.

After the war there was still a daily branch freight, shown in the 1953 working timetable as a Class G freight that ran out to Langholm from Carlisle Canal Yard at 11.20am SX, arriving in Langholm at 12 noon. It then returned at 12.45pm SX and called to shunt at Gilnockie and Canonbie. In addition, the first up passenger service of the day, the 7.5am from Langholm to Riddings Junction, was run as a mixed service as required and was allowed extra time for attaching wagons at Gilnockie and Canonbie.

On closure of the passenger service, in 1964, the track layout at Langholm was rationalised, but the freight services then ran twice daily. Prior to this there had been just one dedicated freight service, as outlined above. The 18.32 SO and 18.22 SX from Langholm to Carlisle also used to pick up RAF traffic in the form of vans from Harker; withdrawal of the passenger service meant that a trip working had to be instated specially for this traffic.

In August 1965 the line's working was the E118 trip, Carlisle-Langholm-Newcastleton-Carlisle. On 1 December 1965 this was powered by BR Standard tank No 80113 from Hawick, but more usually it was hauled by an Ivatt Class 4 2-6-0 from Carlisle. Hawick shed closed on 15 January 1966, and it was thus rare to see locomotives from the northern end of the Waverley Route on the line.

Freight traffic was finally withdrawn on 18 September 1967. The vast majority of traffic had been coal inwards and the original intention had been to close the line from August 1967, but the new coal distribution depot at Longtown that was to replace the sidings at Langholm was not ready for service. Thus, the goods service which now ran on only three days per week, continued to run for a further month and seemed to be the preserve of Type 1 diesel locomotives, and during September Nos D8071, D8081, D8093, D8098, D8101 and D8112 were rostered. The Langholm trip had also served Newcastleton as required, and this responsibility was transferred to the new working.

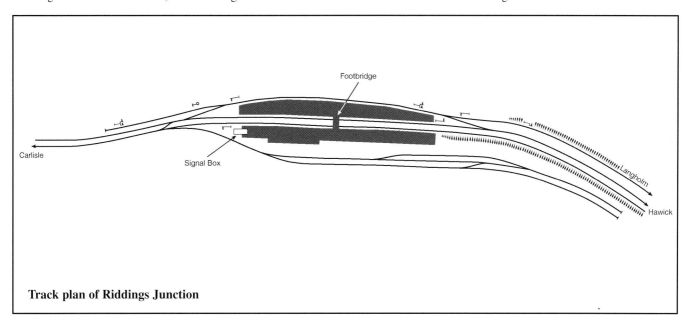

Track plan of Riddings Junction

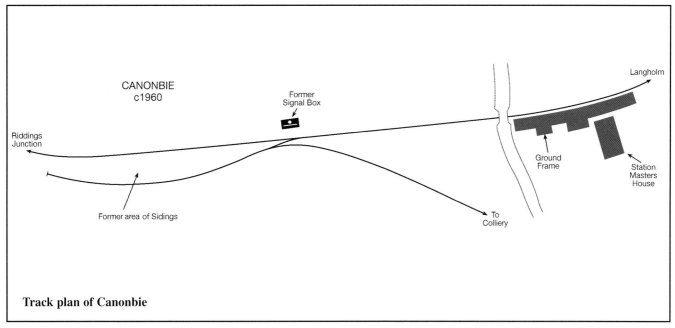

Track plan of Canonbie

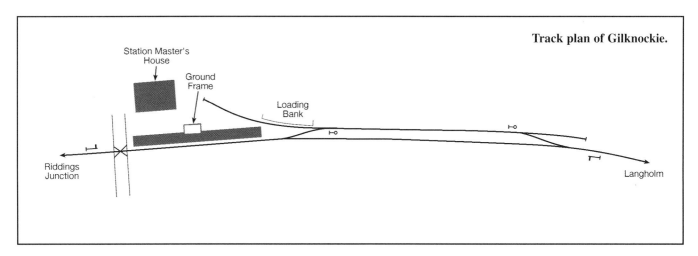

Track plan of Gilknockie.

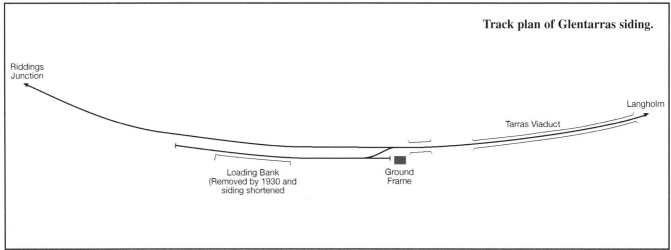

Track plan of Glentarras siding.

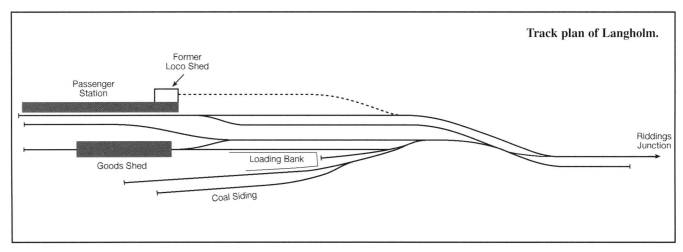

Track plan of Langholm.

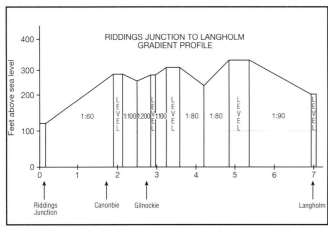

Left:
Gradient profile — Riddings Junction to Langholm.

Right:
Looking down from the footbridge at Riddings Junction, 'A2' class 4-6-2 No 60535 *Hornet's Beauty* and 'J39' No 64932 are present, the Pacific on a train from Edinburgh to Carlisle and the 0-6-0 with the train to Langholm, on 2 June 1960. *J. Spencer Gilks*

Right:
The branch train from Langholm arrives at Riddings Junction behind Ivatt Class 4 2-6-0 No 43000 on 6 April 1963. Note the immaculate appearance of the station — 'pride in the job' meant something on this line. *W. A. C. Smith*

Below Left:
Ex-LNER Thompson 'B1' 4-6-0 No 61221 *Sir Alexander Erskine-Hill* of Haymarket shed has arrived at Riddings Junction with a service from Edinburgh to Carlisle in June 1956. The 'peg' is off for the branch train on the left to depart for Langholm, being hauled by a 'J39' locomotive No 64727. *Ian Allan Library*

Below right:
Looking back at the station, before No 61221's arrival (see above), the train for Langholm is in the platform at Riddings Junction with No 64727 waiting to go. Note the sign, 'Change for Canonbie, Gilnockie and Langholm'. *Ian Allan Library*

Left:
Ivatt Class 4 No 43000 was a regular performer on the line and is seen here crossing the superb nine-arch skew viaduct over Liddel Water (the Border between England and Scotland), with the 5.18 from Carlisle to Langholm on 6 April 1963. Unlike other Anglo-Scottish border crossings, no sign was erected here to inform passengers of the fact.
W. A. C. Smith

Above:
Ivatt Mogul No 43139 arrives at Canonbie with the 5.18pm from Carlisle to Langholm on 3 May 1962. The sidings for the coal traffic to the colliery here can be seen to the left of the train. It was this part of the line which opened first, in 1862, so that coal could be transported, the rest of the route being completed two years later. A small shunting locomotive was once based here for the coal traffic. *David Holmes*

Right:
The previous photograph was taken from the bridge that can be seen at the very smart station at Canonbie on 10 September 1960. There was once a signalbox here but this was closed in May 1921, when Riddings Junction became responsible for the unlocking of the ground frame for the sidings. The station was originally called Canobie as the railway had been confused with the local pronunciation of the name — it was renamed Canonbie on 1 February 1902. *W. A. C. Smith*

Left:
Ivatt Class 4 No 43011 is seen near Gilnockie with the afternoon train to Carlisle on 6 April 1963. Byreburn Viaduct became unstable after only a month of use, and trains were not allowed to cross it; as a result, passengers were brought by train to either side of the viaduct, where they alighted and walked across to another train waiting on the other side! Gilnockie station was opened on 2 November 1864.
W. A. C. Smith

Right:
No 43139 calls at Gilnockie with the 6.32pm from Langholm to Carlisle on 10 September 1960. Gilnockie was renowned for its flowers, having had a stationmaster before World War 2 who was interested in roses, and despite the station having become an unstaffed halt from 2 February 1953, some of these seemed to have survived. The station had a siding which was much used in the war for timber traffic. Behind the photographer was a level crossing operated by a crossing keeper who was based at the station. *W. A. C. Smith*

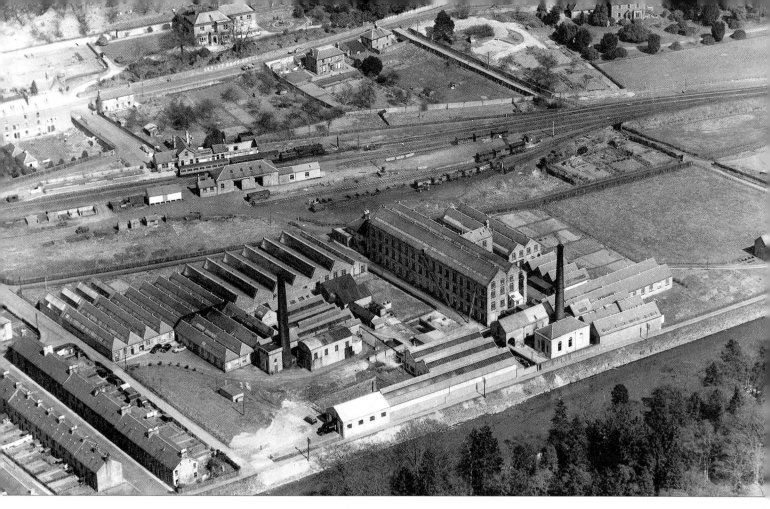

Above:

A panoramic view showing No 43139 at Langholm on 19 April 1955 shows the layout of the station area to good effect. To the rear of the train is the now roofless locomotive shed; the turntable once stood in front of this. As well as the goods shed, the loading bank has some cattle wagons for loading alongside and a line of coal wagons can be seen — one is being unloaded by a local merchant. The scene is dominated by the large mill in the foreground. There were three woollen mills adjacent to the station at this location, these being Buccleuch, Waverley and Kilncleuch woollen mills. These were situated alongside the River Esk, and received coal via the railway to generate power. Just before the entrance of the station limits was Langholm Distillery, which at one time also provided traffic for the railway, although there was no private siding. *Aerofilms*

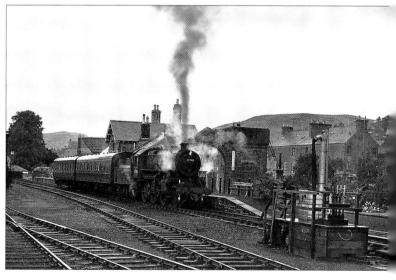

Above left:

Former NBR Class J35 0-6-0 No 64511 waits to leave Langholm with an afternoon service to Carlisle in the early 1950s. These locomotives were later replaced by 'J39s' and Ivatt 2-6-0 tender locomotives. Predictably, there is more goods traffic to be seen in the sidings than with the later photographs. *W. A. Camwell*

Above right:

No 43045 is ready to depart with the 3.30pm to Carlisle on 31 August 1962. The coaches are standing where there was once a small train shed. Note the former locomotive shed to the right of the locomotive and the ground frame that worked the points on the lines served by passenger traffic. *Ian Allan Library*

St. Boswells to Roxburgh Junction, Jedburgh and Berwick

Historical perspective

The first major railway to come to the Border Counties was the Berwick & Kelso Railway, the Act being passed as early as 31 May 1811. This allowed for construction of a line from Tweedmouth Harbour, known as Spittal, to Kelso, but like many such schemes — in this case to link the products of the rich agricultural land to the coast (but not passengers) — it foundered. In 1826 the backers (one of whom would later become well known as Sir Walter Scott) tried to get the line built by extending the route to Melrose. This too failed, and by 1838, as construction had not taken place, the Berwick & Kelso was wound up. On 31 July 1845 new powers were obtained, this time by the Newcastle & Berwick Railway (later the North Eastern Railway), and construction of a route from Tweedmouth to Kelso swiftly commenced, the line reaching as far as Sprouston, opening on 27 July 1849.

From Sprouston a connection was made to the North British branch line from St Boswells that ran through Roxburgh and Kelso, the actual meeting point of the two systems being at Maxwellheugh, one mile and one chain from Sprouston, and opening for through traffic from 1 June 1851. The York, Newcastle & Berwick was granted running powers into the station at Kelso — a further 1 mile 20 chains. (It was at this point that the differentiation would later made between the Scottish and North Eastern Regions of British Railways, the working timetables splitting at Carham.)

The line from Tweedmouth to Sprouston Junction was constructed to double-track standards and at that time the line from St Boswells, Kelso Junction was also double-track, thus a 35-mile long branch of double track could be considered a secondary main line. The Kelso to Kelso Junction section was singled in 1933. At Coldstream, the North Eastern Railway's line to Alnwick ran in, opening to traffic on 5 September 1857.

The early services between the North British and the North Eastern ran out and back to Kelso from either St Boswells or Tweedmouth. Initially, there were no through services, despite the NBR's pressing for the through working of locomotives and stock to cut costs. Connections were also badly timed for through passengers; whether or not this was deliberate is unknown, but little co-ordination was achieved, and there were also bad connections at Roxburgh Junction with trains from Jedburgh, moving the latter's town council to complain to the railway companies.

Freight traffic was primarily agricultural, the focus being at Kelso which had a goods yard that catered for livestock, grain and dairy products — it even had a pilot shunting locomotive until 1955, latterly a Sentinel machine, No 68138, this locomotive having replaced horses and a 40hp NBR petrol shunter. Other stations forwarded cattle and other farm products; inward traffic was coal and other general merchandise such as farm machinery, fertiliser and feedstuffs.

From Roxburgh Junction there was a branch to Jedburgh. First planned in 1846, this line was opened by the Jedburgh Railway Co on 17 July 1856. Four years later, in 1860, the North British (which worked the line) assumed ownership. The station at Jedburgh was not close to the centre, and the railway provided a bus service between there and the station, a ¾-mile journey. Passenger services ran to and from Roxburgh Junction where there were connections with Tweed Valley services, but there were also through services to Kelso, and originally a through coach for Edinburgh was provided. Roxburgh Junction at one time employed up to 23 staff: as well as the stationmaster there were porters, signalmen, clerks and lengthmen. The line was well used and at the peak of its carryings, in the early 1900s, transported up to 43,000 passengers per year, before a steady decline set in. In 1932 only 15,000 passengers booked through Jedburgh.

At Roxburgh Junction, the line joined 'end on' with the line from St Boswells. From there the line ran along the valley of the River Teviot to Kirkbank, 1½ miles from Roxburgh, which had a small yard as well as the platform. Kirkbank was originally called Old Ormiston.

From Kirkbank, Nisbet was reached after a further 2½ miles. A level crossing was situated before the station, which had a small wooden building with a grounded coach body used as a lamp room. At Nisbet, the stationmaster was also the local postmaster and had as many as five postmen under his care. The post office was situated in the station building and served the villages of Ancrum and Crailing.

The River Teviot was crossed near Jedfoot on a fine steel lattice bridge supported on brick piers. Jedfoot was the next halt: here were more sidings for local agricultural traffic and inbound coal. The line's course then changed to follow Jed Water to the station at Jedburgh, some seven miles from Roxburgh Junction.

Jedburgh had a single platform, although this was reasonably long and could comfortably take six coaches with enough space left for the engine to run round. Jedburgh had a yard foreman, porter and two signalmen to work the terminus; here too were a cattle dock and loading bank, coal staithes, general goods sidings, a goods shed, a locomotive shed and a water tank.

Passenger services on the Jedburgh branch operated to and from Roxburgh Junction, but some went through to Kelso. The basic service was five trains per day on Mondays to Saturdays, two additional services running Saturdays only. In NBR and LNER days these were worked by the Jedburgh locomotive based

at the small locomotive depot, a sub-shed of St Boswells. Coaching stock comprised three oil-lit four-wheeled coaches, a full brake, a composite and a brake third. The one-time through Edinburgh carriages were six-wheeled composites.

There were daily freight services right to the end of the line's existence, closure coming on 10 August 1964, after the passenger service had been withdrawn on 13 August 1948. The line was flooded at this time but repaired; however, passenger services were not restored, as all the paths on the Tweed Valley line were required for the additional diverted services. From then, a bus was substituted from St Boswells with services connecting Jedburgh with Kelso.

The decline of both freight and passengers using rural lines affected the St Boswells to Tweedmouth route after World War 1 and the western end of the line from Kelso Junction to Kelso was singled in 1933. However, freight traffic had held up well, and there was little rationalisation of services. With the onset of war again in 1939 and the ability of the Luftwaffe to attack the East Coast main line from Norway — the Royal Border Bridge being a prime target that would have put the main line out of action for months if not years — the line's potential use as an alternative route was realised. Thus a loop was constructed at Maxton in 1942, and in December of that year the loop at Roxburgh was extended — of course, this section had originally been double-track.

But it was the weather rather than German air power that brought the line forcibly into its own as a diversionary route, notably in the summer floods of 1948 — would that it were open today! The line itself suffered a landslip at Carham, which was repaired, but the East Coast main line was out of action for some time. This meant that various main line passenger services were rerouted and this, being nonstop services, meant that water could not be taken for 88 miles from Edinburgh Waverley to Lucker troughs — and this with a slog up Borthwick Bank on the Waverley Route in both directions. The East Coast men were well aware that the longest nonstop run in the Britain was set by the rival West Coast main line at 401 miles, and on no fewer than 17 occasions the crews ignored the bankers at Falahill on the Waverley Route as well as the booked water stop at Galashiels with the nonstop 'Capitals Limited' and 'Flying Scotsman'.

Some diverted goods services between Tweedmouth and Edinburgh also used the line, but the cost of these interlopers was the temporary withdrawal of the stopping services from Jedburgh to St Boswells, along with the temporary closure of the stations in between. In the event, the passenger service to Jedburgh was withdrawn altogether and replaced by a bus.

With the normal service restored towards the end of September 1948, after the damage to the line caused by floods had been repaired, it was used by a number of excursions which brought locomotives with power classifications higher than the regular Class 2 variety.

But despite extra traffic in the form of summer excursions and the use of the line for diversions, the 'writing was on the wall' for the local services from 1955. From then, the four passenger trains per day, plus the Saturdays-only Berwick-Coldstream service, were reduced to only two through services, and some of the local stations on the North Eastern section were closed.

On Bank Holiday Monday 3 August 1959 BR Standard Class 2MT No 78049 worked the 4pm from St Boswells as far as Kelso, where the standard two vans were attached as usual and most of

Above:
BR Standard Class 2 2-6-0 No 78048 has arrived at St Boswells with the 18.35 from Berwick on 11 June 1964, two days prior to the withdrawal of passenger services on the route. *David C. Smith*

the passengers left the train. On 4 August a 'V2' 2-6-2 was noted at Roxburgh on a Hawick to Berwick excursion.

July 1960 saw the line particularly busy with holiday traffic, and a correspondent to the *Railway Observer* noted that No 78049 had 'a hectic time reversing at Tweedmouth and St Boswells. A steady 55-60mph was maintained on the double track to Kelso and there was evidence of plenty of freight in the yards. On the same day a freight went down the Wooler branch. The pick-up goods on the Jedburgh branch was in the charge of 'J37' No 64606. Several daily excursions were advertised from Galashiels to Berwick.'

On 23 November 1960 the line was used again for diversions from the East Coast main line due to a derailment at Marshall Meadows. This saw the up 'Talisman' and the down 'Flying Scotsman' diverted via the Waverley Route and Kelso — both trains on this occasion being hauled by Type 4 diesel locomotives.

On 7 August 1961 an up freight hauled by English Electric Type 4 No D261 overran the up loop at Grantshouse and, in so doing, ran through the goods shed and demolished the station buildings. East Coast expresses were once again diverted via Kelso, and on 8 August the up morning 'Talisman' was hauled by no less than 'Deltic' No D9006. This train was held at St Boswells for 35 minutes — having arrived at 9.35am — to wait for Type 4 diesel No D200 on another diverted express to clear the single line from Roxburgh Junction.

Class K3 2-6-0s were also occasional performers. The last 'K3' from St Margarets, No 61968, was used on the 11.20am excursion to Tweedmouth on 14 June 1961, and it also hauled the return working. On 9 July No 61984 from 52D (Tweedmouth) was in charge of another excursion.

On 26 August 1961 'B1' No 61262 of 62B (Dundee Tay Bridge) was used on a factory outing to Berwick and return. On 25 September BR Standard Class 2 No 78046 hauled the 4pm from St Boswells to Tweedmouth, consisting of just one Gresley coach as far as Kelso, where shunting took place and the usual two parcels vans were added to the train. This train returned from Berwick at 6.35pm and was usually well patronised in summer and on bank and local holidays.

Another excursion ran to Tweedmouth on 24 August 1963, hauled by 'V2' No 60952 of 52A (Gateshead), the locomotive running back to St Boswells tender-first. On 13 May 1964 a Type 2 diesel visited the line hauling an S&T engineers' special which ran from Newcastle to Tweedmouth, where it took the St Boswells line before heading to Carlisle and Newcastle via the Tyne Valley. A month later, on 12 June, BR Mogul No 76050 worked the 16.02 from St Boswells to Berwick — a single coach that picked up two parcels vans at Kelso. This locomotive also ran on the last day of passenger services over the line the following day.

Estimates from British Railways in the early 1960s put operating costs at £60,000 per annum. Coldstream was instrumental in illustrating this decline. In 1911 over 22,000 tickets were sold here. This had reduced to only 1,300 by 1951. Against this were set receipts of only £2,000, but as with many routes, no serious rationalisation was attempted. Today a route such as this would have been 'Sprinterised' with significant cuts in operating staff such as signalmen and station staff. But no such philosophy existed at the time, and, in the end, withdrawal of passenger services was instigated quickly, being effected from 13 June 1964. However, notices for the withdrawal of passenger services had been posted for 18 June 1963, but the failure to organise replacement bus services in the area led to services continuing for another year. TUCC approval for closure was finally given after a public meeting in Kelso on 11 October 1963, and 13 June 1964 saw the last passenger trains. The trains were replaced by two bus services a day, subsidised by BR, which had claimed that its costs for operating the line had been nearly 30 times the receipts, approximately £2,500 per annum.

It is interesting to note that the majority of objections had come from passengers who used the services only between Berwick and Tweedmouth.

After the passenger services had ceased, Hawick shed's allocation and diagrams were reduced and only three locomotives were supplied to work Monday to Friday, with a fourth on Saturdays. One of these SX workings was the St Boswells-Kelso/Jedburgh goods and return. The locomotives were Nos 76049, 78047, 78048, 78049 and 80113, the '76s' usually working the Jedburgh goods, which lasted until 10 August 1964.

Passenger services

In the early 1930s, the line was still 'split in two' as far as the organisation of services was concerned. In 1930, on the NER section, the first passenger train on the branch was the 6.5am from Berwick which ran through to Alnwick via Coldstream, arriving at 8.12am. This was followed by a steam railcar which left Tweedmouth at 7.30am and terminated at Coldstream; it worked back to Berwick at 8.10am. Then followed the 8.48am Berwick-Kelso, the steam railcar at 11.40am from Berwick to Kelso, the 2.15 Berwick-Kelso and then the 4.10pm from Tweedmouth to Alnwick, where it arrived at 6.6pm. The last train was the 5.30pm Berwick-Kelso/St Boswells.

The LNER steam railcar used on the Berwick-Kelso services was usually *Royal Charlotte* or *Hero*. These were known in contemporary working timetables as 'steam coaches'.

In the up direction, the first train from Kelso was the aforementioned steam coach for Berwick. Then came the 9.55am Kelso-Berwick, the 12.55pm steam coach from Kelso to Berwick, the 3.18pm from Coldstream to Tweedmouth that had started from Alnwick at 1.50pm, the 3.25pm Kelso-Tweedmouth and the 4.50pm from Kelso to Berwick that came from St Boswells and waited at Kelso for 30 minutes(!), the last train being the 8.14pm from Coldstream to Tweedmouth that originated at Alnwick, which it left at 6.45pm.

In 1939, on the NBR Kelso-St Boswells portion, trains left for St Boswells at 7.35am; there was then an 8.40 to Jedburgh, a 10.11 to St Boswells, an 11.21pm to Jedburgh that was 'mixed', a 12.15pm SO to St Boswells, a 2pm SX to St Boswells, a 2.6 SO to Galashiels, a 4.12 to St Boswells that was extended to Galashiels on Saturdays, and the through train from Berwick (5.30), at 6.27, followed by a 7.50 SX or on Saturdays only, an 8pm. The last Jedburgh service left at 8.55pm SO, with another service to St Boswells at 9.26pm SO.

In the up direction trains for Kelso left St Boswells at 6.20, 8.37 and 11.17am which came from Hawick, and on MSO, Edinburgh. Then came a 1.16 SO, 3.40 and 5.57pm through to Berwick, 7.7 and 8.47pm SO. Services to Jedburgh left Roxburgh at 7.36, 10.14am, 2.5 and 8.33pm SO.

The LNER passenger service from September 1944 showed three trains from Berwick upon Tweed to Kelso that left Tweedmouth at 6.50am, 2.44 and 6.25pm. In addition, another service ran out to Coldstream from Berwick, leaving Tweedmouth at 9.40am. The return services left Kelso at 7.50am, 2.30pm (a through service from Jedburgh, where it departed at 1.48pm) and 8.10pm. There was also a departure back from Coldstream at 10.23pm. During this period only the 6.50am from Tweedmouth and the 7.35pm from St Boswells were through trains, all other through journeys necessitating a change at Kelso, with some lengthy waits.

The Jedburgh passenger service that linked into the line at Roxburgh had five passenger services per day. Trains left Jedburgh at 7.12am for Kelso, 9.57am for Roxburgh, 1.48pm for Berwick and 5.50 and 7.28pm for Roxburgh. In the return direction there was an 8.40am from Kelso to Jedburgh, with departures from Roxburgh for Kelso at 11.56am, 4.30 and 7pm, with the last train at 8.18pm SX, 8.20pm SO.

The Kelso-St Boswells service at the western end of the line saw departures from St Boswells at 6.18, 8.37, 11.32am, 1.16 SO,

4pm, 6.10 and 7.35pm, calling at all stations, save that the 6.18am did not call at Maxton and Rutherford. From Kelso, trains for St Boswells departed at 7.40, 10.11am, 12.9pm SO all stations except Maxton, 2pm SO, 2.20pm SX, 4.40pm, 6.50pm and 8.10pm, not Maxton SX.

By September 1948 there were two through trains, as there had been before the war. The timetable shows the end-on connections between the two regions, and while there were now two through services in the St Boswells to Tweedmouth direction connections at Kelso were lengthy, but were reasonable in the other direction with a maximum of only 15 minutes between

trains, with four through journeys a day being possible, together with the Coldstream mid-day and evening SO service from Berwick. Intermingled with this service was the Jedburgh service — this was five trains a day, six on Saturdays, with 8.38am, 4.40, 6.47pm being through services that left from Kelso, others at 11.59am, 8.13 and 9.45pm SO from Roxburgh.

In the return direction, Jedburgh had departures at 7am, 10.16am, 1.50 SO, 2.5 SX, 5.30, 7.25 and 8.50pm SO, of which the 7am was a through service to Kelso and Berwick, the 1.50 SO/2.5pm SX running through to Kelso, as did the 5.30pm.

Upper right:
LNER passenger services timetable, 22 May 1944 — Berwick and Kelso, Kelso and St Boswells and Kelso, Roxburgh and Jedburgh.

Right and below:
BR ScR passenger services timetable, 31 May to 26 September 1948 — St Boswells, Kelso, Coldstream and Berwick and Kelso, Roxburgh and Jedburgh.

Table 168 — BERWICK and KELSO; Table 169 — KELSO and ST. BOSWELLS; Table 170 — KELSO, ROXBURGH, and JEDBURGH; Table 44 — Kelso, Roxburgh, and Jedburgh; Table 47 — St. Boswells, Kelso, Coldstream and Berwick

Miles	Table 77 BERWICK and KELSO — WEEKDAYS	A am	A am	SO am	A pm	A pm	SO pm
	3 Newcastle .. dep	4 17	6 46	9 28	12 21	4B18	7 29
	3 Edinburgh (Wav.) .. „	..	6 55	10 15	2 0	5 14	8 0
—	**BERWICK** .. dep	6 30	9 20	11 40	3 20	6 40	9 40
1½	**Tweedmouth** arr	6 33	9 23	11 43	3 23	6 43	9 43
	Tweedmouth dep	6 40	9 28	11 48	3 30	6 48	9 50
5½	Velvet Hall .... „	6 47	9 35	11 55	3 37	6 55	9 57
7¾	Norham .. „	6 52	9 40	12 0	3 42	7 0	10 2
10¾	Twizell .... „	6 57	9 45	12 5	3 47	7 5	10 7
13½	Coldstream .. „	7 7	9 54	12 12	3 57	7 14	10 14
16¾	Sunilaws ...... „	7 13	10 0	—	4 3	7 20	—
19	Carham .. „	7 18	10 5	..	4 8	7 25	..
21½	Sprouston...... „	7 23	10 10	....	4 13	7 30	....
23½	**KELSO** .. arr	7 28	10 15	..	4 18	7 35	..
35	St. Boswells .. arr	8 7	10 56	....	4 56	8 10	....

Miles	WEEKDAYS	A am	A am	SO pm	A pm	A pm		
	St. Boswells .. dep	6 37	8 33	..	4 5	7 15	..	..
—	**KELSO** ...... dep	7 35	9 30	....	4 40	7 55	....	....
2¼	Sprouston .. „	..	9 35	..	4 45	..	..	..
4½	Carham ...... „	....	9 40	....	4 50	....	....	....
6¾	Sunilaws .. „	7 47	9 45	..	4 55	8 7	..	..
10	Coldstream .. „	7 57	9 54	1 15	5 5	8 16	....	....
12¾	Twizell .. .. „	8 3	10 0	1 21	5 11	8 22	..	..
15¾	Norham ...... „	8 9	10 6	1 27	5 17	8 28	....	....
18¼	Velvet Hall .. „	8 16	10 13	1 33	5 24	8 35	..	..
22¼	**Tweedmouth** arr	8 23	10 20	1 40	5 31	8 42	....	....
	Tweedmouth dep	8 29	10 25	1 45	5 37	8 47	..	..
23½	**BERWICK** .. arr	8 32	10 28	1 48	5 40	8 50	....	....
81	3 Edinburgh ..arr	....	12 40	3 30	9 5	....	..	..
90½	3 Newcastle .. „	10C45	12 50	4 25	7 45	11X 6	....	....

A—Through Trains between Berwick and St. Boswells.
B—Connection at Tweedmouth.
C—Connection at Tweedmouth. On Saturdays arrives Newcastle 10.48 am.
SO—Saturdays only.
X—On Saturdays arrives Newcastle. 10.48 pm. Connection at Tweedmouth.

Left:
BR NER passenger services timetable, 25 September 1950 — Berwick and Kelso.

Table 54

BERWICK-UPON-TWEED and KELSO

Miles	WEEKDAYS ONLY	Through Train— Berwick to St. Boswells am	Through Train— Berwick to St. Boswells pm		
	2 Newcastle.. dep	6 55	4M30	....	....
	2 Edinburgh (Wav.) .. „	8G 0	5 8	..	..
—	**BERWICK-upon-TWEED** .... dep	9 59	6 35	....	....
1½	**Tweedmouth** arr	10 2	6‡38	..	..
	Tweedmouth dep	10 9	6‡45	....	....
7¾	Norham .. „	10 20	6‡56	..	..
13½	Coldstream .. „	10 29	7 9	....	....
23½	**KELSO** .. arr	10 45	7 26	..	..
35	St. Boswells .. arr	11 10	8 0	....	....

Miles	WEEKDAYS ONLY	Through Train— St. Boswells to Berwick am	Through Train— St. Boswells to Berwick pm				
	St. Boswells dep	8 25	4 2	..	..	..	..
—	**KELSO** ...... dep	8 50	4 49	....	....	....	....
10	Coldstream .. „	9 9	5 13	..	..	..	..
15¾	Norham ...... „	9 19	5 23	....	....	....	....
22¼	**Tweedmouth** arr	9 30	5‡34	..	..	..	..
	Tweedmouth dep	9 37	5‡41	....	....	....	....
23½	**BERWICK-upon-TWEED** arr	9 40	5 44	..	..	..	..
81	2 Edinburgh arr	12D14	9F 0	....	....	....	....
90½	2 Newcastle „	1L 7	7E32	..	..	..	..

For other trains between Berwick-upon-Tweed and Tweedmouth, see Table 2.

D—On Mondays to Fridays from 15th July to 23rd August arrives Edinburgh 11.38 am. On Saturdays from 20th July to 17th August arrives Edinburgh 11.30 am.
E—Arrives Newcastle 7.21 pm on Fridays and Saturdays.
F—On Saturdays arrives Edinburgh 8.40 pm.
G—On Saturdays also on Monday, 5th August, departs Edinburgh 6.50 am.
M—Connection at Tweedmouth. On Saturdays departs Newcastle 4.40 pm.
‡—No staff in attendance.

Lower left:
BR NER Passenger Services Time Table 7 June to September 8 1963, Berwick upon Tweed and Kelso

By 1950 the two main changes to the passenger timetable were the withdrawal of passenger services from Jedburgh (since August 1948) and the introduction of more through working from Berwick to St Boswells. Trains left Berwick at 6.30, 9.20am, 3.30 and 6.40pm with two other Saturdays-only services to Coldstream that departed at 11.40am and 9.40pm.

In the opposite direction, trains for Berwick left St Boswells at 6.37, 8.33am, 4.5 and 7.15pm. There was also a Coldstream to Berwick service on Saturdays only at 1.15pm. A local service ran into St Boswells from Kelso on a daily basis, leaving St Boswells at 11.38am and arriving at Kelso at 11.59am, returning at 12.21pm SX (12.7 SO).

The timetable for 20 September 1954 to 12 June 1955 saw the withdrawal of the local services at the eastern end of the line. The passenger service on offer was now four through trains in each direction, leaving Berwick at 6.30, 9.20am, 3.28 and 6.47pm, the other direction seeing departures from St Boswells at 7.35, 9.30am, 4.40 and 8pm. There was still a mid-day local service that ran out and back between St Boswells and Kelso.

There was a dramatic reduction in passenger services from 1955 with the through services were reduced to only two. At the same time, stations were closed on the North Eastern section, at Sprouston, Carham, Sunilaws, Twizell and Velvet Hall, from 4 July 1955.

The Kelso-St Boswells section retained two local services as well as the through trains, but this was certainly the first sign that the BR regions were looking to rationalise and cut costs, even before Beeching. One of these local services was an evening DMU from Edinburgh Waverley that had run via Peebles and Galashiels, arriving at Kelso at 7.2pm.

By 1963 the service was a shadow of its former self, with only two trains per day, plus a mid-day local service between St Boswells and Kelso.

These through trains left Berwick at 9.59am and 6.35pm, the return trains leaving St Boswells at 8.25am and 4.2pm. Only Norham, Coldstream, Kelso and Roxburgh were served en route.

Freight services

The Tweed Valley line passed through rich agricultural land, and traffic consisted of products such as grain, dairy produce and other items; Norham, for instance, forwarded a variety of countryside products, and, in addition to vegetables, milk, grain and sugar beet also forwarded eggs, game and rabbits. Not surprisingly, inward traffic to stations on the line comprised commodities such as domestic coal, agricultural machinery, fertiliser and feedstuffs for animals.

Livestock had always been an important traffic on the line, being centred on Kelso, where there was a large goods yard that forwarded grain, turnips and potatoes, livestock, dairy products and received inwards, coal, farm machinery, general goods and agricultural feedstuffs. Thus there were cattle wagons collected from local stations, and these formed trains to Kelso and also from there out of the area. Other traffic was carried to Kelso, which had a locomotive shed; based there was a North British Railway 40hp petrol shunter, but this was later replaced by 'Y1' Sentinel steam shunter No 68138.

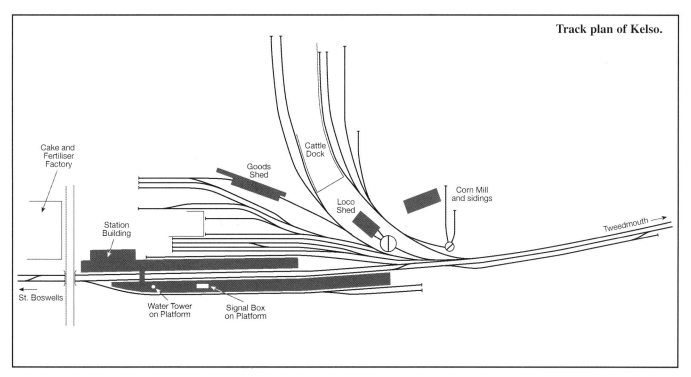

Cake and Fertiliser Factory

Cattle Dock

Goods Shed

Corn Mill and sidings

Loco Shed

Station Building

Tweedmouth →

St. Boswells

Water Tower on Platform

Signal Box on Platform

Above:
BR ScR working timetable, Kelso branch, 21 September 1953.

In pre-Second World War days there were no fewer than five 'Q' paths timetabled for cattle trains (one mixed with a general goods) running out of the area for the coast. One of these paths was from Wooler, on the Cornhill branch, to Alnwick. In the opposite direction there was a path inwards between Tweedmouth and Wooler. Cattle wagons would also be returned on other general freights. In addition to the 'Q' paths there were two timetabled goods services in both directions from Kelso to Tweedmouth daily. There was also a Kelso to Wooler freight that delivered cattle empties and other merchandise. This ran back as required, otherwise the rest of the Cornhill line's traffic returned via Alnwick and Alnmouth.

While the NER freights centred on Tweedmouth, the NBR end of the line focused on Galashiels, Hawick and Edinburgh Portobello. As well as a daily trip to and from Hawick to Jedburgh, there was a daily service from Edinburgh to Kelso, which conveyed livestock on Tuesdays. One passenger train, the 7.7pm from St Boswells, ran as mixed, while there was another goods from Jedburgh to Kelso (for onward shipment to Tweedmouth).

At Coldstream the connection was made with the former NER line to Alnwick. This line had been freight-only from 1933 and

was another to be damaged by floods in 1948, being consequently truncated at Wooler. Trips were worked from Tweedmouth to Wooler and passed through Coldstream on a daily freight, latterly reduced to three days a week. This traffic was primarily coal inwards, the empties being returned along with the odd wagon of agricultural produce.

As well as agricultural traffic there was military business for the RAF and Royal Navy. World War 1 saw troop trains to the training areas in the Borders, plus additional supply trains to the East Coast ports. Between the wars in 1933 the track was singled from Kelso to Kelso Junction, but World War 2 saw such an increase in traffic with troops and equipment (and the need to have the line ready as a diversionary route) that the loop at Maxton was reinstated. This was also necessary because of the construction of an ammunition depot for the War Department at Charlesfield, near St Boswells. Charlesfield opened in 1942 and had a siding, together with a 60-wagon loop. Originally used by the RAF, it was closed in 1946 but later reinstated by the Royal Navy, before closing in 1961. For passengers the depot had a halt on the Waverley Route.

After the war, freight traffic declined with much of the livestock moving to road transport. The Scottish Region working

timetable from 21 September 1953 showed the first up freight working from St Boswells at 6.45am, the branch freight to Kelso. The train arrived at 7.15am at Roxburgh Junction, where it shunted and then left at 7.50am for Kelso, shunt before running back to Roxburgh at 8.30am and departing for Jedburgh at 9am. This working, Reporting No 519, arrived at Jedburgh at 9.55am, after calling at Kirkbank, Nisbet and Jedfoot as required; it then shunted at Jedburgh before departing at 12.30pm. The traffic here was from the Jedburgh Rayon Mill. The train was back at St Boswells at 1.55pm. On Saturdays excepted there was another freight, Reporting No 528, which left St Boswells at 1.20pm and ran to Roxburgh arriving at 2.54pm. This worked back, Reporting No 760, leaving Kelso at 3.40pm and arriving back at Roxburgh at 3.50 before departing at 4.5pm for a nonstop run to Jedburgh, which it reached at 4.35pm. It returned (as No 522) at 5.15pm, arriving back at St Boswells at 6.40pm. On Saturdays the train left St Boswells (No 535) at 2.55 for Kelso, arriving at 4.20 after shunting for half an hour at Roxburgh. It returned at 5pm for a 5.55 arrival into St Boswells. A through freight (No 1307) from St Boswells to Tweedmouth departed at 4.55pm, serving Roxburgh, Kelso, Coldstream and Norham and reaching Tweedmouth at 7.31pm.

In the down direction there was a 7.30am (No 1300) from Tweedmouth to Kelso, arriving at 9.55am. A through freight ran at 1.50pm SX from Tweedmouth to St Boswells, arriving at 3.39pm; on Saturdays this train ran an hour earlier, leaving Tweedmouth at 12.50pm and arriving at St Boswells at 2.54pm.

By 1961 there was only one through freight train service per day along the whole route. Livestock continued go be carried on 'special' trains and within the timetabled goods services, as did other agricultural commodities. The main commodity was coal.

pm
12.50 SO Class H Tweedmouth-St Boswells
1.50 SX Class H Tweedmouth-St Boswells
3.55 SO Class H St Boswells-Tweedmouth
4.30 SX Class H St Boswells-Tweedmouth

Jedburgh was served by a trip from St Boswells until 10 August 1964, while at the eastern end of the line there was the Tweedmouth-Wooler trip, which lasted until 29 March 1965.

BR Standard Class 3 2-6-0 No 77002 from Tweedmouth shed, which was closed from 14 June 1965, worked the last goods on 27 March 1965, and from Monday 29th goods services were formally withdrawn from Velvet Hall, Norham, Coldstream, Sunilaws, Akeld and Wooler. No 77002 and a sister also worked the 7.30am Tweedmouth-Reston-Duns freight on Mondays, Wednesdays and Fridays and the track-lifting train, which was removing one of the tracks between Kelso and Tweedmouth, on Tuesdays, Thursdays and Saturdays.

The Kelso-St Boswells service lasted as a trip working on an 'as required' basis until 1 April 1968. Although this service was worked latterly by a Class 08 diesel shunter, the last train was hauled by 'Clayton' Type 1 No D8500.

Left:
'C16' class 4-4-2T No 67489 stands in the bay at St Boswells with the 16.05 to Kelso and Berwick train on 3 September 1955. This ex-North British locomotive was based at St Boswells and it is interesting to note that the line also saw NER power from Tweedmouth, at this time 'G5' class 0-4-4T. 'Scott' class 4-4-0s were also common on the line in this period, which was before the influx of BR Standard types that came in from the late 1950s. *W. A. C. Smith*

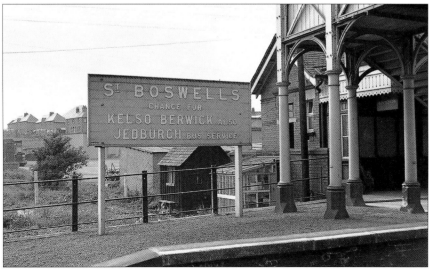

Lower left:
St Boswells station sign on 22 May 1961. By August 1948 the Jedburgh passenger service had been withdrawn due to flooding on the East Coast main line, hence the reference to a bus service, which was altered after the floods had closed the line to passengers.
Edwin Wilmshurst

Right:
Leaving St Boswells with the goods to Kelso on 7 July 1962 is 0-6-0 diesel shunter No D3582. The train has just left the Waverley Route at Kelso Junction and the line is now single for the run to Roxburgh and Kelso. The original double-track formation to Maxton is well illustrated here, with the stub end of the line terminating at a buffer-stop.
Roy Hamilton

Left:
BR Standard Class 4 No 76050 of Hawick arrives at Kelso Junction with the 11.52 SO Kelso to St Boswells local service on 11 April 1964. A single brake composite coach of various parentages was the standard coaching diagram for all services on this line at this time. The line closed to passengers within a month of this photograph being taken, on 4 May 1964. Between Kelso Junction and Maxton, Charlesfield Siding was opened to serve an RAF factory in 1942. After the war it was taken over by the Royal Navy, lasting until 1961, even having its own diesel shunting locomotive. *M. Dunnett*

Below:
The last North British 4-4-0 'Glen' class locomotive in traffic, No 62484 *Glen Lyon,* leaves Maxton, Roxburghshire, with a goods from Jedburgh to Galashiels on 1 August 1961. *D. E. Esau*

Left:
BR Mogul No 78048 is seen at Maxton with the 2.21pm from Kelso to St Boswells on 26 August 1960. The loop line here (once part of the double track to Kelso Junction and extended during World War 2), was now out of use. This locomotive, together with No 78049, was a regular performer on the line's passenger services, usually hauling a one coach train. The signalbox at Maxton was reduced to just a crossing box by early 1932, but World War 2 saw a siding opened at Charlesfield for the RAF, which resulted in it reopening as a full block post, staying open until 29 March 1965. This locomotive hauled the last 18.35 Berwick upon Tweed-St Boswells, carrying the headboard 'Kelso Laddie'. *Hugh Ballantyne*

Above left:
Ex-LNER Class 'J39/2' 0-6-0 No 64917 passes through Maxton with a train of hoppers and mineral wagons from Tweedmouth to St Boswells on 26 August 1960. It is likely that this service had been diverted from the East Coast main line and was ultimately running to Niddrie Yard. Hopper wagons were tripped to Norham for unloading in the former locomotive shed; this train may convey some of these.
Hugh Ballantyne

Above right:
The next station was Rutherford which had two sidings for local traffic and small station buildings at ground level away from the platforms. It was reduced to one platform from 1933 when the line was singled through to St Boswells from Kelso. *Ian Allan Library*

Lower left:
Before the line became dominated by the BR Standard Moguls, 'V1'/'V3' 2-6-2Ts sometimes worked services, notably No 67606 from Hawick. On this occasion, sister locomotive No 67617 leaves Roxburgh with a service to Berwick in the late 1950s, together with the usual brake composite coach. From Roxburgh, the line passed over Teviot Viaduct and then climbed towards Kelso, which was reached by a short descent of 1 in 72. *D. F. Tee*

Above:

Regular engine No 78049 has arrived at Roxburgh with the 11.46am to Kelso on 18 July 1963. This means that Ivatt 2-6-0 No 43138, on the left, can depart for St Boswells with the 12.30pm goods from Jedburgh. The station looks extremely smart, as does the condition of the track and signalling. Roxburgh is one of the original Royal Burghs of Scotland, and was originally a walled city, with a Royal Mint castle which was the scene of many an Anglo-Scottish dispute. *J. Spencer Gilks*

ROXBURGH TO JEDBURGH

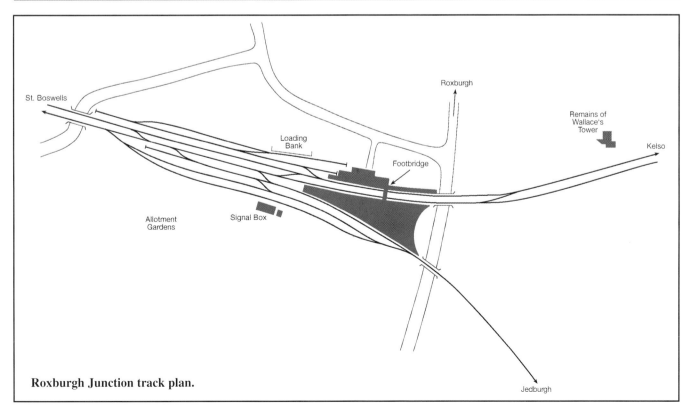

Roxburgh Junction track plan.

Above:

Roxburgh was 25 miles 25 chains from Tweedmouth and 'Glen' 4-4-0 No 62471 *Glen Falloch* is by the Jedburgh line platform with a Branch Line Society special — the 'Scott Country Railtour' for Jedburgh, among other destinations such as Greenlaw and Selkirk, on 4 April 1959. *Roy Hamilton*

Right and above right:

RCTS 'Borders Railtour' notice.

Below:

A second special — the RCTS 'Borders Railtour' — visited the line on 9 July 1961, this time hauled by 'J37' 0-6-0 No 64624 and preserved 'D34' 4-4-0 No 256 *Glen Douglas*. The pair have arrived back at Roxburgh with the special train, having left Jedburgh at approximately 4.30. Opened on 17 July 1856, the Jedburgh line lost its passenger services from 12 August 1948 due to flood damage on the East Coast main line, which saw the diverted expresses requiring the paths that the Jedburgh trains had occupied on the now single-track Kelso-St Boswells section. *John Langford collection*

SCHEDULE

Mileage M. Ch.			Schedule a.m.	Mileage M. Ch.			Schedule p.m.
0.00	LEEDS CITY (SOUTH)	dep.	9-50	199.63	KELSO JCT.	pass	3-11
10.57	SHIPLEY (LEEDS JCT.)	pass	10-05	208.00	ROXBURGH	pass	3-25
17.00	KEIGHLEY	pass	10-12	215.00	JEDBURGH	arr.	3-48
25.01	SNAYGILL	pass	10-20				
26.15	SKIPTON STN.	pass	10-22	221.60	ROXBURGH JCT.	arr.	4-25
36.15	HELLIFIELD	pass	10-35			dep.	4-35
39.35	SETTLE JCT.	pass	10-38	224.60	KELSO	pass	4-41
53.35	BLEA MOOR	pass	10-56	229.26	CARHAM	pass	4-48
64.50	AIS GILL	pass	11-08	234.52	COLDSTREAM	pass	4-58
82.15	APPLEBY WEST	pass	11-22	247.08	TWEEDMOUTH	arr.	5L21
111.35	DURRAN HILL S.S.	pass	11-46			dep.	5L31
112.25	PETTERIL BRIDGE JCT.	arr.	11L48	261.21	BELFORD	pass	5-47
		Noon		278.04	ALNMOUTH	pass	6-03
		dep.	12L00	296.23	MORPETH	pass	6-20
			p.m.	312.73	NEWCASTLE	arr.	6L43
112.48	CARLISLE No. 7	pass	12-02			dep.	6L51
112.71	CARLISLE No. 10	pass	12-06	313.41	KING EDWARD		
113.10	CARLISLE No. 11	pass	12-08		BRIDGE	pass	6-54
114.05	CARLISLE No. 3	pass	12-13	327.78	DURHAM	pass	7-11
114.16	CANAL JCT.	pass	12-15	335.14	WILLINGTON	pass	7-26
122.35	LONGTOWN JCT.	pass	12-24	339.07	BISHOP AUCKLAND	pass	7-34
126.72	RIDDINGS JCT.	pass	12-29	342.01	SHILDON	pass	7-41
137.07	NEWCASTLETON	pass	12-42	351.03	DARLINGTON	arr.	7-58
145.16	RICCARTON JCT.	pass	12-58			dep.	8-00
147.29	WHITROPE SDG.	pass	1-03	365.17	NORTHALLERTON	pass	8-15
158.17	HAWICK	arr.	1L19	373.15	SINDERBY	pass	8-24
		dep.	1L29	379.00	RIPON	pass	8-32
170.39	ST. BOSWELLS	pass	1-47	390.37	HARROGATE	pass	8-48
—	RAVENSWOOD JCT.	pass	1-50	399.36	ARTHINGTON	pass	9-01
185.00	GREENLAW	arr.	2-20	408.58	LEEDS CITY (SOUTH)	arr.	9-20
		dep.	2-32				
—	RAVENSWOOD JCT.	pass	3-02				
199.41	ST. BOSWELLS	arr.	3-05				
		dep.	3-10				

Above:

'D34' class No 62471 *Glen Falloch* **again, this time at Kirkbank with the 'Scott Country Railtour' on 4 April 1959. Kirkbank's sidings are clearly visible: note the loading bank alongside the passenger platform.**
W. A. C. Smith

Below:

On 15 April 1963 'B1' 4-6-0 No 61324 hauled another special to Jedburgh, which will be seen again at other places but is pictured here passing the small station at Nisbet, complete with a post office. *W. A. C. Smith*

Above:

The locomotive for the pick-up goods on the Jedburgh branch came from a diagram which saw a St Boswells locomotive run to Carlisle with the 7.19pm goods, from where it returned at 1am. On arrival at St Boswells, the locomotive took the branch freight to Kelso and Jedburgh, thus some interesting types could be seen occasionally on the branch. Perhaps the most unusual was 'Jubilee' 4-6-0 No 45696 *Arethusa*, which paid a visit on 29 May 1964 and is seen at Nisbet. *J. Spencer Gilks*

Below:
No 62471 *Glen Falloch* calls at Jedfoot with the 'Scott Country Railtour' on 4 April 1959. This locomotive was in immaculate condition and, together with three BR Mk1 coaches in carmine and cream, looked extremely smart.
W. A. C. Smith

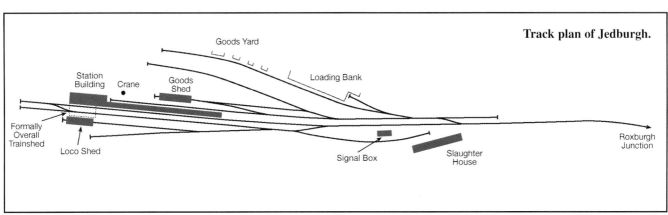

Track plan of Jedburgh.

Goods Yard

Station Building

Crane

Goods Shed

Loading Bank

Formally Overall Trainshed

Loco Shed

Signal Box

Slaughter House

Roxburgh Junction

Right:
Another view of No 62471
Glen Falloch as it runs round the
'Scott Country Railtour' at
Jedburgh. Freight traffic lasted
here until 10 August 1964.
Roy Hamilton

Centre right:
'B1' No 61324 has the road at
Jedburgh with the 'Scottish
Rambler No 2' on 15 April 1963.
The foreground shows where a
siding has been lifted which had
led to the loading bank.
W. A. C. Smith

Lower right:
Former North British 'Glen'
No 256 *Glen Douglas* and 'J37'
No 64624 are seen at Jedburgh.
This train was organised by the
Railway Correspondence & Travel
Society (RCTS) on 9 July 1961
and left Leeds City at 9.50am
hauled by no less than Stanier
Pacific No 46247 *City of Liverpool*;
there followed a run to Carlisle in
just over 113 minutes for the 112
miles. At Carlisle two 'B1s', Nos
61290 and 61242 *Alexander Reith
Gray* — replaced the 4-6-2 for the
run to Hawick, where they arrived
10 minutes late after an
uninspiring performance. At
Hawick Nos 256 and 64624 took
over the train and travelled to
Greenlaw. The train returned to
St Boswells and then ran via
Roxburgh Junction to Jedburgh,
where it reversed once again
before travelling to Roxburgh,
Kelso and Tweedmouth, arriving
24 minutes late due to a points
failure at Roxburgh. At
Tweedmouth, 'A1' No 60143
Sir Walter Scott (how appropriate!)
took over for the run to Newcastle
Central. From there, Leeds
Neville Hill 'A3' No 60074
Harvester worked the train on to
Leeds via Ripon (the Bishop
Auckland part of the tour being
dropped in favour of the main
line), where a near on-time arrival
at 9.20pm was achieved. The cost
for all this? 46 shillings, or £2.30.
David Holmes

KELSO TO TWEEDMOUTH AND BERWICK UPON TWEED

Left:
On 29 May 1964, the 2.20pm Kelso-St Boswells leaves the viaduct which crossed the Teviot near Roxburgh. The passenger service had only two weeks to go, being discontinued from 15 June.
J. Spencer Gilks

Centre left:
The rural nature of this section of the line is well illustrated as BR 2-6-0 No 78049 approaches Roxburgh with the 9.56am from Kelso to St Boswells on 4 September 1962. *M. Dunnett*

Lower left:
No 78049 pauses at Kelso with the 4pm from St Boswells to Berwick upon Tweed on 7 July 1962. Kelso was the largest station on the line and had a considerable goods yard as well as a locomotive shed (closed 1955), which at one time had a 45ft turntable.
Roy Hamilton

Above:
North British 'Scott' 4-4-0 No 62440 *Wandering Willie* **calls at Kelso with a service for St Boswells on
5 September 1954. It remained gas lit until closure.** *W. A. Camwell*

Below:
**Ex-NER 'G5' 0-4-4 tank No 67268 stops at Kelso with the 3.28pm from Berwick to St Boswells on 12 June 1954.
It is interesting to note that, even well into BR days, power from the NER and NBR worked the line in many
cases only as far as the Regional 'borderpost' at Kelso!** *W. A. C. Smith*

Above:

The 4.5pm from St Boswells to Berwick upon Tweed sets back to collect a van from the bay at Kelso, as was usual for this service. 'V1' 2-6-2T No 67659 is in charge. *N. R. Knight*

Centre left:

BR No 78049 and a sister are seen in the yard at Kelso on 4 August 1964. This yard was always busy and generated much traffic for the line. Mainly catering for agricultural and livestock traffic, as well as domestic coal and general merchandise, the yard was worked until the mid-1950s by a Sentinel shunter, Class Y1/2 No 68138. Before this, a petrol shunter was used, and before that horses, known locally as 'hairy pilots'! *J. W. Armstrong*

Lower left:

Class V3 2-6-2T No 67606 of Hawick has arrived at Kelso with a train for St Boswells. 'J39' 0-6-0 No 64917 of Tweedmouth has also worked in from that direction and is preparing to return there with a pick-up goods in May 1958. *Peter J. Robinson*

Above:

BR Standard Class 4 No 76050 leaves Kelso with the 09.59 train from Berwick to St Boswells on 11 April 1964. This locomotive, allocated to Hawick, became a regular performer on the line in the last years of passenger services. *M. Dunnett*

Right:

No 78046 at Kelso with the 4pm service from St Boswells to Berwick on 25 September 1961. The train was allowed 26 minutes to attach itself to the two parcels vans in the bay to the left. A number of cattle wagons can be seen in the siding, Kelso being the destination for livestock from the surrounding area. The goods yard was over to the left and there was also a livestock market next to the station. *W. A. C. Smith*

Above:

No 78048 leaves Sprouston with the 8.25am St Boswells-Berwick on 7 July 1962. From Kelso the line was double-track to Tweedmouth, which proved very useful when it was used as diversionary route for the East Coast main line. Sprouston was one of three stations built in Scotland by an English company, (the others being Carham (see below), and Annan Shawhill) which was reached after a short climb. Sprouston 'Junction' was 20 miles 6 chains from Tweedmouth and was the end-on connection between the North British and the North Eastern. Because of this there was a locomotive shed, but this was closed on 14 July 1916. However, during World War 2 the shed was home to preserved GWR 4-4-0 No 3717 *City of Truro*, which arrived from York via Tweedmouth on 18 July 1941, hauled by 'D49' 4-4-0 No 220. *Roy Hamilton*

Left:

A view of the locomotive shed at Sprouston that housed *City of Truro* during World War 2, recorded on 26 April 1952. To the right is a wagon on the coal-drop road — there were drops here for hopper wagons to unload.

J. W. Armstrong Trust

Right:
Sprouston again, this time from the rear of a freight train; the engine shed and yard are visible on the left. The LNER placed a camping coach here in the 1930s.
J. W. Armstrong Trust

Centre right:
Another Class 2 2-6-0, this time of the earlier Ivatt LMS design: No 46473 with brake van at Carham on 7 July 1962. Note the staggered platforms either side of the level crossing. From Carham the line passed Sunilaws, named Wark until 1 October 1871. Between Carham and Sunilaws the line passed from Scotland into England and there was an appropriate sign put up in the 1950s. Sunilaws had a siding and loading bank together with up and down platforms and a signalbox, the latter having been expanded in 1912. A further siding served Shidlaw Tileworks.
Between Sunilaws and Coldstream was also Learmouth Sidings, the signalbox here closing as early as 1907. *Roy Hamilton*

Lower right:
Coldstream, looking towards Kelso, showing the junction signals for the line to Wooler and Alnwick. The impressive signalbox was built in the 1920s, having replaced a smaller, 1888-built structure. The 'box had 38 levers and controlled the Wooler line and sidings in the immediate vicinity, the branch to Wooler surviving for freight until 29 March 1965. *J. W. Armstrong*

Above:
No 78046 calls at Coldstream with the 4pm St Boswells to Berwick on 25 September 1961. The fine signalbox stands guard — Coldstream was still the junction for the former Alnwick line, but this was now open only for freight as far as Wooler. *W. A. C. Smith*

Left:
A good number of passengers await the 9.56am from Berwick to St Boswells, hauled by BR Standard 2MT No 78048 at Coldstream, where the junction with the line to Alnwick was made. *Roy Hamilton*

Upper right:
Class B1 No 61324 calls at Coldstream on 15 April 1963 with the 'Scottish Rambler No 2' railtour. The train is ready for a trip down the Alnwick line as far as Wooler, hauled by Ivatt '2MT' No 46474 just seen on the rear. Coldstream station was actually situated at Cornhill (its name until 1 October 1873), south of the River Tweed, thus putting it in a different country from Coldstream itself. It was 12 miles 36 chains from Tweedmouth and was equipped with a goods yard.
W. A. C. Smith

Centre right:
Twizell was a small halt and is seen from the train on 26 April 1952. It had a siding and a small loading bank, to the right of the photograph. Originally, there were no sidings here, but in June 1882 one was put in and another was added in May 1885, together with a crossover linking the up and down lines, in the summer of 1900. This also involved the construction of a new signalbox in the same year. In the 1930s, there was an LNER camping coach here. *J. W. Armstrong Trust*

Lower right:
Norham station, looking west on 15 April 1963. This was 6 miles 53 chains from Tweedmouth and had a signalbox that had been rebuilt from the original wooden cabin of 1902, with a brick structure housing a 20-lever frame. There was a goods shed here too which was originally a small locomotive shed — this was for a small shunting locomotive that worked the sidings of all the stations on this section, from Kelso to Tweedmouth. After closure, the station was converted into a railway museum. This included the goods shed, signalbox and station buildings. *W. A. C. Smith*

Above:
No 78049 calls at Norham with a passenger service on 20 July 1963.
J. Spencer Gilks

Centre left:
A rare view of Velvet Hall is had from the rear of a freight train on 26 April 1952. This station was closed on 4 July 1955 when there was a general rationalisation of passenger services and most of the smaller stations on the NER section were closed. This was another station where there was a camping coach in the 1930s.
J. W. Armstrong Trust

Lower left:
No 78047 is seen between Velvet Hall station and Tweedmouth with the 4pm from St Boswells to Berwick upon Tweed on 1 June 1962. Velvet Hall was not a village but the station was named after a local farm near the village of Horncliffe, over a mile away. At Velvet Hall there was a signalbox which controlled the line up to Tweedmouth and down to Kelso.
Michael Mensing

St. Boswells to Duns and Reston

Historical perspective

The line from Reston (on the East Coast main line) to Duns — 8½ miles in length — was given approval on 26 June 1846. It took only three years to build, to double-track standards (as with the Alnwick-Alnmouth branch), and opened on 13 August 1849. The trains replaced a once-a-day horse-drawn coach service which linked the town with the East Coast main line at Reston, this latter route having been completed in June 1846. Not content with this section of line, a link to the Waverley Route at St Boswells was projected in order to carry the large amounts of agricultural produce and livestock that the area generated, as well as bringing in raw materials such as coal. The Berwickshire Railway Company obtained approval to extend the line from Duns on 17 July 1862. The North British Railway, which, of course, owned both the East Coast main line at Reston and the Waverley Route at St Boswells, sponsored the Berwickshire Railway with 50% of the investment required, the rest coming from backers from the area itself. The Reston to Duns section did not generate the expected traffic levels and certainly did not carry enough to warrant the double track formation that it enjoyed. By 1857 things were proving so uneconomic that the line was reduced to single-track.

West of Duns, the Berwickshire Railway was constructed from Greenlaw, where there was a ceremony to mark the occasion on 14 October 1862. Opening in stages, the railway reached Earlston from where it opened as far as Duns on 16 November 1863. The final section to St Boswells needed to cross the magnificent Drygrange Viaduct over the River Tweed at Leaderfoot. Initial problems with the structure moving during construction called for much remedial work to be done, which meant that opening of the whole route was delayed until 2 October 1865. The line joined the Waverley Route at Ravenswood Junction approximately one mile from St Boswells, which now had two branches to the East Coast main line — the other being to Kelso and Tweedmouth.

Train services

Passenger services from Reston to Duns were originally only three trains a day, with an extra on Mondays, but they did at least offer four classes of travel! The most curious arrangement on this section of the line, however, was the access to Reston station. The Duns line arrived at Reston on the down side of the East Coast main line and to reach the station, a passenger train had to set back into the platform, that is if it was not making a run directly to Berwick.

On the opening of the line from St Boswells to Duns there were two passenger trains per day on this section, with a daily branch freight that came out from St Boswells to Reston, together with a cattle service that ran Mondays only from Berwick to Duns and back. Initially, there were only two timetabled goods services every week on the Duns to Reston line. Grain to Edinburgh was carried on the back of the 3.45pm passenger service which ran to

Reston as mixed, on Tuesdays only. Here wagons were detached for Edinburgh. On Mondays only, a cattle train ran to Berwick. As well as the cattle and grain forwardings from Duns, there was intermediate traffic to Chirnside, where there was esparto grass traffic for a paper mill, while at Edrom there were forwardings of beet and potatoes. Another siding was provided at Crumstane, near Duns.

Opening on 2 October 1865, the new Berwickshire-line extension to St Boswells was operated by the NBR, using coaching stock purchased from that company by the Berwickshire Railway. Roughly half the income was paid to the NBR for its trouble.

Freight services increased in number as traffic grew — up to three daily return services and two extras were run on Mondays. In 1865 services were timed as follows:

---

am
5.30 MO — Berwick-Reston-Duns — cattle service
7.5 — Reston-St Boswells — passenger
9.13 — Reston-St Boswells — passenger
12.00 — Berwick-Reston-St Boswells — passenger
pm
3.00 — Reston-St Boswells — goods
3.15 — Berwick-St Boswells — passenger
6.19 — Reston-St Boswells — passenger

am
6.30 — Duns-Reston — passenger and mails
7.5 — St Boswells-Reston — passenger
8.30 MO — Duns-Berwick — cattle service
8.42 — St Boswells-Berwick — passenger
10.46 — St Boswells-Reston — goods
11.5 — St Boswells-Berwick — passenger
pm
4.16 — St Boswells-Reston — passenger
5.35 — St Boswells-Duns — passenger

The Berwickshire Railway was finally taken over by the NBR on 25 October 1876.

The last year before the Grouping saw four through services along the whole line from St Boswells to Berwick and three return workings. There was a further evening service from St Boswells as far as Reston, and in the opposite direction there was a 7.10am from Duns to St Boswells as well as two evening locals from Reston to Duns only.

Goods services ran at:

---

am
4.55 MO — Berwick-Duns-Greenlaw on certain dates only
5.45 MX — Berwick-Duns
9.30 MO — Reston-Duns

---

pm
12.10 — Duns-St Boswells
2.50 — Reston-Duns
5.5 — Duns-St Boswells
7.26 — Greenlaw-Duns — cattle
7.58 MO — Duns-Reston — cattle and other traffic
9.15 — St Boswells-Duns
11.50 — Duns-Reston
pm
1.20 — St Boswells-Berwick
2.50 — St Boswells-Duns
5.45 — Duns-Berwick
6.15 — St Boswells-Duns — ran 'mixed', as required

Following the Grouping the line passed into the ownership of the LNER. Initially the service, although a through service between St Boswells and Reston/Berwick, was known for delays that were timetabled to occur at Duns, most through services experiencing lengthy waits.

Before World War 2, the line saw special trains from Peebles and Hawick that ran to Whitley Bay. This service ran weekly, alternately via Duns then Kelso and Reedsmouth Junction, and all for 2s 6d return. These trains had ceased by 1939 and the war years saw three through services from Berwick to St Boswells supplemented by a St Boswells-Reston through service. There were two others, a 7.6am from Duns to St Boswells and an 8.25pm from Reston to Duns. The shed at Duns provided the power for the line at this time, but the LNER transferred responsibility for the motive power to Tweedmouth shed rather than St Boswells.

The line passed into British Railways ownership on 1 January 1948. In the timetable in operation that year four trains ran from St Boswells to Berwick; a fifth ran through to Reston where there was a connection for Berwick. The first train from St Boswells arrived at Duns at 7.6am, exactly the same time the first train back to St Boswells departed (this having been stabled overnight at Duns); it then formed the 8.25am St Boswells-Berwick, where it arrived at 10.41am. This had been preceded by the 6.10am from St Boswells, the stock for this service being stabled, along with the locomotive, at St Boswells. Further services followed at 11.35am, 4pm and 6.5pm, the last train going only as far as Reston. Trains came from Berwick at 8.8am, 12.50, 3.25 and 5.50pm for St Boswells — the last departure was at 8.30pm from Reston, the return working of the 6.5pm ex St Boswells, the stock and locomotive then staying overnight at Duns for the 7.6am departure the following morning. The locomotive allocation was transferred from Tweedmouth to Hawick, on the Scottish Region.

This timetable was the last to offer through services, as on 12 August 1948 the bridge over the Langton Burn, between Marchmont and Duns stations, was destroyed in floods, one of many bridges in the area that were swept away. Langton Burn flows eventually into Blackadder Water, which itself flows into Whiteadder Water, a tributary of the River Tweed. The Duns line also crossed Blackadder Water just to the east of Greenlaw and there, the small masonry viaduct was also damaged by the 1948 floods. Thus all services were suspended with buses replacing trains. The part of the line from Greenlaw to Duns was never reopened. Goods services only returned to the Ravenswood Junction-Greenlaw section, but further to the east the Duns-Reston Junction section reopened for freight traffic in the autumn of 1948, passenger trains recommencing on 1 August 1949. With access to St Boswells now cut off, except by means of a long detour, responsibility for providing power for the line was transferred back to Tweedmouth.

ST. BOSWELLS, DUNS, RESTON, and BERWICK.—North British.

Down. Week Days only.

Miles		mrn	mrn	mrn	aft	aft		
	St. Boswells .... dep.	6 23	8 33	11 10	4 5	6 15	...	...
4¼	Earlston	...	8 42	11 20	4 15	6 27	...	...
10¼	Gordon	...	8 54	11 32	4 27	6 41	...	...
14½	Greenlaw	...	9 3	11 41	4 39	6 55	...	...
18¾	Marchmont	...	9 10	11 49	4 47	7 5	...	...
22	Duns { arr.	7 2	9 17	11 57	4 55	7 15	...	...
	Duns { dep.	7 12	10 0	12 40	5 1	7 25	...	...
25¼	Edrom	7 20	10 8	12 48	5 9	7 33	...	...
26¾	Chirnside	7 24	10 12	12 52	5 13	7 37	...	...
30¼	Reston * 776 { arr.	7 33	10 21	..	5 22	7 46	...	...
	Reston { dep.	7 36	10 24	1 6	5 26		...	...
34¾	Ayton	7 43	10 32	1 14	5 33		...	...
36¾	Burnmouth	7 49	10 38	1 20	5 39		...	...
42	Berwick .... arr.	7 57	10 46	1 28	5 48		...	...

Up. Week Days only.

Miles		mrn	mrn	aft	aft	aft	aft
	Berwick .... dep.	...	8 30	12 50	3 28	...	...
5¼	Burnmouth	...	8 41	1 2	3 39	...	...
7¾	Ayton	...	8 46	1 7	3 44	...	...
11½	Reston { arr.	...	8 54	1 14	3 52	...	...
	Reston { dep.	...	8 58	1 18	3 56	6 40	8 2
15¼	Chirnside	...	9 8	1 28	4 6	6 50	8 12
16½	Edrom	...	9 12	1 32	4 10	6 54	8 17
20	Duns { arr.	...	9 20	1 40	4 18	7 2	8 25
	Duns { dep.	7 10	9 29	1 43	4 21		
23½	Marchmont	7 18	9 37	1 51	4 29		
27¼	Greenlaw	7 27	9 46	2 0	4 38		
31½	Gordon	7 36	9 55	2 9	4 47		
37¼	Earlston ...... [and below]	7 49	10 8	2 22	5 0		
42	St. Boswells 780,781 arr.	7 59	10 18	2 32	5 10	...	...

* Station for Coldingham (3¼ miles) and St. Abbs (4¼ miles).

☞ For **LOCAL TRAINS** between Reston and Berwick, see **page 776.**

Above:
Bradshaw's guide Timetable July 1922, Berwick, Reston and Duns.

Right:
LNER timetable 22 May 1944 until further notice, Berwick and St Boswells.

Table 175	BERWICK and ST. BOSWELLS								

Week Days only

Miles		mrn	mrn b	aft b	aft b	aft	aft
—	Berwick .... dep		8 8	12 50 3 20		6 10	..
¾	Burnmouth	..	8 19	1 33 34		6 29	..
7¼	Ayton	..	8 24	1 33 39		6 35	..
11½	Reston, for St. Abbs arr	..	8 31	1 15 46		6 42	..
—	157 Edinburgh (W.) dep	..	6 40	10 40 11 40		3 50 6 30	
—	Reston .... dep	..	8 33	1 17 3 53		6 50 8 25	
15¼	Chirnside	..	8 42	1 24 0		6 58 34	
16½	Edrom	..	8 46	1 28 4		7 2 39	
20	Duns { arr / dep	7 6	8 52 / 9 44	1 34 10 / 1 36 4 20		7 8 45 / 7 20	
23½	Marchmont	7 14	9 52	1 44 36		7 28	
27¼	Greenlaw	7 23	10 1	1 52 34		7 38	
31½	Gordon	7 31	10 10	2 04 42		7 47	
37¼	Earlston	7 42	10 23	2 11 52		7 59	
42	St. Boswells .... arr	7 50	10 33	2 20 5 1			
9¾	167 Carlisle ...... arr	10 22	12 46	5 55 9 10		1 25	
82½	167 Edinburgh (W.) arr	9 48	12 40	4 49 7 30		10 p 9	

Week Days only

Miles		mrn	mrn b	mrn b	aft	aft
—	167 Edinburgh (W.) dep	..	6 25 9 55		2 25 4 10	..
—	167 Carlisle .... "	..	5 55 8 58		1 50 8 40	..
—	St. Boswells .... dep	6 10	8 25 11 30		4 0 6 8	..
4¼	Earlston		8 35 11 43		4 10 6 19	..
10¼	Gordon		8 47 11 58		4 22 6 32	..
14½	Greenlaw		8 56 12 8		4 35 6 41	..
18¾	Marchmont	6 48	9 3 12 17		4 49 6 58	..
22	Duns { arr / dep	6 56 / 7 6	9 10 12 24 / 9 58 12 34		4 55 57 20	..
25¼	Edrom	7 13	10 3 12 41		5 27 28	..
26¾	Chirnside	7 17	10 7 12 45		5 37 33	..
30¼	Reston, for St. Abbs ...	7 26	10 16 12 54		5 17 42	..
77	157 Edinburgh (W.) arr	9 15	12 47 3 38		8 32	..
—	Reston .... dep	7 29	10 19 12 58		5 32 18	..
34¾	Ayton	7 36	10 27 1 6		5 39 28	..
36¾	Burnmouth	7 42	10 33 1 13		5 44 31	..
42	Berwick	7 50	10 41 1 21		5 52 41	..

a Mrn.   b Thro' Trains between Berwick and St. Boswells.   f Arrive 3 19 aft on Saturdays.
I Depart 1 50 aft on Saturdays.   N Arrive 6 21 aft.   p Aft.
For **OTHER TRAINS** between Berwick and Burnmouth, see **Table 171**—Berwick and Reston, **Table 157.**

Table 43 — St. Boswells, Duns and Berwick

Mls			a.m	a.m	a.m	n'n	a.m	p.m	p.m	p.m	p.m	p.m (Sats only)	p.m
	Glasgow (Queen Street) lev.		—	—	—	—	8 35	—	—	1 0	—	—	2 25
	Edinburgh (Waverley) "		6 20	·	·	—	1010	·	·	2 35	·	—	4 10
	Carlisle "		4 53	·	·	—	9 5	·	·	1 25	·	—	3 30
	St. Boswells lev.	6 10	·	8 25	·	1135	·	·	4 0	·	—	6 5
4¼	Earlston		—	8 35	—	1148	·	·	4 10	·	—	6 16
10	Gordon		·	8 47	·	12 3	·	·	4 22	·	—	6 29
14¼	Greenlaw		—	8 56	—	1213	·	·	4 34	·	—	6 38
18¼	Marchmont	6 48	9 3	1222	·	·	4 41	·	—	6 47
22	Duns arr	6 56	9 10	1229	·	·	4 48	·	—	6 55
	Duns lev.	7 6	9 56	1239	·	·	4 55	·	—	7 3
25¼	Edrom	7 13	10 3	1246	·	·	5 2	·	—	7 11
26½	Chirnside	7 17	10 7	1250	·	·	5 8	·	—	7 18
30½	Reston (for St. Abbs) arr	7 26	1016	1259	·	·	5 17	·	—	7 25
	Edinburgh (Wav.) via Reston ar	9 15	1248	3 26	·	·	9 20
	Glasgow (Queen Street) arr	11 9	2 10	5 0	1113
	Reston lev.	7 29	8 30	1019	12J0	1 33	3 35	4 49	5 19	5 28	A	8 22
34¾	Ayton	7 36	8 37	1027	1 11	3 57	5 35	8 29
36¾	Burnmouth	7 42	8 42	1033	12J9	1 18	3 43	4 9	5 40	8 23	8 36
42	Berwick arr	7 50	8 51	1041	1218	1 26	3 52	4 16	5 34	4 18	3 35	8 44

			a.m	a.m	a.m	a.m	p.m	p.m	p.m	p.m	p.m	p.m	p.m (Sats only)
	Berwick lev.	7 18	—	8 8	1118	1250	1 30	2 13	3 25	5 50	7 6	9 30
	Burnmouth	7 31	·	8 19	1 5	1 40	3 38	6 3	7 25	9 41
	Ayton	7 36	·	8 24	1 10	1 45	3 43	6 8	7 31	H
	Reston (for St. Abbs) arr	7 44	·	8 31	1136	1 17	1 53	2 32	3 50	6 15	7 41
	Glasgow (Queen Street) lev.		9 5	1 0	5 0
	Edinburgh (Wav.) & Reston lev.		6 40	1035	2 30	3 45	6 35
	Reston lev.	8 33	1 20	3 56	6 30	8 30
	Chirnside	8 42	1 28	4 4	6 38	8 39
	Edrom	8 46	1 33	4 8	6 42	8 44
	Duns arr	8 52	1 39	4 14	6 48	8 50
	Duns lev.	7 6	8 44	1 43	4 19	7 10
	Marchmont	7 14	9 52	1 51	4 25	7 18
	Greenlaw	7 23	10 1	2 0	4 44	7 28
	Gordon	7 31	1010	2 8	4 44	7 37
	Earlston	7 42	1022	2 18	4 54	7 49
	St. Boswells arr	7 52	1032	2 27	5 2	7 59
	Carlisle arr	1022	1254	5 54	8 42	1228
	Edinburgh (Waverley) "	9 32	1205	4 20	7 10	9 49
	Glasgow (Queen Street) "	11 9	2 10	6 27	10:26

Table 79 — BERWICK, RESTON and DUNS

Miles			WEEKDAYS							
			am	am	am	am J	pm	pm	pm	pm
—	BERWICK dep	6 10	7 5	....	11 10	2 27	....	....	7 10
5¼	Burnmouth "		7 18	....	2 39	..	7 26
7¼	Ayton "		7 23	....	2 44	..	7 29
11¼	Reston arr for St. Abbs	6 29	7 34	..	11 28	2 51	..	7 35
—	Edinburgh dep	....	....	6 55	....	....	2 30	3 45	6 35
—	Reston dep	6 31	7 41	8 40	11 38	2 53	3 55	5 33	8 10
15¼	Chirnside "	6 39	7 49	8 48	11 46	3 1	4 3	5 41	8 18
16½	Edrom "	6 43	7 53	8 52	11 50	3 5	4 7	5 45	8 22
20	DUNS arr	6 49	7 59	8 58	11 56	3 11	4 13	5 51	8 28

Miles			WEEKDAYS							
			am	am	am	J pm	pm	pm	pm	J pm
—	DUNS dep	7 12	8 11	..	5 12 35	3 22	4 58	7 10	8 51
3¼	Edrom "	7 19	8 15	11 12	12 42	3 29	5 5	7 17	8 58
4½	Chirnside "	7 23	8 19	11 16	12 46	3 33	5 9	7 21	9 2
8½	Reston arr for St. Abbs	7 32	8 28	11 25	12 55	3 42	5 18	7 30	9 11
55	Edinburgh arr	9 7	..	12p40	3 30	....	....	9 5	....
—	Reston dep	..	8 32	11 50	12 58	3 47	5 23	8 5	9 14
12¼	Ayton "	..	8 39	..	1 6	....	5 30	8 12	....
14½	Burnmouth "	..	8 43	12 1	1 13	4	15	5 36	8 18	....
20	BERWICK arr	..	8 51	12 10	1 24	4 10	5 44	8 26	9 33

J—Through trains between Berwick and Duns. | p—pm.

Above:
BR ScR timetable, 31 May to September 1948, Berwick, Reston and Duns.

Left:
BR NER timetable, 25 September 1950, Berwick, Reston and Duns.

This last service pattern for passenger trains showed eight return workings per day on the line. However, these were worked on an out-and-home basis from Tweedmouth shed, as the depot at Duns had closed, the first train leaving Berwick at 6.10am and arriving at Duns at 6.49am. This train then worked the branch until the 12.35 departure, which took it back to Berwick for a crew change and a fresh engine. This working then left Berwick at 2.27pm, with an arrival at Duns at 3.11pm. After working the branch during the afternoon the service returned to Berwick from Duns at 8.51pm. Passenger services on the remaining Duns-Reston section were withdrawn from Monday 10 September 1951, the last train being the 7.25pm Duns-Berwick with 'D20' 4-4-0 No 62351 as the train engine. However, freight remained worked as two separate services, one from St Boswells to Greenlaw, the other from Tweedmouth to Duns.

By January 1963 the Reston-Duns section was operated as 'one engine in steam' and the signalboxes at Chirnside and Duns were closed. Traditional freight forwardings such as livestock and farm produce had declined significantly since the war, and by the 1960s only one daily service was needed on the line, sugar beet and potatoes being forwarded from places like Edrom; coal was the main inward commodity, along with animal feedstuffs. However, the line did carry a quantity of

'intervention' traffic, commodities such as sugar and grain for storage.

The branch freight shunted the yard at Berwick until departure time at 8.10am. After possibly calling at Ayton, the train arrived at 8.45am at Reston, which, after shunting (and what is now called a PNB), it left by 10am for Chirnside and Duns; departure from Duns was at 11.10am, the train returning to Reston and Berwick. While the branch goods was normally hauled by steam power from Tweedmouth, on Whit (Bank Holiday) Monday 1965 the power was provided by Haymarket, Type 4 diesel No D360 being used. This was because Tweedmouth did not steam locomotives on holiday weekends but Scotland worked, as it did not observe the holiday. On August Bank Holiday that year the motive power was Gateshead 'Peak' diesel No D181, which promptly derailed at Duns, where it was left with its train until the next day!

On Boxing Day 1965 the branch freight was cancelled, next running on the Tuesday with BR Standard Class 3 No 77004. The next diesel to work the line was an 0-6-0 shunter with 14 wagons on Easter Monday 1966. The locomotive struggled and the train came to a stand four times, eventually reaching Duns and returning later on in the day. The freight service from Duns to Reston ceased from 4 November 1966; by this time it was a MWFO service out and back from Tweedmouth.

At the western end of the line the daily St Boswells to Greenlaw freight survived until 19 July 1965. Closure of this end of the line from Ravenswood Junction to Greenlaw had been under consideration from the Scottish Region for a number of years. But even at this late hour, the farming industry still relied on the railway for both inward traffic such as feedstuffs, equipment and coal, as well as outward transportation of animals and other produce. With Earlston a railhead for this business (even for Lauder after that line had closed), services continued as long as the infrastructure could be cheaply maintained. About 600 loaded wagons were handled on the line in the late 1950s, but apparently this was not enough to justify the costs of service provision at that time, as well as the maintenance of expensive structures such as Drygrange Viaduct — as much as twice the annual income generated by the line.

RESTON JUNCTION AND DUNS BRANCH

UP TRAINS		WEEKDAYS		DOWN TRAINS	
No.	334		No.	334	
Description			Description		
Class	K		Class	K	
Departs from	Tweedm'th 8.16 a.m.		Departs from	Tweedm'th 8.16 a.m.	
Previous Times on Page	W 19		Previous Times on Page	W 78	

M. C.		am		M. C.		am	
1 69	Reston Junction ⊕ ..	*	.. .. ..	2 0	Duns	*	.. .. ..
2 6	Auchincrow	..	.. .. ..	3 20	Crumstone	*	.. .. ..
3 77	Billiemains	*	.. .. ..	4 63	Edrom	*	.. .. ..
5 40	Chirnside	*	.. .. ..	8 60	Chirnside	*	.. .. ..
8 60	Edrom	*	.. .. ..		Reston Junction ..	*	.. .. ..
	Duns	*	.. .. ..				

Arrives at	Tweedm'th *		Arrives at	Tweedm'th *	
Forward Times on Page	W 78		Forward Times on Page	W 9	

RAVENSWOOD JUNCTION AND GREENLAW BRANCH

UP TRAINS		WEEKDAYS		DOWN TRAINS	
No.	532		No.	540	
Description			Description		
Class	K		Class	K	
Departs from	St. Boswells 6.10 a.m.		Departs from		
Previous Times on Page	W 78		Previous Times on Page		

M. C.		am		M. C.		am	
4 4	Greenlaw	8 10	.. .. ..	1 28	St. Boswells	6 10	.. .. ..
7 75	Gordon	8 35	.. .. ..	4 39	Ravenswood Junction .. ⊕..		.. .. ..
9 75	Fans Loonend	9 35	.. .. ..		Earlston	6 50	.. .. ..
13 6	Earlston		.. .. ..	10 30	Brownlie Siding		.. .. ..
14 34	Ravenswood Junction ⊕..		.. .. ..	14 34	Gordon	7 10	.. .. ..
	St. Boswells	9 50	.. .. ..		Greenlaw	7 20	.. .. ..

Arrives at			Arrives at	St. Boswells 9.50 a.m.	
Forward Times on Page			Forward Times on Page	W 78	

Above:
BR ScR working timetable September 21 1953, Reston Junction-Duns branch and Ravenswood Junction-Greenlaw branch that once formed a through route between Reston and Ravenswood Junction.

Below:
Track plan — Reston Junction.

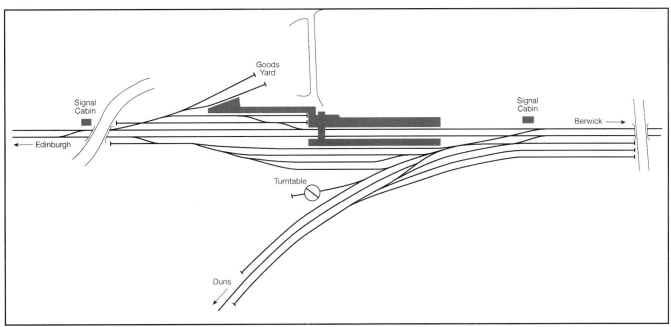

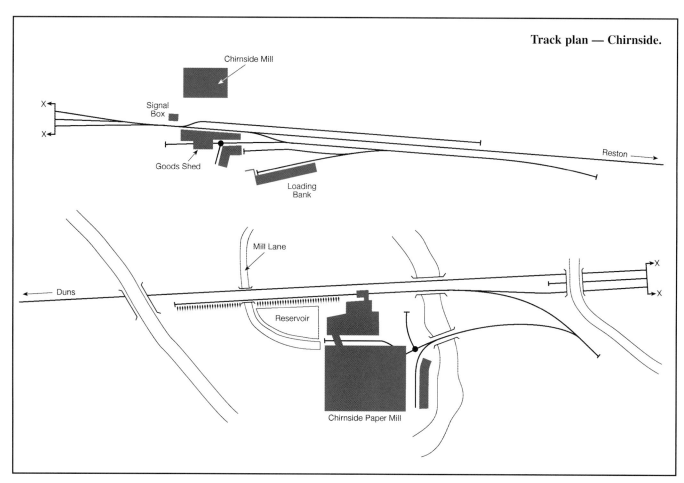

Track plan — Chirnside.

Chirnside Mill

Signal Box

X

X

Goods Shed

Loading Bank

Reston

Mill Lane

Duns

Reservoir

Chirnside Paper Mill

X

X

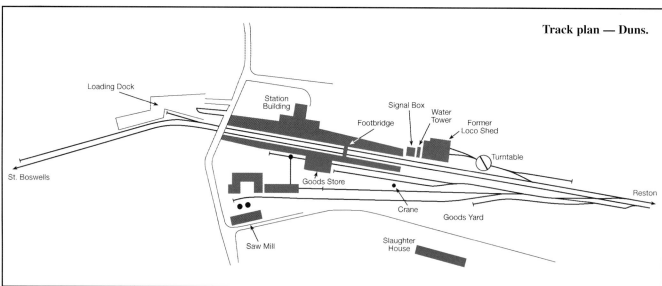

Track plan — Duns.

Loading Dock

Station Building

Signal Box

Water Tower

Footbridge

Former Loco Shed

Turntable

St. Boswells

Goods Store

Crane

Goods Yard

Reston

Saw Mill

Slaughter House

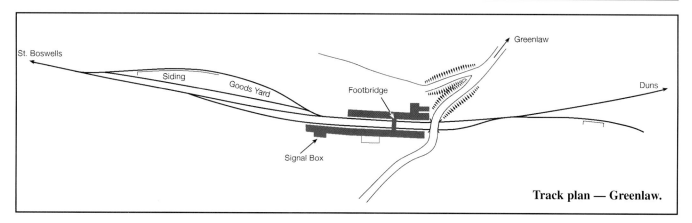

St. Boswells

Greenlaw

Siding

Goods Yard

Footbridge

Duns

Signal Box

Track plan — Greenlaw.

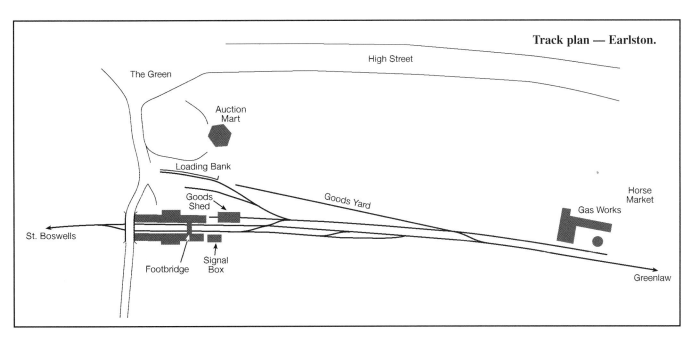

Track plan — Earlston.

High Street

The Green

Auction Mart

Loading Bank

Goods Shed

Goods Yard

Horse Market

Gas Works

St. Boswells

Footbridge

Signal Box

Greenlaw

Right:
BR ScR timetable, 15 June to 6 September 1964 — replacement bus services for the Berwickshire Railway.

Below:
Trains for the Greenlaw and Duns line ran down the Waverley Route for a mile before reaching Ravenswood Junction. Here, the signalman returns to his cabin after having handed the token to the branch freight for Greenlaw on 29 May 1959. What a wonderful job it must have been to work here! Note too the smartness of the permanent way, lineside equipment, the condition of the box, the tidy embankments, etc. What a contrast to now, as the embankment that once formed the Greenlaw line is now obliterated by a road.
J. Spencer Gilks

Table 65

DUNS and RESTON

SCOTTISH OMNIBUSES LTD., NEW STREET, EDINBURGH

Outward from Duns	S pm	E pm							Inward to Duns	am							
Duns Square .. .. dep	1240	5 10	..	..	..	..	..	..	Reston .. .. .. dep	8 20	..	..	..	..	..	..	..
Chirnside Cross Hill.....	1 0	5 30	....	....	....	....	....	....	Chirnside Cross Hill....	8 35	....	....	....	....	....	....	....
Reston .. .. .. arr	1 15	5 45	..	..	..	..	..	..	Duns Square .. .. arr	8 55	..	..	..	..	..	..	..

E Except Saturdays.   S Saturdays only

Table 66

GALASHIELS, MELROSE, GORDON and DUNS

SCOTTISH OMNIBUSES LTD., NEW STREET, EDINBURGH

Outward from Galashiels	am	am	pm	pm	E pm	pm		Inward to Galashiels	am	am	pm	pm	
Galashiels Market .. dep	8 25	10 0	2 45	5 0	6 30	..	Duns Market .. .. dep	6 55	1125	4 5	8 30	..
Melrose Market.........	8 40	1015	3 05	5 15	6 45	..	Greenlaw Post Office	7 15	1145	4 25	8 50	....
Leaderfoot	8 47	1022	3 6	5 22	6 52	..	Gordon East End	7 29	12 0	4 40	9 5	..
Earlston Square	8 55	1030	3 13	5 30	4 2 7 0	....	Earlston Square	7 47	1221	5 0	9 25	..
Gordon East End	9 15	1050	3 31	.. 6 1	7 20	..	Leaderfoot	7 54	1229	5 8	9 33	..
Greenlaw Post Office	9 30	11 5	3 45	.. 6 15	7 35	..	Melrose Market.........	8 0	1236	5 15	9 40	..
Duns Market .. .. arr	9 50	1125	4 5	.. 6 35	7 55	..	Galashiels Market .. arr	8 15	1251	5 30	9 55	..

E Saturdays excepted.   S Saturdays only

RAVENSWOOD JUNCTION

Left:
Class J35 No 64494 crosses Drygrange Viaduct (often called Leaderfoot Viaduct), consisting of 19 arches built in 1865 by the Berwickshire Railway. It suffered from instability in some of its piers during construction and went over budget by approximately £44,000 even before any remedial work. Thankfully it attracted a Grade B listing and is still standing today but carries no trains. The 0-6-0 has the returning 'Berwickshire goods' from Greenlaw and, in addition to the normal traffic, has some permanent way ballast wagons. From the viaduct the line passed through Lauderdale to Earlston. *Stuart Sellar*

Centre left:
Despite this portion of the line being freight only at the time, ex-North British 'Glen' No 62471 *Glen Falloch* is seen returning to Earlston from Greenlaw with the Branch Line Society's 'Scott Country Railtour' on 4 April 1958. Earlston had a passing loop and, after the closure of the Lauder Light Railway, was the nearest railway to Lauder until its services were withdrawn in 1948. *Roy Hamilton*

Lower left:
No 62471 is seen tender first in the station at Earlston on the outward journey with its special train for Greenlaw on 4 April 1958. At Earlston there was a reasonably sized goods yard which carried stone traffic from a local quarry operated by King & Company. Even after closure to passengers Earlston still had a stationmaster and three staff. It was important as it was the railhead for a wide area, especially for coal and agricultural users and had a livestock market near the station. *Roy Hamilton*

The more normal scene on the branch was freight traffic. Class J36 No 65233, formerly named *Plumer,* is seen at Earlston on 29 May 1959. It was at Earlston where the line from Duns had terminated until the final link to St Boswells had been completed, delayed due to problems with Leaderfoot Viaduct. Thus the authorities demanded that a turntable be provided here, so the Berwickshire Railway built one, but of only 18ft diameter! This did not prove to be acceptable and the railway was given three months to extend it. In the event this was not done as through running commenced shortly afterwards. *J. Spencer Gilks*

Right:
Class J37 No 64591 has arrived at Earlston with the branch freight on 31 May 1963. The 'smalls' are being checked by the stationmaster who has a consignment note in his hand as he tallies up the number of boxes on the platform. *John Langford collection*

Above:
Class J35 No 64494 gets away from Earlston with the Berwickshire-branch freight to Greenlaw on 15 May 1958. The area either side of the railway line seems to be quite untidy — it has since been landscaped.
Stuart Sellar

Below:
From Earlston the line crossed Leader Water on a three-arch viaduct before reaching a siding at Fans Loanend. Three miles on from there came Gordon, where No 62471 *Glen Falloch* is seen calling with the Branch Line Society's 'Scott Country Railtour' on 4 April 1958, having worked to Greenlaw. The structure to the right is the former whinstone aggregates plant, which forwarded traffic. Agricultural products were sent and received at the station, where coal was also received. *W. A. C. Smith*

Right:
Class J37 No 64591 at Gordon with the Greenlaw goods on 31 May 1963. A new-looking Ford Popular waits in the yard, a car being a necessity for local transport, as the passenger service on this section was never reinstated following the 1948 floods. *John Langford collection*

Centre right:
The paperwork done, No 64591 leaves Gordon after having paused with the goods for Greenlaw on 31 May 1963.
John Langford collection

Below:
No 64494 has stopped near Greenlaw to allow the crew to dig up peat for the station garden at Melrose. As this was the only train of the day, at least nothing would be held up while this important activity took place!
Stuart Sellar

Having run round its train, the Branch Line Society's 'Scott Country Railtour', No 62471 *Glen Falloch* **prepares to leave Greenlaw and head back to St Boswells on 4 April 1958. Greenlaw once had a footbridge, which led to the platform on which the photographer is standing, and a signalbox that controlled sections to Duns and Earlston.** *W. A. C. Smith*

No 64591 shunts at Greenlaw with the 7.30am goods from St Boswells on 31 May 1963. The photographer is looking towards St Boswells, with the sidings to the right. In this era of no vandalism, the station has survived well and the station house is still occupied by railway staff. At this time, the traffic is mainly coal and other general merchandise, hardly any livestock was forwarded. *John Langford*

No 64494 has deposited some wagons at Greenlaw, having brought them in earlier from Galashiels, on 15 May 1958; it has now shunted and is preparing to leave with the balancing working back to St Boswells. Locomotives for the Greenlaw branch were once based at St Boswells, but on that shed's closure, on 16 November 1959, they were transferred to Galashiels, itself a sub-shed of Edinburgh St Margarets (64A). *Stuart Sellar*

Above:

The very last passenger service to run on the Berwick to Greenlaw section was hauled by No 256 *Glen Douglas* **and 'J37' No 64624, seen on 9 July 1961 at 2.42pm on arrival at Greenlaw with the RCTS special.** *David Holmes*

Right:

Duns station, seen from the road bridge to the west end of the station on 15 April 1963. One of the platform roads has been lifted following the demise of the passenger service over ten years previously. There is still a large amount of goods traffic here, including grain and sugar, as well as inwards coal. The occasion was the passing of what was to be the last passenger train — the 'Scottish Rambler No 2' hauled by 'B1' No 61324. Duns was once a large receiver and forwarder of livestock, with a slaughterhouse and market situated close to the station. *W. A. C. Smith*

Upper left:
No 61324 has set back the stock of the railtour into Duns station on 15 April 1963. *W. A. C. Smith*

Upper right:
Ivatt 2-6-0 No 46475 heads the daily branch freight from Tweedmouth at Duns on 31 May 1963. *John Langford collection*

Centre right:
Duns also had a locomotive shed situated on the up side of the tracks to the east of the station. At the Grouping, in exchange for Carlisle London Road, the North Eastern Area of the LNER took over three former NBR sheds from the Scottish Area, Duns, Reedsmouth and Rothbury, while Berwick was incorporated into Tweedmouth. As a result, the shed at Duns housed various NER locomotives; in 1930 it had 'D23' 4-4-0 No 258, in 1934/5 'H1' 4-4-4T No 2160 and from 1945 to 1948 'D20' 4-4-0 No 2028, later No 2357. The shed was returned to the Scottish Region on 13 June 1948. In the 1960s the branch freight was worked by a variety of motive power from Tweedmouth; here, on 23 April 1960, 'J39' No 64843 has arrived with a goodly number of wagons. The train is standing in the down platform road, which had been lifted by the time of No 61324's visit in 1963. *Stuart Sellar*

Lower left:
No 64843 has now shunted the yard and is preparing to leave Duns station for Berwick on 23 April 1960. Note the considerable quantity of freight traffic, both in the train and still in the yard. *Stuart Sellar*

Lower right:
'B1' No 61324 on the 'Scottish Rambler No 2' calls at Chirnside station on its way back to Reston on 15 April 1963. Chirnside had a large paper mill and this attracted much inwards coal and raw materials for the manufacture of paper. *Ian Allan Library*

Left:
Chirnside station, seen from the back of the brake van of the Duns-Reston freight on 31 May 1963. Note the large goods shed which was latterly used to store 'intervention grain'. The signalbox here was closed in September 1962, after which the line was worked by 'one engine in steam' from Reston.
John Langford

Above:
No 64843 exchanges the tablet at Chirnside having arrived from Berwick and Reston on 23 April 1960. It is amazing to think that Chirnside was the target of a raid by Zeppelins during World War 1. *Stuart Sellar*

Galashiels to Selkirk

Historical perspective

The Selkirk & Galashiels Railway was authorised on 31 July 1854, the line running along the Tweed Valley for much of its distance before turning into Ettrick Water. Six miles long, it was opened on 5 April 1856.

The line's backers saw the opportunity to transport woollen and tweed products from the mills in Selkirk to the central belt of Scotland and to England, and as well as this, there was passenger traffic to and from Galashiels and Edinburgh.

The line also passed close to Abbotsford, the home of Sir Walter Scott. This was open for visitors and a station was provided at Abbotsford Ferry whence passengers could reach the house.

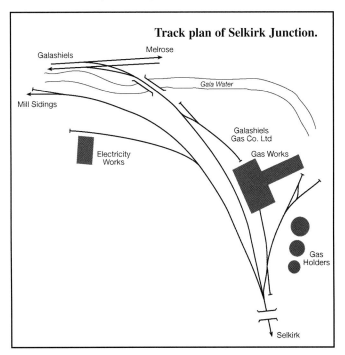

Track plan of Selkirk Junction.

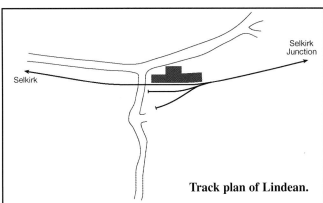

Track plan of Lindean.

Other freight traffic, such as inward coal, agricultural supplies and general merchandise, plus the outward movement of livestock, meant that the line had potential — until it opened — but, as with other small branch lines, arrangements had to be made to send traffic to Galashiels and the new Waverley Route by road.

The line diverged from the Waverley Route at Selkirk Junction — approximately one mile south of Galashiels station. Almost immediately it passed the Galashiels & District Electricity Supply Co, where there was a siding, with a further siding to Netherdale Woollen Mill. Next came the Galashiels Gas Company works where sidings were also provided. The line then ran alongside the north bank of the River Tweed after having passed over Gala Water by Selkirk Junction. The first station reached, after approximately 1½ miles, was Abbotsford Ferry, where a rowing boat provided access for tourist passengers to Scott's house. Although the station closed as early as 5 January 1931, the platform remained, and it was reopened occasionally for passengers from the annual Braw Lads Gathering. The ferry boat, known locally as the Boleside Ferry, was guided across the river by overhead wires and continued to operate until the end of World War 2.

Having crossed the River Tweed by means of a five-span steel bridge, the line reached the station at Lindean, four miles from Galashiels; like the station at Abbotsford Ferry, this had a single platform, but it also had a siding and loading bank. The route then followed Ettrick Water before arriving at Selkirk.

At Selkirk, the station had a large building complete with an entrance canopy over the street. It had one lengthy platform, and adjacent to this was a substantial goods yard, with sidings for coal, cattle and general merchandise, while two cranes were provided for unloading items such as farm machinery.

Train services

The initial service was four trains per day to and from Galashiels, Mondays to Saturdays, with two on Sundays. By the 1920s the service had expanded to eight trains a day, with an extra service on Saturdays. There was also a daily branch freight to serve the many mills and other sidings with both inward and outward traffic.

Passenger services were operated initially by NBR 0-6-0 tank locomotives and four-wheel carriages. Traffic was buoyant until after the end of World War 1 when the advent of the motorbus started to make an impact. With numbers falling, the LNER continued this general service pattern, but, as with the Langholm-Riddings Junction services, passenger traffic was generally light, and as an economy measure the LNER introduced steam railcars to the line from 5 January 1931. The railcars most commonly used were *Nettle* and *Flower of Yarrow*. These operated up to seven services on weekdays, with nine on Saturdays. But the railcars were withdrawn by World War 2, and services were then operated by an engine and coaches.

By 1948, such was the sparseness of passenger traffic that the service had been much reduced, to only two trains per day. These survived until 8 September 1951, when the trains were replaced

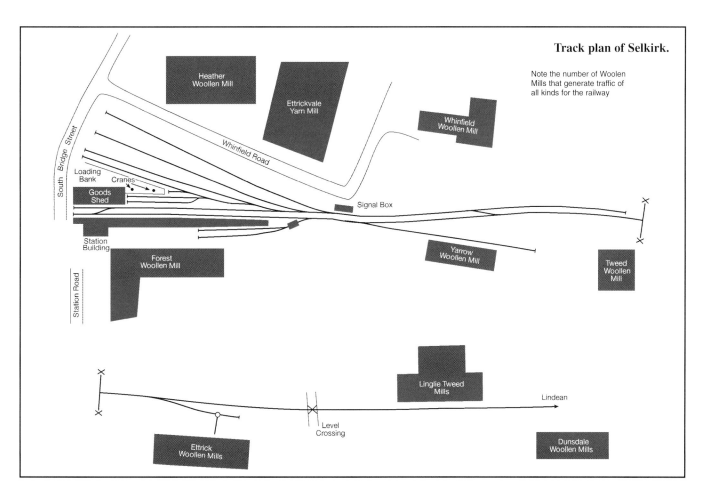

Track plan of Selkirk.

Note the number of Woolen Mills that generate traffic of all kinds for the railway

Heather Woollen Mill

Ettrickvale Yarn Mill

Whinfield Woollen Mill

South Bridge Street

Whinfield Road

Loading Bank

Cranes

Goods Shed

Signal Box

Station Building

Station Road

Forest Woollen Mill

Yarrow Woollen Mill

Tweed Woollen Mill

Lindean

Linglie Tweed Mills

Level Crossing

Ettrick Woollen Mills

Dunsdale Woollen Mills

GALASHIELS and SELKIRK.—North British.

Miles	Up.	Week Days only.											Miles	Down.	Week Days only.									
		mrn	mrn	mrn	aft	aft	aft	aft	aft	aft						mrn	mrn	mrn	aft	aft	aft	aft	aft	aft
						S														S				
	Galashiels ....dep.	8 45	9 45	1055	2 18	3 30	5 33	7 8	8 30	1051	....	....		Selkirk ....dep.	8 11	9 6	1013	1 30	2 39	4 50	5 54	7 40	1015
2¼	Abbotsford Ferry ‡‡	8 51	9 51	11 1	2 43	3 65	5 39	7 14	....	....	....		2	Lindean	8 18	9 11	1018	1 36	2 45	4 56	6 0	7 46	1021
4¼	Lindean	8 55	9 55	11 5	2 28	3 40	5 43	7 18	8 40	....	....		3¾	Abbotsford Ferry ‡‡	8 07	8 22	9 15	1022	1 40	2 49	5 0	6 4	....
6¼	Selkirk ....arr.	9 1	10 1	1111	2 34	3 46	5 49	7 24	8 47	11 6	....		6¼	Galashiels 780, 781 arr.	8 29	9 21	1028	1 46	2 55	5 6	6 10	7 54	1029

S Saturdays only.   ‡‡ Station for Abbotsford, about 1 mile.

Above:
Timetable — Galashiels and Selkirk (Bradshaw, 1922).

Table 178   GALASHIELS and SELKIRK—(One class only)

Miles		Week Days only										Miles		Week Days only							
		mrn	mrn	mrn		aft	aft	aft	aft	aft				mrn	mrn		aft	aft		aft	aft
						S			E									S	S			
167	EDINBURGH (W.) 177 dep	6 25	8 22	9 55	..		2 25	4 10	5 55	6 50		7 4	1015		Selkirk ....dep	8 20	1026		1230	3 0	..	5 5	6 20	..	7 45	9 5
—	Galashiels............dep	8 0	9 55	1130	..	1 33	3 0	5 38	7 7	8 25		8 33	1130		2¼	Lindean	8 26	1032		1236	3 6	..	5 11	6 26	..	7 51
4	Lindean	..	10 5	1140	..	1 13	3 40	5 48	7 17	8 35		8 43	..		6¼	Galashiels.............arr	8 35	1041		1245	3 15	..	5 20	6 35	..	8 0	9 24
6¼	Selkirk ....arr	8 14	1011	1146	..	1 19	3 46	5 54	7 23	8 41		8 49	1151		39¼	167 EDINBURGH (W.) 177 arr	9 45	1240		1 55	4 49	..	7 30	..	..	10 9	..

E Except Saturdays.   S Saturdays only

Above:
LNER Passenger Services timetable, Galashiels and Selkirk, 22 May 1944.

Table 41 Galashiels and Selkirk—One Class only between Galashiels and Selkirk

Miles			a.m				p.m			Miles			a.m				p.m	
—	GLASGOW (Qu. St.) lev.		—	.	.	.	4 0	.		—	Selkirk — — lev.	8 15		.	.	.	7 55	.
—	EDINBURGH (Wav.) "	6 20	.	.	.	S 53	.		—	Lindean	8 21		.	.	.	8 1	.
—	CARLISLE — — "	4 53	.	.	.	4 38	.		—	Galashiels — — arr.	8 30		.	.	.	8 10	.
—	Galashiels . lev.	7 54	.	.	.	7 0	.		—	CARLISLE — — arr.	1254p		.	.	1225a	
4	Lindean — — .	8 4	.	.	.	7 10	.		—	EDINBURGH (Wav.) "	9 35		—	.	.	9 49	
6¼	Selkirk . . . arr.	8 10	.	.	.	7 16	.		—	GLASGOW (Qu. St.) "	11 9		.	.	.	.	

Above:
BR timetable, Galashiels and Selkirk, 31 May to 26 September 1948.

by buses, although the station remained open to sell tickets and handle documentation for freight and parcels services. Freight remained until 2 November 1964, when the service was cut back to serve Netherdale Siding only.

Bus services between Galashiels and Selkirk were far more frequent than the branch trains — and took 15 minutes, leaving from the Market Place; only one, at 11pm, started from Galashiels station, although it did wait for the 10.5pm train from Edinburgh, which called at 10.54pm on its way to St Pancras.

At Selkirk were no fewer than nine woollen and tweed mills, these being Dunsdale Mill, Linglie Mill, St Mary's Mill, Ettrick Mill, Yarrow Mill, Whinfield Mill, Ettrickvale Mill, Forest Mill and Heather Mill. As well as transporting finished products from the mills, there was coal inwards and other general merchandise traffic for the town. This being a farming area, agricultural machinery was also delivered, as were feedstuffs, fertilisers and other materials; there was also some cattle movement. There was a siding at Lindean, where the main traffic was a wagon of coal, and at the Selkirk Junction end of the line there was a gas and electricity works for Galashiels that received coal. Coal was also delivered to a mill at Netherdale, from where woollen products were manufactured. Latterly, Selkirk sent a tank or two of fuel oil.

The end of World War 1 saw the first major competition to the railway's freight and passenger business. Traffic from the mills reduced as same-day direct deliveries to Glasgow and Edinburgh were possible by road. This trend continued throughout the 1930s and by World War 2 most of the limited livestock business had also gone.

Passenger numbers were also in decline, while freight was limited to the railway's staple business — coal. Many woollen products were transported by passenger train, but due to the heavy nature of most of the traffic, two branch freights were needed to bring in deliveries and remove empties.

Freight services survived and in 1953, two Class K services operated the branch and carried general merchandise and coal plus some woollen products from the various mills. The first ran on weekdays only and left Galashiels at 6.40am, arriving at Selkirk at 7.30am. This train would also shunt the siding at Galafoot Gas Works and Lindean siding, as required. It was not timed to stop at intermediate sidings and would return from Selkirk at 8.35am, arriving back at Galashiels at 9am. A second train ran Saturdays excepted, leaving Galashiels at 1.55pm and calling at Lindean at 2.13pm and Selkirk at 2.25pm. This latter service would also shunt at Galafoot Gas Works and at Netherdale Mill, Galashiels Electric, Ettrick Mill and St Mary's Mill. It returned from Selkirk at 4.25pm, calling at Lindean at 4.40 and was booked at Selkirk Junction at 4.50, with arrival in Galashiels at 4.55. This arrangement continued roughly unchanged until 2 November 1964, when the line was closed between Netherdale Mill and Selkirk. The final section to Selkirk Junction was closed on 3 September 1966.

The station building in Selkirk was demolished in December 1971, and the Galashiels-Selkirk line has been swallowed up by the main A7 road. With the exception of the station area at Lindean, there is now little trace of a railway.

Table 68

SELKIRK and GALASHIELS

SCOTTISH OMNIBUSES LTD., NEW STREET, EDINBURGH

Week Days (Time—15 minutes)

Selkirk Market—Depart—6 55 am, 7 25 am, 8 10 am, 8 30 am, 9 0 am. 9 40 am, 10*0 am, 10 20 am, 11 5 am, 11 30 am, 12S0 noon, 12 30 pm, 1 5 pm, S1*15 pm, 1 30 pm, S1*45 pm, 2 0 pm, S2*15 pm, 2 30 pm, S2*45 pm, 3 5 pm, S3*15 pm, 3 30 pm, S3*45 pm, 4 0 pm, S4*15 pm, 4 35 pm, S4*45 pm, 5 0 pm, S5*15 pm, 5 35 pm, S5*45 pm, 6 5 pm, S6*15 pm, 6 30 pm, S6*45 pm, 7S0 pm, 7E5 pm, S7*15 pm, 7 40 pm, S7*45 pm, 8 0 pm, S8*15 pm, 8 30 pm, S8*45 pm, 9 0 pm, S9*15 pm, 9 30 pm, S9*45 pm, 10 0 pm, 10 30 pm, 11S10 pm, 11S50 pm

Galashiels Market—Depart—6 50 am, 7 30 am, 8 0 am, 8 30 am, 9 0 am, 9*30 am, 10 0 am, 10 30 am, 11 10 am, 11 30 am, 12 0 noon, 12 30 pm, 1 5 pm, S1*15 pm, 1S30 pm, 1E40 pm, S1*45 pm, 2 0 pm, S2*15 pm, 2 30 pm, S2*45 pm, 3S0 pm, E3*0 pm, S3*15 pm, 3 35 pm, S3*45 pm, 4 0 pm, S4*15 pm, 4 30 pm, S4*45 pm, 5 0 pm, S5*15 pm, 5 30 pm, 5*45 pm, 6 0 pm, S6*15 pm, 6 30 pm, S6*45 pm, 7 0 pm, S7*15 pm, E7*30 pm, 7S30 pm, S7*45 pm, 8 0 pm, S8*15 pm, 8 30 pm, S8*45 pm, 9 0 pm, S9*15 pm, 9 30 pm, 10 30 pm, 11S30 pm

* Runs via Buccleuch Road   † Waits on arrival of train from Edinburgh

E Saturdays excepted   G Starts from Galashiels Station   S Saturdays only

Left:
BR timetable, Selkirk-Galashiels bus service, 15 June to 6 September 1964.

SELKIRK BRANCH

UP TRAINS				WEEKDAYS		DOWN TRAINS		
No.		508	534		No.		508	774
Description					Description			
Class		K	K		Class		K	K
				M. C.			am	SX PM
					Selkirk		8 35	4 25
				2 3	Lindean		..	4 40
				5 14	Selkirk Junction			4 50
				6 12	Galashiels .. .. ⊕ ..		9 0	4 55
Departs from					Arrives at			
Previous Times on Page								
		am	SX PM					
M. C.	Galashiels .... ⊕ ..	6 40	1 55					
0 78	Selkirk Junction	..	2 0					
4 9	Lindean	..	2 13					
6 12	Selkirk	7 30	2 25		Forward Times on Page			

No. 508—Works Gas Works Siding and Lindean, as required.

Sidings—Galafoot Gas Works, Netherdale Mill, Galashiels Electric, Ettrick Mill, St. Mary's Mill.

No. 508—Works Gas Works Siding and Lindean, as required.

Lower left:
BR working timetable, Selkirk branch, 21 September 1953

Above:
Class A3 Pacific No 60099 *Call Boy* **passes Selkirk Junction with the up 'Waverley' for St Pancras on 17 February 1958. The line to Selkirk can be seen curving away on the left. Netherdale Mill and the gas and electricity companies that had sidings off the Selkirk branch are in the valley to the left.** *A. Hamilton*

Left:
The first station on the branch was at Abbotsford Ferry, which closed in 1931. However, the platform remained and No 62471 *Glen Falloch* was able to call there on 4 April 1958 with the Branch Line Society's 'Scott Country Railtour'. The train is heading towards Selkirk. Today, the platform is still there, now in the front garden of a house.
Roy Hamilton

Right:
Lindean station was reached after crossing the River Tweed. It was similar to Abbotsford Ferry but had a siding with a loading bank. A level crossing was at the end of the platform. A small frame to work the points for the siding can be seen in the hut on the extreme left. Although this photograph was taken in 1950, there is still an LNER sign on the poster board attached to the building. Today, the trackbed here is a bridleway.
Ian Allan Library

Left:
Eight years later, and No 62471 *Glen Falloch* passes on 4 April 1958 with the 'Scott Country Railtour'. The platform has been cut back, the station having closed on 8 September 1951.
Roy Hamilton

Right:
Before passenger services were withdrawn from the line, LNER 'D34' 4-4-0 No 2483 *Glen Garry* **of Galashiels shed waits at Selkirk with the 7.55pm service for Galashiels on 21 June 1947.**
W. A. Camwell

Centre right:
Selkirk station is seen from the platform in 1950, looking towards the buffer stops. The loading dock is on the right with coal wagons and a small container. The station was virtually surrounded by textile mills, its main source of business. *Ian Allan Library*

Left:
The rather grand frontage of Selkirk station, situated alongside Station Road and South Bridge Street in Selkirk. The station building was demolished in 1971, and the yard is now occupied by a small industrial site.
Ian Allan Library

The Peebles Loop

Historical perspective

Of all the towns that feature in this book, Peebles was probably the most unfortunate, together with Peeblesshire, in having gained two railways and then lost both of them. There had first been a plan to build a line from Peebles to Edinburgh in the 1840s. However, this failed, and other options were considered, one being a route from Berwick to Ayr via Peebles, part of which was eventually built as the Caledonian route from Peebles to Symington. The nearest railway was the line that the North British Railway built from Edinburgh to Hawick, which eventually became the Waverley Route and which had opened on 1 November 1849. However, the town of Peebles was not on this route, much to the disappointment of its inhabitants. Not to be outdone the people sought to open a railway through the town and Parliamentary approval was given to the Peebles Railway Company on 8 July 1853 for a line that left the Hawick route at Hardengreen. The line was opened on 4 July 1855, 18¾ miles in length from Hardengreen Junction to Peebles, where it terminated on the north bank of the River Tweed, and it quickly became a success.

There were stations at Bonnyrigg, Rosewell & Hawthornden, Rosslynlee, Pomathorn, Leadburn (the line's summit, at 930ft) and Eddleston, these being extended as traffic grew. Leadburn became a junction when the line to Dolphinton opened on 4 July 1864, meeting the Caledonian line from Carstairs, which opened on 1 March 1867. Two more branches were also constructed from the Peebles Loop, one from Esk Valley Junction (between Hardengreen Junction and Bonnyrigg) to Polton, which opened on 12 October 1868, the other the Penicuik line from Rosewell & Hawthornden, opened on 2 July 1872.

The line terminated at Peebles at a small station which had a single platform, with train shed, sidings and locomotive shed. It was initially proposed that the line would be operated under contract to the North British, but satisfactory terms were not reached. This meant that the Peebles Railway Co operated the line in its own right, and traffic receipts were encouraging, with nearly 3,000 passengers a week using the service. However, within two years operating and maintenance costs had risen and the company found itself having to raise additional share capital to keep running. It again looked to the NBR as a solution and this time negotiated a lease of the line from 1861, in perpetuity.

It was always hoped that the line could be extended further, and an extension to Galashiels, Kilnknowe Junction, (the Galashiels & Peebles Railway) was approved on 28 June 1861, opening as far as Innerleithen on 1 October 1864, but not until

Right:

'B1' No 61234 of Edinburgh St Margarets depot passes Kilnknowe Junction at Galashiels (17½ miles from Peebles East) with the 8.5am from Hawick to Edinburgh Waverley in July 1963. This train was travelling via the Waverley Route as the Peebles Loop had closed in February 1962. The demolition gang has been at work and has virtually finished the track lifting — this was done by a demolition train running out from Galashiels and lifting the track back to there. Another train lifted track back from Peebles East to Rosewell & Hawthornden. However, the points for the line are still extant, just to the rear of the train. Six more years and the Waverley Route was to share the same fate.
G. Kinghorn

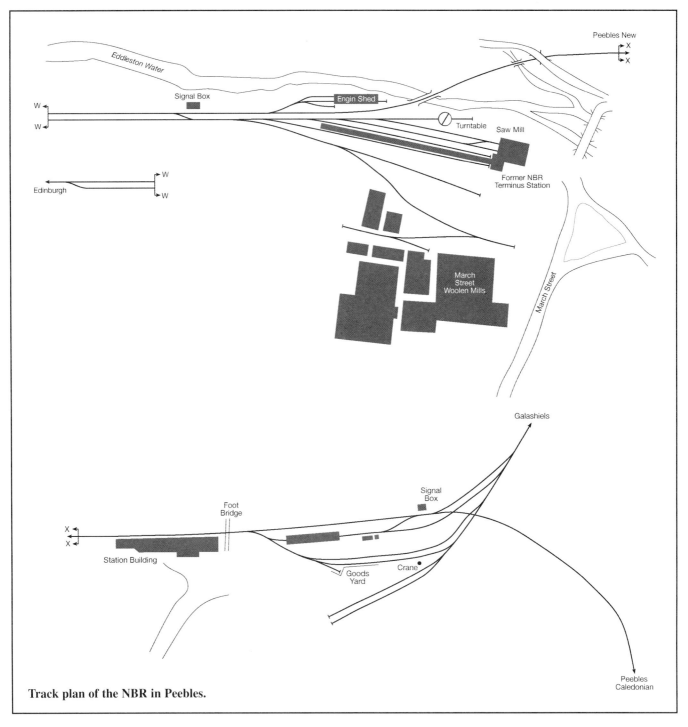

Track plan of the NBR in Peebles.

after the rival Caledonian line from Symington had arrived at Peebles, on 1 February 1864.

The relationship with the Caledonian was not good, and once the Peebles Railway was taken over by the North British any co-operation on connections or even through passenger working was definitely over. This attitude continued right through into BR days, when the connecting spur between the two 'systems' was only rarely used for the transfer of wagons and the occasional passage of the Royal Train.

What became known as the Peebles Loop finally opened from Innerleithen to Galashiels on 1 October 1866, the NBR seeing this section as a baulk towards any further expansion eastwards by the Caledonian. The loop also saw another new station for Peebles — the original station having been a terminus — so the NBR and the Caledonian finally sat facing each other on either side of the River Tweed as there was no possibility of a joint station, such was the competition, the spur that joined the two systems being the only contact.

Passenger services on the line were limited and were hauled by a variety of NBR Reid designs — notably 'C15' and 'C16' 4-42Ts, which were eventually replaced by 'D30' and 'D34' 4-4-0 tender locomotives. While the line was busy between Peebles and Edinburgh, it was lightly used between Galashiels and Peebles. At the Edinburgh end of the line branches from Dolphinton, and more importantly Penicuik and Polton, increased traffic, as these ran local services into Edinburgh. However, local bus services made a significant impact on passenger numbers — in many cases the stations were not conveniently situated for the towns en route. The LNER passenger service was down to only four weekday services in either direction, but there was an extra service on Saturdays, the pattern mainly catering for those travelling to and from Edinburgh.

This general decline and almost retrenchment continued until the mid-1950s, and it looked as though the

Peebles Loop would become a casualty of the many passenger closures that abounded at the time. But at this late stage British Railways used the line to pioneer the general introduction of diesel multiple-units in Scotland. These started from 11 July 1956, with the 7.12am service from Galashiels to Edinburgh. Traffic grew and the DMU service was expected to cut costs and revitalise the line. The three passenger trains that were steam-hauled were replaced by Wickham-built DMUs, and the service was then more than doubled. Rosslynlee Hospital Halt was opened on 11 December 1958 in an effort to boost traffic. Despite this monopoly on passenger workings by DMUs the occasional failure of a unit did see a steam substitute with 'B1' 4-6-0 No 61351 noted working the 7.15am from Galashiels to Peebles and Edinburgh on 27 January 1962.

Notwithstanding the introduction of the DMUs, the line still suffered badly from road competition, and, even though train operating costs had been reduced (and could have been reduced even further with today's signalling technology), the Scottish Transport Users Consultative Committee approved closure from Hawthornden Junction to Peebles and Galashiels at the end of 1961.

The last passenger trains ran on Saturday 3 February 1962 — all DMUs except for a steam special, organised by the Stephenson Locomotive Society, with 'J37' 0-6-0 No 64587 in charge. The last train was the 11.1pm SO to Galashiels, which was well loaded with local people and enthusiasts travelling on the line for a final trip. The DMU experiment had failed.

Official closure was set for 5 February 1962. The only benefit from enthusiasts' point of view was that the 9.10am Sundays from Hawick to Edinburgh and the 11.25am Waverley-Hawick reverted to steam haulage from 11 February, having previously been worked as a filling-in turn by a Peebles-line DMU.

Two officers' specials traversed the line on 22 February and 14 March 1962. At that time all was still *in situ* — only the tablet instruments had been removed as well as the various offices having been cleared. The reason for the specials was to assess the award of contracts for track lifting and demolition. The first section to be removed was from Peebles to Innerleithen. Demolition began of the Hawthornden-Peebles Yard stretch on 7 May 1962 and of Peebles Gas Works-Kilnknowe Junction on 30 April. Trains ran through from Hawthornden and Galashiels and gradually lifted the line back towards both of these locations. The track was in good condition, and much of it was destined for the West Highland line. By January 1963 the track was lifted between Cardrona and Leadburn.

Following closure of the loop, a passenger service from Rosewell & Hawthornden to Edinburgh was retained. This was also approved for closure by the Scottish TUCC in June 1962 and closed from 10 September that year, the last service train running on 8 September. An SLS railtour on 29 August 1964 hauled by 'J36' class 0-6-0 No 65234 was the last passenger train as far as Rosewell & Hawthornden and also visited Penicuik.

Passenger services

By the mid-1900s there were six trains running on the line in either direction, with two on Sundays — these Sunday trains were discontinued from 1923. One of the weekday trains was the 'Peebles-shire' which left Galashiels at 8.1am, called at Peebles East at 8.44 and arrived in Edinburgh at 9.37am. This service returned from Edinburgh at 5.31pm, and was rivalled by the Caledonian's own train called the 'Tinto' which also connected via Symington for Edinburgh Princes Street, as well as for Glasgow.

In 1924 trains left Galashiels at 6.51, 8.12, 10.8am, 12.50, 4.34 and 7.6pm and in the return direction left Edinburgh at 7.12, 10.30am, 1.22 SO, 2.15, 4.30, 5.22 SX and 8.2pm. Motive power was dominated by the 4-4-0 'D34' 'Glen' locomotives as well as the 'D30' 'Scott' class. A major casualty of this period was the branch that ran from Leadburn to Dolphinton, which closed on 1 April 1933, replaced by a bus. The 1930s also saw an initiative to bring more traffic to scenic lines, including a camping coach which was provided at the Tweed Valley station at Cardrona. This was one of a number of conversions from old rolling stock that were placed around the system; another route that received them was the Coldstream-Alnwick line.

The boom years of the 1930s had seen an influx of tourist traffic to Peebles and other stations on the line, but, nevertheless, there was also a significant growth in road competition, and by the end of the 1930s traffic levels had fallen. The war years saw traffic stagnate, and the number of regular trains was reduced to an almost token service. By 1944 the service had been reduced to only three weekday trains, with an extra on Saturdays, trains leaving Galashiels at 7.9, 10.10am, 1.2 SO and 4.6pm. From Edinburgh Waverley, Peebles Loop services departed at 7.59am, 1.17, 4.58 and 8.25pm SO.

With pressure on both costs and passenger numbers after the war, the future of the service looked bleak, especially between Peebles and Galashiels. Thornielee station closed from 6 November 1950, as well as the Peebles West to Symington passenger service. But the loop survived with a meagre passenger service, still steam-hauled, usually by former NBR types, but also supplemented by LNER 'B1' 4-6-0s and even BR Standard 2-6-0s. The 1953 working timetable shows the extent of the service, with only three weekday up services, two extra trains running on Saturdays and four down services on weekdays, with another on Saturdays. This timetable also shows the greater extent of the service at the Edinburgh end of the line.

From July 1956 attempts were at last made to modernise the service. The use of the then new Wickham DMUs was extended to the line and these quickly replaced steam haulage and coaches on all services. By 1959 there were seven down weekday DMU services with eight up trains — a ninth ran on Saturdays as a late evening departure from Edinburgh. But, as mentioned above, despite an initial increase in patronage, the service was to last only until 1962.

Freight services

The line was very much a two-section route when it came to freight services, the vast majority of forwarded traffic coming from the following locations:

Bonnyrigg
    Hopefield Siding
    Philip's Siding
    Polton No 2 Colliery
    Graham Yool's Siding

Rosewell & Hawthornden
    Rosewell Sand Siding
    Dalhousie Siding
    Whitehill Colliery Siding

Rosslynlee
    Holmbank Siding

Peebles
    Scottish Gas Works
    Ballantyne's Mill
    Dyers Saw Mills
    March Street Mills
    Peebles Old Goods Station Sidings

Innerleithen
    Waverley Mill
    MAFF Siding

In addition, most of the stations had small yards with facilities for forwarding and receiving agricultural traffic, livestock and coal.

EDINBURGH, ESKBANK, LEADBURN, and GALASHIELS.—North British.

Miles	Up.	Week Days only. mrn	mrn	aft (Saturdays only)	aft	aft	aft (Except Saturdays)	aft
	Edinburgh (Wav.)...dep.	7 12	1030	1 22	2 13	4 30	5 22	8 2
1	Abbeyhill	...	...	...	...	...	...	...
1¾	Piershill	...	...	...	...	...	...	...
3	Portobello	7 18	...	...	...	...	...	...
6¾	Millerhill*	...	...	...	...	...	...	...
8	Eskbank	7 28	1044	...	2 29	4 44	...	8 16
9½	Bonnyrigg	7 33	1049	...	2 34	4 49	...	8 21
11½	Hawthornden †	7 39	1056	...	2 41	4 56	5 43	8 29
12½	Rosslynlee	7 43	...	...	...	5 0	...	...
15	Pomathorn	7 50	11 6	...	2 51	5 7	...	8 39
17½	Leadburn 789	8 2	1117	2 0	2 59	5 15	5 59	8 47
23	Eddleston	8 14	1129	2 12	3 11	5 30	6 11	8 59
27	Peebles ‡ 846	8 24	1141	2 22	3 22	5 42	6 21	9 10
30½	Cardrona	8 31	1149	2 29	3 29	5 49	6 28	9 17
33½	Innerleithen	8 41	1155	2 36	3 36	5 56	6 36	9 24
35½	Walkerburn	8 46	12 0	2 41	3 41	6 1	6 41	9 29
38¾	Thornielee	8 53	12 5	2 48	3 48	6 8	6 48	9 36
42½	Clovenfords	9 3	1216	2 57	3 57	6 18	6 58	9 45
45½	Galashiels 780......arr.	9 11	1224	3 5	4 5	6 26	7 6	9 53

Miles	Down.	Week Days only. mrn	mrn	mrn	aft	aft	aft
	Galashiels......dep.	6 51	8 12	10 8	1250	4 34	7 6
3½	Clovenfords	7 0	8 21	1017	1259	4 43	7 15
6¾	Thornielee	7 7	8 28	1024	1 6	4 50	7 22
10½	Walkerburn	7 14	8 35	1031	1 13	4 57	7 29
12	Innerleithen	7 19	8 40	1036	1 18	5 2	7 34
15½	Cardrona	7 26	8 47	1043	1 25	5 9	7 41
18½	Peebles ‡ 846	7 35	8 56	1052	1 35	5 18	7 50
22½	Eddleston	7 46	9 6	11 2	1 45	5 29	8 0
28½	Leadburn 789	8 1	9 21	1116	1 59	5 44	8 13
30½	Pomathorn	8 6	...	1121	2 4	5 53	8 18
33½	Rosslynlee	8 11	...	1126	2 9	5 58	...
34½	Hawthornden † 806	8 15	...	1130	2 13	6 1	8 29
36½	Bonnyrigg	8 20	...	1135	2 19	6 6	8 35
37½	Eskbank	8 25	9 38	1139	2 25	6 10	8 40
39½	Millerhill* [794	...	...	...	2 30	...	...
42½	Portobello 778, 788,	8 34	...	...	2 37	6 19	8 49
43½	Piershill [808	...	...	...	...	...	...
44½	Abbeyhill [786 to 795,	...	...	...	...	...	...
45½	Edinburgh (W.) 782, arr.	8 40	9 50	1151	2 43	6 25	8 55

* Station for Edmondstone. † Station for Rosewell. ‡ Nearly ¼ mile to the Caledonian Station.

For **OTHER TRAINS** between Edinburgh, Eskbank, and Galashiels, see page 781; between Edinburgh, Millerhill, and Hawthornden, see page 806; between Edinburgh and Portobello, see pages 778, 781, 788, 794, and 806.

Above:
Bradshaw's **1922 guide, Edinburgh to Galashiels via Peebles.**

Table 177 **EDINBURGH and GALASHIELS, via Peebles**

Miles		Week Days only mrn	aft	aft	aft S
—	Edinburgh (Waverley) dep	7 59	1 17	4 58	8 25
1¾	Piershill	..	..	..	..
3	Portobello	8 7	..	..	8 31
6¾	Millerhill	..	..	..	..
8	Eskbank	8 18	1 32	5 11	8 41
9½	Bonnyrigg	8 23	1 37	5 16	8 46
11½	Rosewell and Hawthornden	8 29	1 43	5 22	8 53
12½	Rosslynlee	8 33	1 47	5 26	8 59
15	Pomathorn	8 40	1 53	5 32	9 6
17½	Leadburn	8 47	2 1	5 38	9 13
23	Eddleston	8 57	2 11	5 48	9 24
27	Peebles	9 8	2 20	5 56	9 33
30½	Cardrona	9 14	2 26	6 2	..
33¼	Innerleithen	9 21	2 33	6 8	9 48
35½	Walkerburn	9 25	2 37	6 12	9 53
39	Thornielee	9 31	2 43	6 18	..
42½	Clovenfords	9 38	2 50	6 25	..
45½	Galashiels arr	9 45	2 57	6 32	1015
110½	167 CARLISLE arr	1246	5 56	9 10	1 25

Miles		Week Days only mrn	mrn	mrn S	aft
	167 CARLISLE dep	..	5 55	8 58	1 50
—	Galashiels dep	7 9	1010	1 2	4 6
3½	Clovenfords	7 19	1018	1 10	4 14
6	Thornielee	..	1024	1 16	4 20
10½	Walkerburn	7 30	1031	1 22	4 27
12	Innerleithen	7 35	1036	1 27	4 32
15½	Cardrona	7 42	1042	1 33	4 38
18½	Peebles	7 50	1050	1 40	4 45
22½	Eddleston	7 58	1058	1 47	4 52
28	Leadburn	8 11	1110	2 2	5 4
30½	Pomathorn	8 16	1115	2 7	5 8
33	Rosslynlee	8 21	1120	2 12	5 13
34½	Rosewell and Hawthornden	8 25	1124	2 16	5 17
36	Bonnyrigg	8 29	1128	2 20	5 21
37½	Eskbank	8 34	1132	2 24	5 25
39½	Millerhill	..	..	2 29	..
42½	Portobello	8 42	1140	2 35	5 33
43½	Piershill	..	..	..	5 37
45½	Edinburgh (Waverley). arr	8 48	1148	2 43	5 42

S Saturdays only.

For OTHER TRAINS between Edinburgh and Portobello, see Tables 157 and 186—Edinburgh and Rosewell and Hawthornden, Table 179—Edinburgh and Galashiels, Table 167.

Above:
LNER timetable 22 May 1944, Edinburgh and Galashiels via Peebles.

Below:
ScR timetable 31 May to 26 September 1948, Edinburgh and Galashiels via Peebles.

Table 46 **Edinburgh, Peebles and Galashiels**

Miles	Leave GLASGOW (Queen St.)	a.m —	a.m 1125	p.m 2A25	Sats only p.m 6 0
.	Edinburgh (Wav.) lev	8 1	1p18	5 4	8 25
1	Abbeyhill	—	—	—	—
3	Portobello	8 7	.	.	8 31
6¾	Millerhill	—	—	—	—
8	Eskbank	8 18	1 33	5 17	8 41
9½	Bonnyrigg	8 23	1 38	5 22	8 46
11½	Rosewell and arr.	8 28	1 43	5 27	8 51
—	Hawthornden lev.	8 29	1 44	5 28	8 53
12½	Rosslynlee	8 33	1 48	5 32	8 59
15	Pomathorn	8 40	1 54	5 38	9 6
17½	Leadburn	8 47	2R2	5 44	9 13
23	Eddleston	8 57	2R12	5 54	9 24
27	Peebles arr.	9 6	2R19	6 0	9 31
—	Peebles lev.	9 8	2R21	6 2	9 33
30½	Cardrona	9 14	2R27	6 8	.
33½	Innerleithen	9 21	2R34	6 14	9 45
35½	Walkerburn	9 25	2R38	6 18	9 50
39	Thornielee	9 31	2R44	6 24	—
42½	Clovenfords	9 38	2R51	6 31	.
45½	Galashiels arr.	9 45	2R58	6 38	1012
.	EDINBURGH (Wav.) "	1225	4R20	8 34	.

Leave EDINBURGH (Wav.)	a.m —	a.m 8 24	Sats only n'n 12 0	p.m 2 35
Galashiels lev.	7 10	1010	1 5	4 10
Clovenfords	7 20	1018	1 13	4 18
Thornielee	.	1024	1 19	4 24
Walkerburn	7 31	1031	1 25	4 31
Innerleithen	7 36	1036	1 30	4 36
Cardrona	7 43	1042	1 36	4 42
Peebles arr.	7 49	1048	1 42	4 48
Peebles lev.	7 51	1050	1 43	4 49
Eddleston	7 59	1058	1 50	4 56
Leadburn	8 12	1110	2 5	5 8
Pomathorn	8 17	1115	2 10	5 12
Rosslynlee	8 22	1120	2 15	5 17
Rosewell and arr.	8 25	1123	2 18	5 20
Hawthornden lev.	8 26	1124	2 19	5 21
Bonnyrigg	8 30	1128	2 23	5 25
Eskbank	8 35	1132	2 27	5 29
Millerhill	.	.	2 32	.
Portobello	8 43	1140	2 38	5 38
Piershill	.	.	.	5 41
Edinburgh (Wav.) arr	8 49	1146	2 44	5 47
GLASGOW (Queen St.)	10 8	2K10	5 0	7 37

EDINBURGH to GALASHIELS, via PEEBLES, POLTON and PENICUIK BRANCHES

UP TRAINS — WEEKDAYS

Distance from Edinburgh M.C.		No.	695‡	340	342		344	520‡	751		346	348	348	348	350
		Description													
		Class	K	B	B		B	K	K		B	B	B	B	B
		Previous Times on Page													
			am	am	am		am	am	am	PM	PM	SX PM	SO PM	SO PM	SX PM
		EDINBURGH (Wav.) .. 1		7 10	7 35		7 56			12 42	1 18	1 18	1 18		1 37
		Abbeyhill .. 2		7 13											1 40
		Piershill .. 3		7 16	7 40										1 43
3 0		Portobello .. 4		7 19	7 43		8 2			12 48	1 24	1 24	1 24		1 49
4 33		Niddrie South Junction .. 5		7 22	7 46		8 5			12 51	1 27	1 27	1 27		1 49
6 19		Millerhill Junction .. 6		7 25											1 52
7 59		Glenesk Junction .. 7													
7 76		Eskbank .. 8		7 30	7 52		8 11			12 57	1 33	1 33	1 33		1 57
8 21		Hardengreen Junction .. 9	6 0	7 31	7 53		8 12		8 35	12 58	1 34	1 34	1 34		1 58
8 59		Esk Valley Junction .. ⊕ 10		7 32	7 54		8 13			12 59	1 35	1 35	1 35		1 59
9 31		Broomieknowe .. 11													
9 65		Lasswade .. 12													
10 49		Annandale's Siding .. 13													
10 69		Polton .. ⊕ 14													
9 31		Bonnyrigg .. 15		7 35	7 57		8 16				1 2	1 38	1 38	1 38	2 2
9 33		Polton No. 2 Siding .. 16													
10 57		¶Graham Yool's Siding .. 17													
11 15		Rosewell & Hawthornden .. 18			8 2		8 22		8 56	1 807	1 43	1 43	1 43		2 7
		Rosewell & Hawthornden .. 19							9 5						
11 24		Hawthornden Junction .. ⊕ 20													
12 42		Rosslyn Castle .. 21													
13 57		Dalmore Mill .. 22													
13 75		Auchendinny .. 23													
14 60		Harper's Brae Siding .. 24										Ceases after 3rd October	Commences 10th October		
15 15		Esk Mill .. 25													
15 30		Valleyfield .. 26													
15 52		Penicuik .. 27							9 35						
11 15		Rosewell & Hawthornden .. 28					8 26				1 45	1 45	1 45		
11 34		Hawthornden Junction .. ⊕ 29													
11 44		Whitehill Siding .. 30													
12 46		Rosslynlee .. 31					8 30				1 50	1 50	1 50		
15 6		Pomathorn Halt .. 32					8 36				1 57	1 56	1 56		
17 •1		Leadburn Junction .. 33					8 41					2 12			
		Leadburn Junction .. ⊕ 34	*				8 42				2 2	2 3	2 3		
22 7l		Eddleston .. 35	*				8 52					2 13			
26 68		Peebles Engine Shed .. ⊕ 36													
27 9		Peebles East .. 37	*				8 59				2 17	2 20	2 18		
27 69		Peebles East.. 38					9 2	9 20			2 19	2 22	2 20		
28 44		Peebles (L.M.S.) .. 39						9 35							
30 30		Peebles Gas Works .. 40					9 n10	9 50							
33 35		Cardrona .. 41					9 16	9 57			2 30	2 33	2 31		
		Innerleithen .. ⊕ 42													
35 25		Innerleithen .. ⊕ 43					9 17	10 53			2 31	2 34	2 32		
38 73		Walkerburn .. 44					9 21	11 5			2 35	2 38	2 36		
42 24		Thornielee .. 45									2 47				
44 44		Clovenfords .. 46					9 33	11 28			2 52	2 54	2 52		
		Klinknowe Junction .. 47					9 38	11 35			2 52				
45 47		Galashiels .. ⊕ 48					9 40	11 40			2 54	2 56	2 54		

EDINBURGH to GALASHIELS, via PEEBLES, POLTON and PENICUIK BRANCHES

UP TRAINS — WEEKDAYS

	756‡	456	354	356		358	578‡	360	364	370
	K	B	B	B		B	K	B	B	B
	SX PM	SO PM	HC PM	PM		PM	SX PM	SO PM	PM	SO PM
1		2 43	5 5	5 27		6 26		8 50	10 30	10 55
2				5 30						
3				5 33						
4		2 49	5 11	5 36		6 32		8 56	10 36	11 4
5		2 52	5 13	5 39		6 35		8 59	10 39	
6				5 42						
7										
9	2 10	2 58	5 19	5 47		6 41	7 0	9 5	10 45	11 10
10	2 16	2 59	5 20	5 48		6 42	9 6	9 6	10 46	11 11
			5 21	5 49			9 7		10 47	
15			5 24	5 52		6 46		9 10	10 49	11 15
18	2 25	3 6	5 29	5 57			7 19	9 15		11 20
19	2 35									
27	3 10									
28			5 30			7 25	9 16			11 21
31			5 34				9 20			11 25
32			5 40							11 31
33			5 45			7 59				
34			5 46			8 6	9 31			11 37
35			5 56							
37			6 3			8 38	9 46			11 52
38			6 5				9 47			11 54
42			6 11				9 58			12 5
43			6 17				9 59			12 6
44			6 21							12 11
47			6 37				10 17			12 27

GALASHIELS to EDINBURGH, via PEEBLES, PENICUIK and POLTON BRANCHES

DOWN TRAINS — WEEKDAYS

Distance from Galashiels M.C.		No.	405	379	482	216	389		222	222	222	751‡	695‡	574‡	411
		Description													
		Class	B	B	B	B	B		B	B	B	K	K	K	B
		Departs from											Hardeng'n 6.0 a.m.		
		Previous Times on Page											W80		
			HC am	am	HC am	HC am	am		SX am	SO am	SO am	am	am	SO PM	HC PM
1 3		Galashiels .. ⊕ 1				7 10			10 16	10 16	10 16			12 4	
3 23		Klinknowe Junction .. 2				7 12			10 18	10 18	10 18			12 19	
6 54		Clovenfords .. 3							10 24	10 24	10 24			12 25	
10 22		Thornielee .. 4													
12 12		Walkerburn .. 5				7 28			10 36	10 36	10 36			12 51	
		Innerleithen .. ⊕ 6				7 32			10 40	10 40	10 40			12 56	
15 17		Innerleithen .. ⊕ 7				7 33			10 41	10 41	10 41			1 45	
18 38		Cardrona .. 8				7 44			10 47	10 47	10 47			2 0	
		Peebles East .. ⊕ 9							10 53	10 53	10 53			2 10	
18 62		Peebles East .. 10				7 46			10 55	10 55	10 55		*		
22 56		Peebles Engine Shed .. ⊕ 11											*		
28 6		Eddleston .. 12				7 54			11 3				*		
		Leadburn Junction .. ⊕ 13				8 6			11 11	11 15	11 13		*		
		Leadburn Junction .. 14				8 7							*		
30 41		Pomathorn Halt .. 15				8 12							*		
32 31		Holme Bank Siding .. 16													
33 1		Rosslynlee .. 17				8 17			11 22	11 24	11 22		*		
34 3		Whitehill Siding .. 18													
34 13		Hawthornden Junction .. ⊕ 19											*		
34 32		Rosewell & Hawthornden .. 20				8 20			11 25	11 27	11 25		*		
From Penicuik															
0 22		Penicuik .. ⊕ 21										10 45			
0 37		Valleyfield .. 22													
0 72		Esk Mill .. 23													
1 57		Harper's Brae Siding .. 24													
1 75		Auchendinny .. 25						Ceases after 3rd October							
3 10		Dalmore Mill .. 26						Commences 10th October							
4 18		Rosslyn Castle .. 27													
4 37		Hawthornden Junction .. ⊕ 28													
		Rosewell & Hawth'nden .. 29							11 55						
From Gala.															
34 32		Rosewell & Hawthornden .. 30		7 41		8 22	8 48		11 26	11 28	11 26		*		1 8037
35 31		Dalhousie Siding .. 31													
35 64		Polton No. 1 Siding .. 32													
36 10		Philips No. 2 Siding .. 33													
36 14		Polton No. 2 Siding .. 34													
36 16		Bonnyrigg .. 35	6 57	7 45		8 26	8 52		11 30	11 32	11 30				1 42
From Polton															
0 30		Polton .. ⊕ 36													
1 4		Annandale Siding .. 37					Eskbank to Niddrie SO							
1 38		Lasswade .. 38													
		Broomieknowe .. 39													
From Gala.															
16 68		Esk Valley Junction .. ⊕ 40													1 44
17 26		Hardengreen Junction .. 41	6 59	7 47		8 29	8 54		11 32	11 34	11 32		*		1 46
17 51		Eskbank .. 42	7 1	7 49	8 7	8 31	8 56		11 34	11 36	11 34				1 46
		Glenesk Junction .. 43													
19 28		Millerhill Junction .. 44	7 8	7 53	8 12	8 39	9 1		11 39	11 41	11 39				1 50
11 14		Niddrie South Junction .. 45	7 8	7 56	8 15	8 42	9 4		11 42	11 44	11 42				1 56
12 47		Portobello .. 46	7 11	7 59	8 18	8 45	9 7		11 45	11 47	11 45				1 59
		Piershill .. 47	7 14	8 2											2 0
		Abbeyhill .. 48	7 17	8 5	8 20										2 3
15 47		EDINBURGH (Wav.) .. 49	7 21	8 8	8 23	8 48	9 10		11 48	11 50	11 48		*		2 6

GALASHIELS to EDINBURGH, via PEEBLES, PENICUIK and POLTON BRANCHES

DOWN TRAINS — WEEKDAYS

	574‡		231	413	756	776	246	246		419	275
	K		B	B	K	K	B	B		B	B
	SX PM		SO PM	PM	SX PM	SX PM	SX HC PM	SO HC PM		HC PM	HC PM
1	12 15						4 4	4 8			7 15
2	12 40		1 4				4 10				7 17
5	1 5		1 22				4 26	4 26			7 35
7	1 30		1 26				4 30				7 36
8	1 45		1 27				4 31				
9	1 55		1 39				4 37				7 47
10			1 40				4 43				7 48
11					3 0		4 45				
12			1 57		3 15		4 53				
13			2 2		3 42		5 4				8 6
14					3 52		5 5				
15							5 10				
17			2 11		4 10		5 15				8 S015
20			2 14		4 20		5 18				8 16
21					3 45						
29					4 30						
30			2 15	3 32	4 50		5 19				8 17
35			2 20	3 36	5 1		5 23			7 25	8 21
41			2 22	3 38	5 8		5 25			7 27	8 23
42			2 24	3 44			5 27			7 29	8 25
44				3 46			5 31				
45				3 48			5 38			7 34	8 30
46			2 32	3 50			5 38			7 37	8 33
47				3 52			5 42				
48							5 45				
49			2 38	3 57			5 45			7 43	8 39

ScR working timetable 21 September 1953, Edinburgh to Galashiels via Peebles.

Table 219—

CARLISLE, HAWICK, GALASHIELS AND EDINBURGH

Week Days

Miles	Miles	Miles		am	am DE	pm ZE	pm ZS	am D	am	am D	am D	am	am A	am A	am AE	am D	noon D	am D	am	am	pm D	noon S	pm D	pm	pm D	pm D
			London (St. Pancras) dep			9L 0	9F 0																			
				am	am	am	am	am	am	am	am	am	am	am	am	am	noon	am	am	am	pm	noon	pm	pm	pm	pm
—	—	—	Carlisle dep			5 1	5 10												9 5							
9¾	—	—	Longtown																9 22							
			Riddings Junction arr																9 30							
14	—	—	Riddings Junction dep									7 45							9 31	9 56						
—	—	1¼	Canonbie									7 50								10 1						
—	—	2¾	Gilnockie (for Clay Gate)									7 57								10 8						
—	—	7	Langholm arr									8 6								1017						
16¾	—	—	Penton dep									Stop							9 37							
21½	—	—	Kershope Foot																9 45							
24¼	—	—	Newcastleton			5 33	5 42												9 53							
28¾	—	—	Steele Road																10 3							
32½	—	—	Riccarton Junction																10 13							
38½	—	—	Shankend																10 29							
41½	—	—	Stobs																10 36							
45½	—	—	Hawick arr			6 13	6 22					am							10 42							
			Hawick dep	5 35		6 18	6 27		6H45			8 2							10 55			12 0				
49¾	—	—	Hassendean									8 9							11 2			12 7				
53	—	—	Belses ¶									8 15							11 8			12 14				
57¾	—	—	St. Boswells arr	5 51		6 34	6 43		7 7			8 22							11 15			12 21				
			St. Boswells dep	5 56		6 39	6 47		7 9			8 27							11 19			12 22				
61	—	—	Melrose	6 4		6 47	6 54		7 16			8 34							11 26			12 29				
64¾	—	—	Galashiels arr	6 10		6 53	7 0		7 22			8 40							11 32			12 35				
			Galashiels dep	6 15		6 59	7 5		7 24	7 15		8 42				9 58		1115	11 36			12 37				2 6
—	3¼	—	Clovenfords													10 6		1123								2E14
—	10¼	—	Walkerburn							7 30						10 15		1132								2 23
—	12	—	Innerleithen							7 35						10 26		1137								2 34
—	15	—	Cardrona							7 41						10 32		1143								2 40
—	—	—	Peebles arr							7 47						10 38		1149								2 46
—	18½	—	Peebles dep							7 48						10 40		1151								2 47
—	22½	—	Eddleston							7 56						10 48		1159								2 55
—	30½	—	Pomathorn Halt							8 12						11 4		1215								3 11
—	32½	—	Rosslynlee Hospital Halt			TC London to Edinburgh	TC London to Edinburgh			8 15						11 7		1218								3 14
—	33	—	Rosslynlee							8 18						11 10		1221								3 17
—	34½	—	Rosewell and Hawthornden arr							8 22						11 14		1225								3 21
			Rosewell and Hawthornden dep		7 5			7 52		8 25	8 47		9 30	1025	1058	11 15	12 0	1226			1 17		1 38		2 35	3 22
—	36	—	Bonnyrigg		7 8			7 55		8 28	8 50		9 33	1028	11 1	11 18	12 3	1229			1 20		1 41		2 38	3 25
71¼	—	—	Stow						7 39			8 57										12 53				
75¾	—	—	Fountainhall						7 47			9 5										1 1				
79¼	—	—	Heriot						7 56													1 9				
80¼	—	—	Tynehead						8E 3																	
86¼	—	Miles	Gorebridge						8 10													1 23		2 5		
88¼	—		Newtongrange						8 15													1 29		2 11		
90¾	37¼		Eskbank and Dalkeith	6 58	7 12			7 59	8 20	8 32	8 54		9 37	1032	11 5	11 23	12 7	1233			1 24	1 35	1 45	2 15	2 42	3 29
95¾	42¼	0	Portobello	7 8	7 22			8 9	8 31	8 42	9 4		9 47	1042	1115	11 33	12 17	1243			1 34	1 46	1 55	2 25	2 52	3 39
—	—	1¼	Piershill	7 11	7 25			8 12					9 50				12 20				1 37		1 58			
—	—	2¼	Abbeyhill		7 28			8 15					9 53				12 j27				1 40		2 1			
98¼	45¼	3¼	Edinburgh (Wav.) arr	7 16	7 31	7 52	7 57	8 18	8 37	8 49	9 10	9 41	9 56	1048	1121	11 39	12 30	1249	12 27		1 43	1 52	2 4	2 31	2 58	3 45

For notes see page 775

Table 219—
continued

CARLISLE, HAWICK, GALASHIELS AND EDINBURGH

Week Days—*continued* / **Sundays**

	pm D	pm E	pm S	pm E	pm S	pm DS	pm E	pm S	am E	am S	pm E	pm D	pm	pm S	pm DS	pm E	pm	pm D	pm D	pm E	pm S	pm S	pm S	Sun. pm Z	Sun. am	Sun. pm
London (St. Pancras) dep									9 15	9 15														9K 0		
	pm	pm	pm	pm	pm	pm	pm	pm	pm	pm	pm	pm	pm	pm	pm	pm	pm	pm	pm	pm	pm	pm	pm	am	am	pm
Carlisle dep		1 28	1 45				3 22	3 30	4 16	4 35			5 8			6 13				7 44	7 44	8 30	9 19	5 1		
Longtown		1 43	2 1				3C37	3 45					5U23			6 33				7 59	7 59	8 49				
Riddings Junction arr		1 51	2 9				3C45	3 53					5U31			6 41						8 57				
Riddings Junction dep		1 52	2 10	2 0	2 20		3C46	3 54					5U32			6 42						8 58				
Canonbie				2 5	2 25								5U37									9 3				
Gilnockie (for Clay Gate)				2 12	2 32								5U44									9 10				
Langholm arr				2 21	2 41								5U53									9 19				
Penton dep				Stop	Stop		3C52	4 0					Stop			6 48							9 46			
Kershope Foot		2 4	2 22				4C 0	4 8								6 56							9 54			
Newcastleton		2 11	2 30				4C 7	4 15	THE WAVERLEY	THE WAVERLEY						7 3				8 20	8 20		10 1			
Steele Road		2 21	2 40				4C17	4 25															1011			
Riccarton Junction		2 31	2 50				4C27	4 35						7 5		7 21	Through Train from Kelso dep 7 20 pm			8 39	8 39		1021			
Shankend		2 43	3 1				4C41	4 49						7 17		7 33							1034			
Stobs		2 49	3 8	pm			4C47	4 55					pm	7 23		7 39										
Hawick arr		2 55	3 14	E			4C53	5 1	5 24	5 43			E	7 29		7 45				9 1	9 1		1044	6 13		
Hawick dep		3 0	3 19	4 15			4C59	5 14	5 29	5 48			6 10	Stop		Stop				9 5	9 5			6 18	9 0	6 30
Hassendean				4 23			5C 6	5 21					6 17													
Belses ¶				4 30			5C12	5 27					6 23								9 17					
St. Boswells arr		3 16	3 35	4 37			5C19	5 34	5 45	6 4			6 30				7 45			9 21	9 24			6 34	9 16	6 46
St. Boswells dep		3 19	3 40	4 38			5C21	5 38	5 47	6 7			6 32				7 47			9 25	9 27			6 39	9 19	6 48
Melrose		3 26	3 47	4 44	pm		5C28	5 45	5 54	6 14			6 39	pm			7 54			9 32	9 34			6 47	9 26	6 55
Galashiels arr		3 32	3 53		D		5C34	5 51	6 0	6 20			6 45	DE			8 0			9 38	9 40			6 53	9 32	7 1
Galashiels dep		3 44	3 58	Stop	4 5		Stop	5 56	6 3	6 24	6 16	6 7		7 15	7 15		Stop	8 35		9 43	9 43			6 59	9 35	7 4
Clovenfords					4E13																					
Walkerburn					4 22							6 22						8 50								
Innerleithen					4 28							6 27						8 55								
Cardrona					4 34																					
Peebles arr					4 40							6 37						9 5								
Peebles dep					4 42							6 42						9 6								
Eddleston					4 50				RC and TC London to Edinburgh	RC and TC London to Edinburgh		6 50												TC London to Edinburgh		
Pomathorn Halt					5 11							7 16						9 34								
Rosslynlee Hospital Halt					5 14																					
Rosslynlee				pm	5 17		pm					7 20				pm	pm	9 38								
Rosewell and Hawthornden arr				D	5 21		D					7 24				D	D	9 42								
Rosewell and Hawthornden dep	3 47			4 32	5 22	5 45	6 38					7 25				8 18	9 15	9 43	10 7							
Bonnyrigg	3 50			4 35	5 25	5 48	6 41					7 29				8 21	9 18	9 46	1010							
Stow								6 12			6 32			7 28	7 28											
Fountainhall								6 20			6 40			7 36	7 36											
Heriot								6 28			6 48				7 44											
Tynehead																										
Gorebridge								6 42			7 2			7 51	7 54											
Newtongrange								6 48							8 0											
Eskbank and Dalkeith	3 54			4 39	5 29	5 52	6 45	6 53			7 11	7 37		8 0	8 3	8 25	9 22	9 50	1014							
Portobello	4 4			4 49	5 39	6 2	6 55	7 4			7 22	7 48		8 10	8 13	8 35	9 32	10 0	1024							
Piershill							6 58									8 38										
Abbeyhill																8 41										
Edinburgh (Wav.) arr	4 10	4 34	4 48	4 55	5 45	6 8	7 3	7 10	6 53	7 17	7 28	7 54		8 16	8 19	8 44	9 38	10 6	1031	1035	1035			7 50	1027	7 56

A Through Diesel train to Corstorphine
C Runs 2 minutes later on Fridays
D Diesel Service
E or **E** Except Saturdays
F Friday nights
j Arrives 5 minutes *earlier*
K Saturday nights
L Runs also on Sunday nights
H Depart 6 50 am on Saturdays
RC Restaurant Car
S or **S** Saturdays only
TC Through Carriages
U Runs 4 minutes later except Saturdays
Z Sleeping Cars London (St. Pancras) to Edinburgh (Waverley); does not convey Edinburgh Sleeping Car passengers from London (St. Pancras)

¶ For Ancrum and Lilliesleaf

Millerhill, Bowland and Leadburn served by road services operated by Scottish Omnibuses Ltd.

Above:

LMR timetable 15 June to 13 September 1959, Carlisle, Hawick, Galashiels and Edinburgh. Shows both Waverley and Peebles loop services

Table 219— *continued*

EDINBURGH, GALASHIELS, HAWICK AND CARLISLE

Week Days

Miles	Miles	Miles		am	am	am	am	am D	am D	am D	am D	am E	am D	am D	am S	am
			Edinburgh (Wav.) ... dep				6 40	7 15	7 40	7 54	8 40		9 5	9 40	9 50	10 5
—	—	1	Abbeyhill				6 43	7 18								
—	—	1½	Piershill				6 46	7 21								
3	3	3½	Portobello				6 49	7 24	7 46	8 0	8 46		9 11	9 46		
8	8	—	Eskbank and Dalkeith				7 0	7 33	7 55	8 9	8 55		9 20	9 55		
9¾	—	—	Newtongrange													THE WAVERLEY
12	—	—	Gorebridge				7 11									
16	—	—	Tynehead													
19	—	—	Heriot				7 29									
22½	—	—	Fountainhall				7 35									
26½	—	—	Stow				7 44									
—	9½	—	Bonnyrigg					7 38	8 0	8 14	9 0		9 25	10 0		
—	11¼	—	Rosewell and Hawthornden arr					7 42	8 4	8 17	9 4		9 28	10 4	Runs 27th June to 22nd August inclusive	RC and TC Edinburgh to London
			Rosewell and Hawthornden dep							8 23			9 29			
—	12¼	—	Rosslynlee							8 28			9 34			
—	13¼	—	Rosslynlee Hospital Halt							8 31			9 37			
—	15	—	Pomathorn Halt							8 38			9 42			
—	23	—	Eddleston							8 52			9 56			
—	27	—	**Peebles** arr							8 59			10 3			
			Peebles dep							9 2			10 8			
—	30½	—	Cardrona							9 10			10 16			
—	33¼	—	Innerleithen							9 16			10 22			
—	35¼	—	Walkerburn							9 20			10 26			
—	42¼	—	Clovenfords							9 30			10 36			
33½	45½	—	**Galashiels** arr				7 54			9 36			10 42		1046	1058
			Galashiels dep				7 57			Stop					1049	11 1
37½	—	—	Melrose				8 4								1056	11 8
40½	—	—	St. Boswells arr				8 10								11 2	1114
			St. Boswells dep				8 15								11 5	1119
45¼	—	—	Belses ¶				8 23									
48¼	—	—	Hassendean				8 30									
52¾	—	—	**Hawick** arr				8 40								1120	1134
			Hawick dep		6 30		8 46								1126	1137
56¾	—	—	Stobs				8 55								Through Train to Sheffield (Mid.) arr 4 33 pm	
59¾	—	—	Shankend				9 3									
65¼	—	—	Riccarton Junction		7 5		9 19									
69¼	—	—	Steele Road				9 25									
74	—	—	Newcastleton		7 17		9 33									
77	—	—	Kershope Foot		7 23		9 40			am						
81¼	—	Miles	Penton		7 30		9 47			S						
—	—	—	**Langholm** .... dep	7 5		9 2				1038		1042				
—	—	4¼	Gilnockie (for Clay Gate)	7 18						1049						
—	—	5½	Canonbie	7 24						1054		1054				
84½	—	7	Riddings Junction arr	7 28	7 36	9 17	9 53			1058		1058				
			Riddings Junction dep		7 38		9 54			11 0		11 0				
88½	—	—	Longtown		7 48		10 3			11 9		11 9				
98¼	—	—	**Carlisle** arr		8B 6		1023			1126		1126			1240	1245
409½	—	—	**London** (St. Pancras) arr													8B 0

	am AE	am A	am A	noon	pm D	pm D	pm S	pm	pm D	pm DS	pm DE	pm S	pm	pm AE	pm DS
Edinburgh (Wav.) ... dep	1025	11 15	1145	12 0	1220	1242	1252	1 2	1 18	1 50	1 52	2 17	2 36	3 13	3 13
Abbeyhill	1028									1 53	1 55				
Piershill	1031							1 7							
Portobello	1034	11 21	1151		1226	1248		1 10	1 25	1 58	2 0			3 19	3 19
Eskbank and Dalkeith	1043	11 30	12 0		1235	1259	1 8	1 21	1 34	2 7	2 9			3 28	3 28
Newtongrange							1 13	1 26							
Gorebridge							1 19	1 31							
Tynehead								Stop							
Heriot							1 39								
Fountainhall							1 45								
Stow							1 52						3 22		
Bonnyrigg	1048	11 35	12 5		1240	1 4			1 39	2 12	2 14			3 33	3 33
Rosewell and Hawthornden arr	1052	11 39	12 9		1243	1 7			1 42	2 16	2 18	Runs 27th June to 15th August inclusive		3 37	3 37
Rosewell and Hawthornden dep	Stop	Stop			1244				1 43						
Rosslynlee					1249				1 48						
Rosslynlee Hospital Halt					1252				1 51						
Pomathorn Halt					1257				1 56						
Eddleston									2 10						
Peebles arr					1 16				2 17						
Peebles dep					1 17				2 18						
Cardrona									2 26						
Innerleithen					1 29				2 32						
Walkerburn					1 33				2 36						
Clovenfords									2E46						
Galashiels arr				1253	1 47		2 2		2 52			3 10	3 32		
Galashiels dep				1255			2 5		Stop			3 13	3 35		
Melrose				1 2			2 12					3 20	3 42		
St. Boswells arr				1 8			2 18					3 26	3 48		
St. Boswells dep				1 13			2 21					3 28	3 53		
Belses ¶				1 21			2 29								
Hassendean		pm		1 28			2 36								
Hawick arr		S		1 35			2 43					3 43	4 8		
Hawick dep		12 25		1 38									4 16		
Stobs		12 34											4 25		
Shankend		12 42											4 33		
Riccarton Junction		12 55		2 7									4 49		
Steele Road		1 1		2 13									4 55		
Newcastleton		1 8		2 21									5 2		
Kershope Foot	pm	1 14						pm	pm				5 8		
Penton	S	1 20						S	E				5 14		
Langholm .... dep	1 2							3 23	3 23						
Gilnockie (for Clay Gate)	1 13							3 34	3 34						
Canonbie	1 18							3 39	3 39						
Riddings Junction arr	1 22	1 27						3 43	3 43				5 20		
Riddings Junction dep		1 28						3 44	3 50				5 21		
Longtown		1 38											5 29		
Carlisle arr		1 53		2 53				4 15	4 18				5 48		
London (St. Pancras) arr													a5d15		

For notes see page 777

Table 219— *continued*

EDINBURGH, GALASHIELS, HAWICK AND CARLISLE

Week Days—continued

	pm A	pm	pm D	pm DS	pm D	pm	pm D	pm	pm E	pm D	pm D
Edinburgh (Wav.) .. dep	3 54	4 10	4 21	4 42	5 5	5 11	5 41	5 52		6 26	6 56
Abbeyhill											
Piershill							5 46				
Portobello	4 0	4 16	4 27	4 48	5 11	5 17	5 49			6 32	7 2
Eskbank and Dalkeith	4 9	4 27	4 36	4 57	5 20	5 28	5 58			6 41	7 11
Newtongrange		4 32				5 33					
Gorebridge		4 38				5 39					
Tynehead		4E48									
Heriot		4 58				5 57					
Fountainhall		5 4				6 3					
Stow		5 11				6 10		6 37			
Bonnyrigg	4 14		4 41	5 2	5 25		6 3			6 46	7 16
Rosewell and Hawthornden arr	4 18		4 44	5 6	5 28		6 7			6 49	7 20
Rosewell and Hawthornden dep			4 45		5 29					6 50	
Rosslynlee	Stop		4 50		5 34	Through Train to Kelso arr 7 2 pm	Stop			6 55	
Rosslynlee Hospital Halt			4 53		5 37					6 58	
Pomathorn Halt			4 58		5 42					7 3	
Eddleston			5 13		5 56					7V18	
Peebles arr			5 20		6 3					7 25	
Peebles dep			5 22		6 6					7 36	
Cardrona			5 30		6 14						
Innerleithen			5 36		6 30					7 38	
Walkerburn			5 40		6 35					7 42	
Clovenfords					6645						
Galashiels arr	pm	5 21	5 54		6 52	6 20		6 47		7 56	
Galashiels dep	E	5 26			Stop	6 25		6 56	7 10		
Melrose	5 5	5 33				6 32		7 3	7 17		
St. Boswells arr	5 11	5 39				6 38		7 9	7 23		
St. Boswells dep	5 15	5 43				6 40		7 14	7 25		
Belses ¶	5 28	5 51							7 33		
Hassendean	5 35	5 58			pm	Stop			7 40		
Hawick arr	5 42	6 5			E			7 29	7 47		
Hawick dep		6S10			6 15			7 33			
Stobs		6S19			6 24						
Shankend		6S27			6 32						
Riccarton Junction		6S42			6 45						
Steele Road					6 51						
Newcastleton					6 57			8 12			
Kershope Foot						pm	pm				
Penton						E	S				
Langholm .... dep						6 22	6 32				
Gilnockie (for Clay Gate)						6 33	6 43				
Canonbie						6 38	6 48				
Riddings Junction arr						6 42	6 52				
Riddings Junction dep						6 44	6 54				
Longtown						6 55	7 3	8 32			
Carlisle arr						7 23	7 27	8 47			
London (St. Pancras) arr											

	pm K	pm N	pm S	pm D	pm D	pm AE	pm DS	pm Z	pm S	pm E	pm SD	pm SD	Sundays am D	Sundays pm	Sundays pm Z	Sundays pm
Edinburgh (Wav.) .. dep	7 0	7 0	7 0	8 12	8 44	9 12	9 12	9 55	10 15	10 15	10 43	11 0	1125	8 25	9 55	1015
Abbeyhill																
Piershill	7 5	7 5	7 5													
Portobello	7 9	7 9	7 9	8 18	8 50	9 18	9 18				10 49	11 6				
Eskbank and Dalkeith	7 20	7 20	7 20	8 27	8 59	9 27	9 27		10 31	10 31	11 0	1115				
Newtongrange	7 25	7 25	7 25								11 6					
Gorebridge	7 31	7 31	7 31							10 39	11 11					
Tynehead																
Heriot	7 49	7 49	7 51													
Fountainhall																
Stow																
Bonnyrigg				8 32	9 4	9 32	9 32					1120				
Rosewell and Hawthornden arr				8 36	9 7	9 36	9 36					1123				
Rosewell and Hawthornden dep					9 8							1124				
Rosslynlee					9 13			TC Edinburgh to London				1129			TC Edinburgh to London	
Rosslynlee Hospital Halt					9 16							1132				
Pomathorn Halt					9 21							1137				
Eddleston					9S36											
Peebles arr					9C41							1156				
Peebles dep					9C45							1157				
Cardrona												12V5				
Innerleithen					9C57							1211				
Walkerburn					10C 1							1215				
Clovenfords																
Galashiels arr	8 7	8 7	8 9		10C15			10 48	11 12	11 15		1229	1221	9 21	1048	1110
Galashiels dep	8 11	8 11	8 11		Stop			10 53	11 17	11 20			1223	9 23	1053	1115
Melrose	8 18	8 18	8 18					11 2	11 25	11 26			1230	9 30	11 2	1123
St. Boswells arr	8 24	8 24	8 24						11 31	11 32			1236	9 36		1129
St. Boswells dep	8 26	8 26	8 26						11 33	11 35			1237	9 38		1133
Belses ¶	8 34	8 34	8 34													
Hassendean	8 41	8 41	8 41													
Hawick arr	8 48	8 48	8 48					11 21	11 48	11 50			1254	9 55	1121	1148
Hawick dep		9 20	9 20					11 29	11 59						1129	
Stobs		9 29	9 29						12V 7							
Shankend		9 37	9 37						12V14							
Riccarton Junction		9 49	9 55						12V30							
Steele Road			10 1													
Newcastleton			10 7						12 43							
Kershope Foot					pm											
Penton					S											
Langholm .... dep					9 33											
Gilnockie (for Clay Gate)					9 44											
Canonbie					9 48											
Riddings Junction arr																
Riddings Junction dep																
Longtown																
Carlisle arr								12 40							1240	
London (St. Pancras) arr								9 20							9 20	

A Through Diesel Train from Corstorphine
a am
B Arrive 8 20 pm on Saturdays
C 2 minutes later on Saturdays
D Diesel Service
d Arrive 5 0 am on Sundays
E or E Except Saturdays
¢ Calls by request to set down only
H Arr 8 11 am on Saturdays
K Except Mondays, Wednesdays and Saturdays
N Mondays and Wednesdays
RC Restaurant Car
S or S Saturdays only
TC Through Carriages
V Calls to set down only
Z Sleeping Cars Edinburgh (Waverley) to London (St. Pancras); does not convey London Sleeping Car passengers from Edinburgh (Waverley)

¶ For Ancrum and Lilliesleaf

Millerhill, Bowland and Leadburn served by road services operated by Scottish Omnibuses Ltd.

Above:
LMR timetable 15 June to 13 September 1959, Carlisle, Hawick, Galashiels and Edinburgh.

A daily freight was enough to serve the line's freight needs for the majority of its life. This generally operated in two halves — Peebles to Hardengreen and Peebles to Galashiels. The 1953 working timetable showed a number of freight services running, the first of these being an 'as required' working that left Hardengreen Junction at 6am, running to Leadburn, Eddleston and Peebles East. This service then ran back at roughly mid-day, calling additionally at Pomathorn, Rosslynlee, Rosewell & Hawthornden, Bonnyrigg (as required) and Hardengreen.

A Class K freight ran out from Peebles East at 9.20am, having tripped to Peebles West; it arrived at 11.40am at Galashiels, where it shunted, and then returned at 12.15pm SX, calling at all stations to Peebles East, where it arrived at 1.55pm. On Saturdays it ran at 12.4pm, arriving at Peebles East at 2.10pm. It then ran at 3pm SX to Hardengreen Junction, arriving at 5.8pm, and at 7pm worked back to Peebles, where it arrived at 8.38pm.

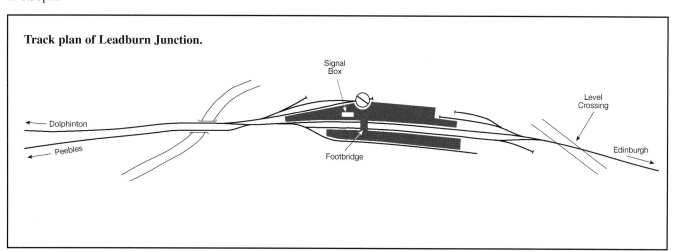

Track plan of Leadburn Junction.

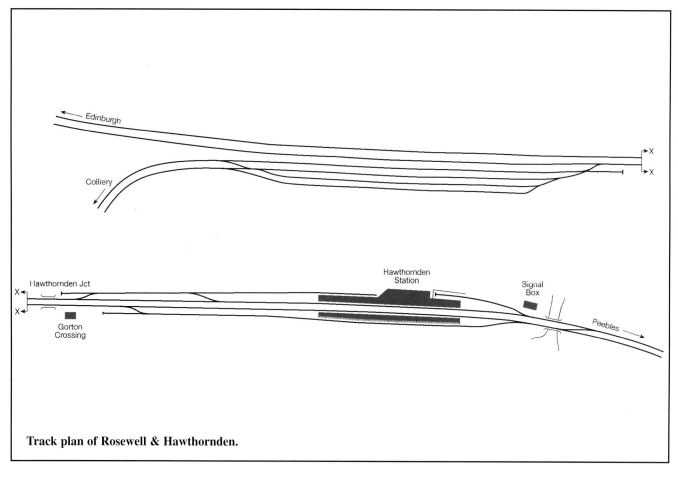

Track plan of Rosewell & Hawthornden.

172

Above:

From Clovenfords the line dropped to Thornielee station — an early casualty, closed on 6 November 1950. It had a single siding and a small loop for recessing the odd wagon. The name of the area it served was actually Thornylee — another example of the railway spelling the station name in a different way. Class B1 No 61351 heads a demolition train on 7 February 1962 to remove signalling equipment; considering the line had been closed only on 3 February, the Scottish Region had certainly lost no time! *Stuart Sellar*

Above:
The same train continues its task at Anglers Bridge Halt on 7 February 1962. Anglers Bridge Halt had originally been provided for the use of fisherman, local arrangements being made to pick up and set down passengers. *Stuart Sellar*

Left.
The line then crossed the River Tweed before arriving at Walkerburn, a single-platform station with two loop sidings and a goods shed with a crane. There was traffic here from the Tweedvale and Tweedholm woollen mills. One of the Wickham DMUs arrives at Walkerburn with a service for Edinburgh Waverley on 27 November 1961. The station here is now a private house.
Roy Hamilton

Right:
Another view of Walkerburn station, looking east towards the level crossing. The area beyond here to the left is shown in the railway line plans as 'Liable to floods'; indeed, this happened on 7 January 1949, when the railway was covered by water and services through the station were suspended for two months.
The small frame to the right of the points was released electrically from Innerleithen. *W. A. C. Smith*

Below:
From Walkerburn the Tweed was crossed again on bridge No 47 before reaching Innerleithen. Two Wickham DMUs are seen crossing at Innerleithen on 27 November 1961; the train to the left is correctly displaying the destination Galashiels, while the other train forms an Edinburgh service. *Roy Hamilton*

Right:
The 2.6pm Galashiels-Edinburgh DMU calls at Innerleithen on 11 November 1961. There was a gasworks here which attracted inward coal traffic in addition to domestic coal, and there were two woollen mills (Waverley and Leithen) near to the station. The goods yard is to the left. The station was also used for storage of 'intervention' traffic by the Ministry of Agriculture. The tall signalbox gave the signalman a fine view of the whole area.
W. A. C. Smith

Left:
Running along the north bank of the Tweed, the railway passed to the south bank over bridge No 41 before arriving at Cardrona station. Immediately to the west of the station was yet another bridge, No 38, which took the railway back to the north bank again. Here, on 20 January 1962, the 1.18pm Edinburgh-Galashiels DMU crosses the bridge at Cardrona and prepares to stop at the station. *W. A. C. Smith*

Above:
Class J37 No 64577 crosses the Tweed at Cardrona with the daily goods from Peebles to Galashiels on 25 August 1960. This is quite a lengthy train with a number of coal wagons, a tank for oil and vans of general merchandise. There were two small sidings here, and one of the LNER's camping coaches was also placed here in the 1930s. *Hugh Ballantyne*

Left:
The 2.6pm Galashiels-Edinburgh DMU pauses at Cardrona on 20 January 1962. The small yard can just be seen to the right. The train will cross the viaduct over the Tweed, which is situated behind the photographer. *W. A. C. Smith*

Running to the north of the Tweed, the line followed the river towards Peebles. To the right came Peebles Gas Works, where there were sidings and unloading facilities for coal traffic. Following this, after a further half mile, Peebles Junction was reached, and it was here that the junction for the link to the Caledonian station at Peebles West was made. The 12.21pm DMU from Edinburgh to Galashiels collects the tablet at Peebles Junction 'box on 20 January 1962. The smaller arm on the signal post was for the branch to the Caledonian.

W. A. C. Smith

Left:
The general goods yard at Peebles was at the east end of the station where there was a goods shed, crane and a loading dock which are all visible in this photograph of 'J37' No 64587 on 3 February 1962. The train was the 'Farewell to Peebles' special, the last full steam passenger working on the line. It has shunted back into the goods yard, while those on the train have a last chance to inspect the deserted sidings.
Stuart Sellar

Right:
Peebles East station on 11 November 1961, with the 2.6pm Galashiels-Edinburgh waiting to leave. This was not the original station, the former terminus station of the Peebles Railway being nearer Edinburgh. The station was renamed Peebles East on 25 September 1950, having been Peebles New after the original terminus closed, to distinguish it from the Caledonian station. *W. A. C. Smith*

Left:
The junction to the former terminus station at Peebles was at Peebles Engine Shed signalbox. The main line to Peebles East and Galashiels runs just in front of the signalbox, the line in the foreground leading to the former terminus where there were private sidings for a sawmill and a woollen mill. The locomotive shed was accessed by a set of points to the right of the signalbox in this photograph, which is dated 11 November 1961.
W. A. C. Smith

Above:

The first crossing away from Peebles on the run to Eddleston was at Winkston Crossing, situated near Winkston Mill. This photograph looks towards Peebles and was taken on 20 January 1962. *W. A. C. Smith*

Below:

Originally there were two platforms in use at Eddleston, and there was a small yard on the up side that contained two sidings with a loading bank and crane. The disused platform can be clearly seen in this photograph of the 2.6pm Galashiels-Edinburgh DMU on 20 January 1962. The signal is located on the disused platform. *W. A. C. Smith*

The 'Farewell to Peebles' special called at Eddleston on 3 February 1962 hauled by No 64587. From Eddleston the line climbed at grades of up to 1 in 61 to the summit of the route at 930ft, on the run to Leadburn Junction. At one time there had been a small station on this section, known as Earlyvale Crossing Gate, but this closed as early as 1857.
Stuart Sellar

Centre left:
Leadburn was the junction for the ten-mile branch to Dolphinton that was closed as early as 1 April 1933. This partially reopened in World War 2 as far as Macbie Hill near Broomlee for freight traffic to and from a Ministry of Supply depot. A DMU for Edinburgh calls at Leadburn on 28 June 1958. There was originally a turntable here, behind the buildings to the left. The platform on the right, for Dolphinton trains, was once accessed by a footbridge. A new brick signalbox was built here in the war, as seen on the left, and the footbridge was situated between this and the station buildings.
Roy Hamilton

Lower left:
No 64587 again, this time on a last-day special at Leadburn on 3 February 1962. From Leadburn the line dropped away towards Pomathorn which was reached after crossing the county boundaries of Peeblesshire and Midlothian. *W. A. C. Smith*

Above:

A change of weather from the previous two photographs shows the heavy snowfall in February 1958. This was too bad for the DMUs, and as a result steam haulage made a brief return on passenger services. St Margarets 'B1' No 61332 is seen at Leadburn Junction on an Edinburgh Waverley-Peebles service on 2 February. The photographer's notes state that the down train it was waiting to cross was headed by a 'D34' ('Scott') 4-4-0.
Stuart Sellar

Above:

Pomathorn station was originally named Penicuik, but this was changed on the opening of the branch to Penicuik in 1872. A single-track station, it once featured a signalbox and a loop, as well as a small, three-siding yard. On 20 January 1962 the 12.21pm Edinburgh-Galashiels prepares to pass over the level crossing situated at the end of the platform. *W. A. C. Smith*

Left:
No 64587 calls at Pomathorn on its way to Peebles with the last-day special on 3 February 1962. *Stuart Sellar*

Centre left:
Rosslynlee Hospital Halt was opened on 11 December 1958, which was late on in the line's life. A very simple affair to serve a local hospital, it still carried enough importance for the last-day special to call there on 3 February 1962, with No 64587 in charge. *Stuart Sellar*

Lower left:
Always one of the smaller stations on the line, Rosslynlee had a single platform and siding. Another view of No 64587 on the last-day special shows the attractive little signalbox design that housed the ground frame for the crossing. *Stuart Sellar*

Upper right:
Rosewell & Hawthornden was reached after a descent from Rosslynlee at 1 in 59. A DMU forms the 10.27am to Edinburgh on 25 August 1962. This was the stub-end service that ran between here and Edinburgh after the rest of the Peebles Loop had closed. The service was finally withdrawn from 10 September 1962. Rosewell & Hawthornden was the junction for the line to Penicuik which ran parallel to the Peebles line before branching off half a mile closer to Rosslynlee. Here too was a mineral railway to Whitehill Colliery that branched off just beyond station limits on the up side as well as the private Dalhousie Siding. From here, the Peebles Loop became single track. *Roy Hamilton*

Lower right:
Looking towards Edinburgh, No 64587 crosses a service train at Rosewell & Hawthornden on 3 February 1962. The smart lattice girder footbridge and rather large buildings were befitting to such a junction. *Stuart Sellar*

Left:
The first train to be hauled by ex-NBR 4-4-0 No 256 *Glen Douglas* following its restoration calls at Rosewell & Hawthornden on 29 August 1959. The locomotive was heading a trip to Glencorse.
Stuart Sellar

Centre left:
A Railway Society of Scotland railtour hauled by 'J36' No 65234 was the last passenger train as far as Rosewell & Hawthornden and also visited Penicuik on 29 August 1964. It is seen at Bonnyrigg, the first station beyond Hardengreen Junction. After Bonnyrigg came Esk Valley Junction where the line to Polton branched off before Hardengreen Junction was reached. Bonnyrigg had two private sidings, one for Polton No 2 Colliery, the other for Philip's. This train also visited Leith Citadel. *Stuart Sellar*

Below:
The start of the Peebles Loop at Hardengreen Junction. 'J37' No 64552 has a train of empty coal wagons for Newbattle Colliery and Lady Victoria Pit and is seen plodding up the Waverley Route on the 20 May 1960. The tall Junction signalbox and junction signal behind the train controlled access to the Peebles line that is seen forking away to the right. The line was double track from here through to Rosewell & Hawthornden.
Stuart Sellar

The 'Lauder Light'

Historical perspective

The Light Railways Act of 1896 allowed the construction of secondary railways to a lower and therefore cheaper specification than normal. One scheme that grew from this was the line that ran from Fountainhall Junction (on the Waverley Route) to Lauder. Incorporated in 1898, the line, at 10 miles 33 chains, was opened on 2 July 1901 and was worked by the North British. A scheme for a line from Fountainhall to Lauder had first been mooted in 1852 but had failed, due mainly to lack of enthusiasm from Lauder itself. More plans followed in 1883, but these too were not taken up. The NBR did, however, serve Lauder by means of a bus connection (the integrated transport policy of the 19th century!), which ran to and from Stow on the Waverley Route, the NBR subsidising a bus operator.

With the Light Railways Act, £15,000 was paid by Lauder Town Council and the County of Berwickshire towards the cost of construction of a light railway that would run from Lauder to Oxton and then Fountainhall, where an interchange was to be provided with the Waverley Route. This was only a third of the capital required, the rest being funded by investors.

Construction started in 1899, on 3 June, a comparatively late start in railway terms, with completion only two years later, on 2 July 1901. Power and rolling stock were provided by the North British, which operated the line on the basis of a profit-sharing scheme with the railway company; in reality this was based on receipts and was split 50:50. The lightweight construction of the track meant that there was a speed restriction of 25mph, and, as a result, trains were slow, taking up to 45 minutes for the journey. The locomotives used were Drummond 4-4-0s introduced for the North British in 1880. Coaching stock was provided in the form of two six-wheeled carriages of both third and first class, with steam heating and incandescent gas lighting.

From a bay platform on the up side at Fountainhall, the line swung across the Galashiels Road over a level crossing, operated by the guard. Other level crossings on the line had cattle grids

Above:
A general view of Fountainhall station on the Waverley Route on 17 August 1968, looking towards Edinburgh — the bay platform for Lauder can be seen to the right. There was a camping coach here in the 1930s.
G. N. Turnbull

instead of gates. Swinging northeast, the line then climbed through the Larriemiur Hills to the summit at 944ft near Eastertown. After the summit, the line descended to Oxton, a small village at the head of Lauderdale, which had goods sidings. Four miles from Oxton came Lauder, reached after following Leader Water. Fountainhall was 700ft above sea level, while Lauder station was 600ft above sea level.

Passenger receipts were not good, but the service did allow anglers and other 'outsiders' to travel with ease to the many trout streams in the area. The main traffic carried was agricultural materials, products and livestock to and from the area, with coal and parcels/general merchandise being conveyed into Lauder. Total income was never more than a few hundred pounds per annum, however, and, after paying out its share with the North British, the Lauder Light Railway Co was barely solvent. Despite this, it managed to hold out against an absorption by the North British, unlike some other lines, but in 1923, when the railways were formed into the 'Big Four', it became part of the London & North Eastern Railway.

The line was repaired following the flood damage sustained in 1948 and reopened on 2 November 1950. Operations continued until 1 October 1958, one train a day making the trip from Galashiels, usually worked by a 'J67' 0-6-0T with a converted wagon for a 'tender'.

Train services

The original passenger service consisted of four trains per day, which ran mixed 'as required'.

	am	am	pm	pm
Edinburgh	6.20	9.27	4.25	6.45
Galashiels	6.50	7.42	3.29	8.00
Fountainhall	7.40	10.28	5.10	8.25
Oxton	8.14	11.2	5.44	8.59
Lauder	8.27	11.15	5.57	9.12
Lauder	6.25	9.30	3.3	7.3
Oxton	6.38	9.43	3.16	7.16
Fountainhall	7.12	10.17	3.50	7.50
Galashiels	7.56	10.43	4.55	8.19
Edinburgh	8.26	12.58	4.57	9.3

Services started from Lauder, where there was a small wooden engine shed which housed the locomotive that ran in from Galashiels on a weekly basis. In NBR and early LNER days these were 1880-built Drummond 0-6-0 tank locomotives (usually No 10427). These were later replaced by ex-NBR 'D51' 4-4-0 tank locomotives. This daily service was later reduced to three trains per day only, with the evening train on Saturdays only.

Above:
Bradshaws 1922 timetable.

Above:
ScR timetable, 31 May to 26 September 1948 — Fountainhall and Lauder services.

LAUDER LIGHT RAILWAY

UP TRAINS			DOWN TRAINS		
	WEEKDAYS			WEEKDAYS	

Above:
ScR working timetable, 21 September 1953, Lauder Light Railway.

The 1922 Bradshaw shows the service to be:

	am	am	pm	pm
Fountainhall	7.22	9.25	5.11	8.5 SO
Oxton	7.50	9.53	5.39	8.33 SO
Lauder	8.3	10.6	5.52	8.46 SO
Lauder	6.35	8.16	3.3	7.14 SO
Oxton	6.48	8.29	3.16	7.27 SO
Fountainhall	7.16	8.57	3.44	7.55 SO

The LNER withdrew the passenger service on 12 September 1932 and bus services were advertised in the railway timetables, which also advised that stations would remain open for parcels and miscellaneous traffic.

The line's weight restrictions led to the appearance of ex-Great Eastern Railway 'F7' 2-4-2Ts, which replaced the 'D51' 4-4-0Ts employed by the North British. Latterly, the line was worked by two ex-GER 'J67' 0-6-0Ts, Nos 68492 and 68511, attached to North British tenders so that the locomotives need not carry water in their side tanks and thus reducing the axle weight. It was reported that an ex-LMS 2-6-0 had worked the line in 1952, but this was apparently not authorised in the longer term.

The Scottish Region working timetable for September 1953 shows a daily weekdays-only freight service (Trip No 958) that ran out from Galashiels at 9.26am. This train called at Fountainhall at 10.35am, stopping as required at Middleton Siding (2 miles 11 chains from Fountainhall) and Hartside Siding (4 miles 53 chains), both serving agricultural purposes, before arriving at the intermediate station of Oxton, 6 miles 38 chains from Fountainhall. The Oxton departure time was 11.25am, with an arrival at Lauder at 11.43. Just over half an hour was allowed for shunting at Lauder, with a departure at 12.15, passing Oxton at 12.30 and arrival back at Fountainhall at 1.5. The train then proceeded to Galashiels, arriving at 1.40pm.

As mentioned above, the line had closed from 12 August 1948 due to flood damage but had reopened for freight on 20 November 1950. The axle load restriction was raised to 14 tons on 15 June 1956 under the British Transport Commission (Dornoch and Lauder Branches) Light Railways (Amendment) Order 1956.

As well as agricultural traffic, freight latterly was coal inwards, and the line was also used for wagon storage. But so small were the receipts that the 'Auld Lauder Light' was closed to all traffic from 1 October 1958 and the nearest station for local people and farmers to use as a freight railhead was Earlston on the St Boswells-Greenlaw line.

The Branch Line Society organised a special train along the line on Saturday 15 November 1958. The train was patronised by many of the local people, including members of the Town Council. BR Standard Class 2MT 2-6-0 No 78049 hauled two ex-LMS coaches (the only time bogie coaches ran on the line), leaving Fountainhall at 2pm and returning at 3.40pm to Lauder, whence it ran to Galashiels.

Above:
No 78049 with the last train on the 'Lauder Light' on 15 November 1958 calls at Oxton. Despite closure a month before, there were still a number of wagons being stored here.
John Langford

Left:
No 68511 arrives at Lauder with a brakevan to form the 12.15pm back to Fountainhall and Galashiels, which comprised two wagons, on 14 October 1954.
W. A. Camwell

Lower left:
A photograph of Lauder station, looking towards the buffer stops and showing the overall layout, on 18 June 1936. To the right is the water tower, the platform with the simple building is on the right, and the small goods shed can be seen to the left. The locomotive shed that was once situated here was in front of the platform ramp, but by now was demolished.
SLS collection

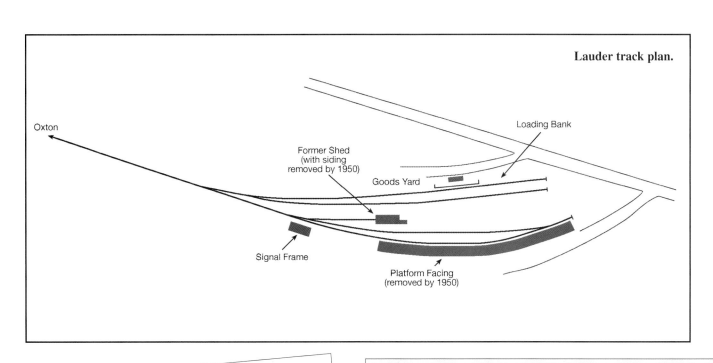

Lauder track plan.

Oxton

Loading Bank

Former Shed
(with siding
removed by 1950)

Goods Yard

Signal Frame

Platform Facing
(removed by 1950)

Above:
**No 78049 and its special train at Lauder on
15 November 1958. The station is crowded with local
people and the train's passengers. A wreath is being
placed on the front of the locomotive as a mark of
respect to the line, and, as part of this ceremony, a
speech made by the Provost.** *Stuart Sellar*

BRANCH LINE SOCIETY

(catering for all interested in minor railways)

SPECIAL LAST TRAIN

on

LAUDER LIGHT RAILWAY

on

15th NOVEMBER, 1958

- - - - - - -

TIMINGS

Fountainhall	dep.	2.00 p.m.
Oxton	arr.	2.30 p.m.
"	dep.	2.45 p.m.
Lauder	arr.	3.10 p.m.
"	dep.	3.40 p.m.
Fountainhall	arr.	4.35 p.m.

The train is being extended to Galashiels
as an ordinary train, tour tickets not being
valid. The arrival time at Galashiels will
be 5.00 p.m.

Above:
**BLS notice 15 November 1958, Lauder Light Railway
special last train.**

The Border Counties and the Wansbeck Valley; Riccarton Junction to Reedsmouth and Hexham; Reedsmouth to Scotsgap, Rothbury and Morpeth

Historical perspectives

Perhaps one of the most remarkable railways of the Borders was that which ran from the isolated Riccarton Junction on the Waverley Route to Hexham (Border Counties Junction), through Bellingham and Reedsmouth — the Border Counties Railway. At Reedsmouth a line from Morpeth via Scotsgap Junction came in — known as the Wansbeck Valley Railway — and from Scotsgap Junction a further branch ran for 13 miles to Rothbury, giving a useful network to serve those small towns and villages for both freight and passenger traffic.

An extension of the Newcastle & Carlisle Railway along the North Tyne Valley from Hexham was first planned in 1839, but this scheme failed as it did not meet the approval of Commissioners who were at the time advising on a number of Anglo-Scottish schemes. The Newcastle & Carlisle Railway, which had opened its main line throughout in 1839, tried again in 1846, this time for the construction of a line from Wooden Bridge at Hexham to Bellingham and thence to Woodburn, where there was to be a further link to the projected line from Newcastle to Hawick, which would connect to the North British's Hawick to Edinburgh line, this latter section having been granted authority in 1845.

The Newcastle-Hawick scheme was never built, but at the same time the North British was trying to extend its Edinburgh-Hawick line to Carlisle and thus gain direct access to and from England without having to rely on the hostile Caledonian or the East Coast main line. It saw the link to the now-authorised (1854) line from Hexham to Falstone and Plashetts — the grandly titled Border Counties Railway — as a way of accessing Newcastle via the independent (from the North Eastern), Newcastle & Carlisle Railway. The extension of the Border Counties line north of Plashetts to Hawick would achieve this for the North British, but in the event its own link to Carlisle — the Border Union Railway — was authorised on 21 July 1859, and the Border Counties extension to Hawick was altered to link to the Border Union at the remote area of Riccarton on 1 August 1860. The North British and the Border Counties succeeded in gaining the rights to run traffic between Hexham and Newcastle, and this was followed by full running powers, the Border Counties line being absorbed into the North British Railway in 1862.

The North Eastern had been formed in 1854 but did not take over the Newcastle & Carlisle until 1862. Despite this takeover, the NBR kept its access to and from Hexham and Newcastle via the Border Counties line. This was a mostly single track line with a ruling gradient of 1 in 100, meaning there were severe constraints on traffic capacity and speed, not at all satisfactory, but it did at least allow access to Newcastle.

The Wansbeck Valley route also allowed the NBR to strengthen its access to the East Coast. It was given Parliamentary approval on 8 August 1859 and ran from Morpeth on the East Coast main line to Reedsmouth, where it met the Border Counties. It was 25 miles long, single track and at the Morpeth end of the line it joined to the Blyth & Tyne Railway, which took coal traffic to the ships on the river. The Blyth & Tyne was taken over by the North Eastern in 1874, the North British retaining the Wansbeck Valley line.

The Wansbeck Valley line (truly a Scottish railway in England) was constructed in a number of constituent parts, being completed by 1 May 1865. At Scotsgap a junction was made, and there was a further extension — known as the Northumberland Central Railway — which was proposed to run to Coldstream on the Tweed Valley line, obtaining powers on 28 July 1863. In the event, the line was only ever built as far as Rothbury, a distance of 13 miles, opening on 1 November 1870. It merged two years later with the North British. Rothbury station had a long platform, as there was excursion and race traffic here, and there was also a locomotive shed with a turntable. The line served stations at Longwitton, Ewesley, Fontburn and Brinkburn and served quarries at Hartington and a colliery and quarry at Longwitton. Limestone was also transported from Ewesley quarries. The freight traffic was much more significant than the local passenger business, the line providing an important railhead for local farmers, but there were also flurries of activity associated with race meetings and other excursion traffic.

With Parliamentary powers being obtained in 1854 for the Border Counties line, a route to link Hexham with coal deposits at Plashetts (which were perceived to be of good enough quality to supply coal to the woollen industry situated in the border towns of the Galashiels area), construction started on 11 December 1855. The first portion of the route, as far as Humshaugh, was

opened on 5 April 1858. The line was completed to Falstone by 2 September 1861, and the stretch from there to Riccarton Junction was opened on 1 July 1862, the same day that the Waverley Route opened throughout from Carlisle to Hawick and Edinburgh. It was later discovered that the coal at Plashetts was suitable only for domestic use, and the other hope — that the line might form a key route between Newcastle and Scotland — was never realised, due not least to the lack of potential for high-speed running and the constraints of a single line.

Passenger services on the Border Counties were worked initially by Beyer Peacock 2-2-2 tender locomotives which had previously seen service on the Edinburgh & Glasgow Railway and dated from 1856. In the main there were three through services provided from Newcastle to Hawick. An additional train ran on Saturdays as far as Bellingham, and this was later extended to and from Kielder Forest for tourists and walkers. No Sunday services ran after World War 2.

In 1924 there were three trains that ran throughout on the line. The first up service ran from Hawick through to Newcastle at 6am, the next two departing Riccarton at 10.2am and 4.48pm. In the return direction there was a 7.4am Hexham-Riccarton, followed by a through Newcastle-Hawick service from Hexham at 11.47am. The last train was no less than a through train from Newcastle to Edinburgh, leaving Hexham at 5.8pm. As well as these services there was a local train that ran from Scotsgap at 3.37pm via Reedsmouth Junction to Bellingham, which it left at 4.5pm to return to Scotsgap.

The loss of the through Edinburgh train aside, the 1944 service was remarkably similar to that of 20 years previously, as is apparent from the extract from the 1944 timetable.

RICCARTON, REEDSMOUTH, and HEXHAM.—North British.

(1922 timetable extract — Up and Down services, Week Days only)

Above:
Bradshaw's **1922 guide — Border Counties.**

Table 163 HEXHAM and RICCARTON JUNCTION

(1944 LNER timetable extract — Week Days only)

A Thro' Train between Newcastle and Riccarton Junction.
B Thro' Trains between Newcastle and Hawick

Bb Calls on Tues. and Sats. at 7 1mrn when required to take up.

Cc Calls at 6 45 mrn. when required to take up on informing the Station Master at Riccarton Junc. before 50 aft the day previous to travel

Above:
LNER timetable, 22 May 1944, Border Counties.

Table 39 Riccarton, Bellingham, Hexham, and Newcastle.

Waverley Stn.	a.m.	.	a.m.	p.m	p.m	p.m	W	SUNDAYS	
EDINBURGH lev.	—	—	6 20	M.	—	2 35	7 p 2	—	—
Hawick . .	6 15	.	8 41	.	.	4 30	1045	.	.
CARLISLE — "	—	—	9 5	—	—	3 30	—	—	—
Riccarton Jn. lev	6 47	.	1027	.	.	5 8	1118	.	.
Deadwater —	6Y56	—	1037	—	—	5 13	1130	—	—
Kielder . .	7 3	.	1043	1 40	.	5 19	1136	.	.
Lewiefield (Halt)	7 8	—	1048	1 46	—	5 24	1143	—	—
Plashetts .	7 11	.	1052	1 51	.	5 28	1148	.	.
Falstone —	7 20	—	11 1	2 0	—	5 36	1155	—	—
Thorneyburn	7 27	U	11 8	2 7	.	5N43	.	.	.
Tarset — —	7 31	—	1110	2 11	—	5 46	—	—	—
Bellingham . (North Tyne)	7 38	.	1117	2 18	4 5	5 53	.	.	.
Reedsmouth arr.	7 42	—	1121	2 22	4 9	5 57	—	—	—
Reedsmouth lev.	7 48	.	1124	2 26	.	6 8	.	.	.
Wark — —	7 57	—	1133	2 35	—	6 17	—	—	—
Barrasford .	8 4	.	1140	2 42	.	6 24	.	.	.
Chollerton —	8 8	—	1144	2 46	—	6 28	—	—	—
Humshaugh .	8 13	.	1148	2 50	.	6 32	.	.	.
Wall — —	8 18	—	1152	2 54	—	6 36	—	—	—
Hexham arr.	8 25	.	1159	3 1	.	6 43	.	—	.
Newcastle arr.	9 11	—	1X12	3 43	.	8 J 2	—	—	—

Central Stn.	a.m	a.m	p.m	p.m	M	SUNDAYS	
Newcastle lev.	5 50	1120	—	4 30	8p30	—	—
Hexham . lev.	6 51	12p7	.	5 10	9 45	.	.
Wall — —	6 59	1215	—	5 18	9 53	—	—
Humshaugh .	7 4	1220	.	5 23	9 58	.	.
Chollerton —	7 9	1224	—	5 27	10 3	—	—
Barrasford .	7 13	1228	.	5 31	10 7	.	.
Wark — —	7 22	1236	—	5 39	1015	—	—
Reedsmouth arr.	7 30	1244	.	5 47	1023	.	.
Reedsmouth lev.	7 46	1248	3 5	6 1	1028	—	—
Bellingham . (North Tyne)	7 51	1253	3 9	6 7	1033	.	.
Tarset — —	7 58	1 0	—	6 13	1039	—	—
Thorneyburn	8 2	1 * 4	.	6 17	.	.	.
Falstone — —	8 10	1H10	—	6 25	1049	—	—
Plashetts .	8 20	1H20	.	6 35	1059	.	.
Lewiefield (Halt)	8 26	1H25	—	6 40	11 4	—	—
Kielder . .	8 34	1H32	.	6 47	1112	.	.
Deadwater —	8 40	1H38	—	—	—	—	—
Riccarton Jn. arr	8 50	1H48	.	7 2	.	.	.
CARLISLE arr.	1022	5 54	—	.	—	—	—
Hawick . .	1049	2Z16	.	7 27	.	.	.
EDINBURGH "	1225	4H20	—	9 49	—	—	—

Above:
ScR timetable, 31 May to 26 September 1948, Hexham and Riccarton Junction.

Table 72 HEXHAM and RICCARTON JUNCTION

Miles		WEEKDAYS A am	SX B am	SO B am		B pm	H pm
	65 Newcastle .... dep	5 52	11 20	11 20	....	4 30	8 30
			pm	pm	pm		
—	HEXHAM.. .. .. dep	6 50	12 6	12 6	..	5 14	9 45
3¼	Wall .... "	6 59	12 15	12 15	....	5 23	9 54
5	Humshaugh .. .. .. "	7 4	12 20	12 20	..	5 28	9 59
6¼	Chollerton .... "	7 9	12 24	12 24	....	5 32	10 4
7¾	Barrasford .. .. .. "	7 13	12 28	12 28	..	5 36	10 8
11¼	Wark .... "	7 22	12 36	12 36	....	5 44	10 16
15½	Reedsmouth .. arr	7 30	12 44	12 44	....	5 52	10 24
	dep	7 46	12 48	12 48	3 5	6X 1	10 29
17	Bellingham (North Tyne) .. "	7 51	12 53	12 53	3 9	6X 7	10 34
20¼	Tarset .... "	7 58	1 0	1 0	—	6X13	10 40
21½	Thorneyburn .. .. "	8 2	..	1 4	..	6X17	..
25½	Falstone .... "	8 10	1 10	1 13	....	6X25	10 50
30¼	Plashetts .. .. .. "	8 20	1 20	1 23	..	6X35	11 0
32	Lewiefield Halt .... "	8 26	1 25	1 28	....	6X40	11 5
33¾	Kielder Forest .. .. "	8 34	1 32	1 35	..	5X47	11 13
36¼	Deadwater .... "	8 40	1 38	1 41	....	....	—
39¼	Saughtree .. .. .. "	..	1U45	1b48	..	..	..
42	RICCARTON JUNC. .. arr	8 50	1N48	1 53	....	7X 2	....
55	Hawick .. .. .. arr	10 47	2C14	2 25	..	7X27	..
107¼	Edinburgh (Waverley) .. "	12p21	4 20	4 23	....	10 24	....

Miles		WEEKDAYS B am	A am	H pm	pm	SX B pm	SO B pm	J pm
	Edinburgh (Waverley) .. dep	....	6 40	....	....	2 35	2 35	7 2
	Hawick .. .. .. "	6 15	8 53	..	..	4 32	4 32	10 57
						pm	pm	pm
—	RICCARTON JUNC. .. dep	6 47	10 27	....	....	5 3	5 5	11 30
2¼	Saughtree .. .. .. "	..	..	..	..	5Z 8	5L10	..
5½	Deadwater .... "	E	10 37	....	....	5y13	5 17	11 42
8¼	Kielder Forest .. .. "	7 3	10 43	1 40	..	5y19	5 22	11 48
10	Lewiefield Halt .... "	7 8	10 48	1 46	....	5y24	5 27	11 55
11¾	Plashetts .. .. .. "	7 11	10 52	1 51	..	5y28	5 31	12 0
16½	Falstone .... "	7 20	11 1	2 0	....	5y36	5 40	12 7
20½	Thorneyburn .. .. "	7 27	F	2 7	..	5y43	5 47	—
21¼	Tarset .... "	7 31	11 10	2 11	....	5y48	5 51	....
25	Bellingham (North Tyne) .. "	7 38	11 17	2 18	4 5	5y55	5 58	..
26¾	Reedsmouth .. arr	7 42	11 21	2 22	4 9	5y59	6 2	....
	dep	7 48	11 24	2 26	Scotsgap (arr 4.48 pm)	6 8	6 8	..
30¾	Wark .... "	7 57	11 33	2 35		6 17	6 17	....
34¼	Barrasford .. .. .. "	8 4	11 40	2 42		6 24	6 24	..
35¾	Chollerton .... "	8 8	11 44	2 46		6 28	6 28	....
37	Humshaugh .. .. "	8 13	11 48	2 50		6 32	6 32	..
38¾	Wall .... "	8 18	11 52	2 54		6 36	6 36	....
42	HEXHAM.. .. .. arr	8 27	12 1	3 3		6 45	6 45	..
62¾	65 Newcastle .... arr	9 11	1K12	3 43	....	8G 0	8G 0	....

A—Through Train between Newcastle and Riccarton Junction.
B—Through Train between Newcastle and Hawick.
C—Arrives 2.19 pm Mondays and Thursdays.
E—Calls 6.55 am when required to take up on informing the Station Master at Riccarton Junction before 5 pm the day previous to travel.
F—Calls at Thorneyburn 11.8 am on Saturdays only to take up passengers and runs 2 minutes later forward to Hexham. thence as booked.

G—Passengers can arrive Newcastle 7.22 pm by changing at Hexham.
H—Runs alternate Saturdays only. Commences October 7th.
J—Runs alternate Saturdays only. Commences September 30th.
K—Passengers can arrive Newcastle 12.41 pm (12.43 pm SO) by changing at Hexham.

L—Calls to set down only.
N—Arrives 1.50 pm on Mondays and Thursdays.
SO—Saturdays only.
SX—Saturdays excepted.
U—Calls to take up only on Mondays and Thursdays.
X—2 mins. later on Saturdays.
Z—Calls to set down only on Mondays and Thursdays.
b—Calls to take up only.
p—pm.
y—1 min. later on Mondays and Thursdays.

Above:
NER timetable, 25 September 1950, Hexham and Riccarton Junction

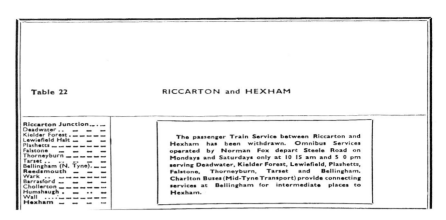

Table 22				RICCARTON and HEXHAM

Riccarton Junction... ..				
Deadwater ..	—	—	—	
Kielder Forest .	—	—	—	The passenger Train Service between Riccarton and
Lewiefield Halt	—	—	—	Hexham has been withdrawn. Omnibus Services
Plashetts	—	—	—	operated by Norman Fox depart Steele Road on
Falstone	—	—	—	Mondays and Saturdays only at 10 15 am and 5 0 pm
Thorneyburn	—	—	—	serving Deadwater, Kielder Forest, Lewiefield, Plashetts,
Tarset ..	—	—	—	Falstone, Thorneyburn, Tarset and Bellingham.
Bellingham (N. Tyne).	—	—	—	Charlton Buses (Mid-Tyne Transport) provide connecting
Reedsmouth	—	—	—	services at Bellingham for intermediate places to
Wark ..	—	—	—	Hexham.
Barrasford .	—	—	—	
Chollerton	—	—	—	
Humshaugh .	—	..	—	
Wall	—	—	—	
Hexham	—	—	—	

The 1948 and 1950 BR services included the three through trains, two of these running to and from Hawick, the other to and from Riccarton Junction. Additional services for walkers and visitors to the area were a 1.40pm return working for Hexham and two evening services — a 9.45pm from Hexham to Kielder Forest which ran on alternate Saturdays and an 11.30pm from Riccarton Junction to Falstone (it came from Hawick), which also ran on the other alternate Saturdays to the Hexham service. It should be noted that the return afternoon working from Bellingham to Reedsmouth continued to operate.

As well as from tourists and walkers, members of the Armed Forces and a significant level of local support, the main passenger traffic came from Forestry Commission workers centred on the Kielder area. However, costs remained higher than income, and in early 1956 the BTC proposed to withdraw passenger services, claiming it would save £20,000 a year. The BTC also claimed that the line cost £750 a mile per annum to maintain and signal, and this did not include the operating costs of the train services. If fares were cut by 25% to encourage patronage then there would have to be an increase of just over 33% in passenger journeys to maintain the income at its existing level. But so poor were the prospects for local buses that even these services had been withdrawn, and taxis became the main source of alternative transport, as well as the private car. To compensate for this lack of patronage a local bus operator was to receive a subsidy of £3,000 per annum to operate a service from Bellingham to connect with Waverley Route services at Steele Road, these being provided by Norman Fox, with any receipts passed to BR. The main reason given for the withdrawal of services was that major repairs needed to be carried out to the Tyne Bridge, to the west of Hexham. (Of course, freight services continued to reach Bellingham via Reedsmouth and the Morpeth/Scotsgap direction). Services for goods on the northern section were to continue to Barrasford only.

Passenger services were withdrawn from Saturday, 13 October 1956. Class K1 2-6-0 No 62022, complete with wreath on the smokebox door, hauled the last through train from Newcastle to Hawick and return. This train left Newcastle at 11.10am and comprised six coaches, two more being added at Hexham.

There was a problem with the single-line tablet apparatus that day at Hexham which meant that the tablet for the 10.39am SO from Hexham to Kielder Forest had not been released, thus necessitating the need for a pilot, which delayed the train for 56 minutes. The 10.22am from Riccarton Junction had to be held at Reedsmouth Junction until 1.6pm so that it could cross the 11.10am Newcastle to Hawick; it eventually arrived at Hexham 100 minutes late.

Because of the short platforms the 11.10am to Hawick had to draw up at most stations, while from Riccarton to Hawick the train was partially banked by 'J37' No 64539. The engine found it difficult to keep to time with an eight-coach train, and arrival at Hawick was 30 minutes behind schedule.

The return working departed from Hawick at 4.32pm, this train also being banked — this time by a real treat, as it was 'D30'

No 62440 *Wandering Willie*. Many locals were there to see the passing of the last train and, not surprisingly, the biggest turn-out was at Bellingham.

After formal closure to passengers a number of excursions continued to run, usually DMUs, and all were associated with the agricultural fairs at Bellingham. The last train to run on the route throughout was a ramblers' excursion which ran from Newcastle to Hawick on Sunday 7 September 1958. This was formed by a number of DMU sets and was well patronised.

The Border Counties line did see other traffic, such as saplings which were then planted as the area was exploited for forestry, Kielder Forest having a siding for this traffic that had been brought in from Aviemore to forest the area. The armed forces had training areas nearby which saw a large number of troop trains, many of these going through to Woodburn via Reedsmouth; some even ran through from the 'Port Road' from Stranraer — joining the line at Hexham — especially in the war years. A halt was constructed at Lewiefield for a camp used for providing unemployed people with training; this was later used by the military. The line also served the local agricultural community, with the transportation inwards of supplies such as animal feedstuffs and equipment and outwards of produce and livestock to market.

Between Wall and Hexham was Acomb Colliery. This enjoyed a freight service from Carlisle (see the working timetable extract) until 1952. Cattle markets were situated at Hexham, Bellingham and Scotsgap to consolidate livestock traffic. Indeed, this was the case with other lines such as Kelso and Earlston.

Some general freight and domestic coal continued to be carried until final closure, which took place in stages, long after passenger services had been withdrawn. The destination of this traffic, Bellingham, was latterly served via Reedsmouth Junction, Scotsgap and the Wansbeck Valley line from Morpeth (the link to Hexham having closed to passengers in October 1956), which joined the Border Counties at Reedsmouth Junction and had opened throughout on 1 May 1865.

Freight services were withdrawn between Hexham and Reedsmouth and between Riccarton Junction and Bellingham from 1 September 1958. The Bellingham-Reedsmouth section remained open and was served by a twice-weekly goods train from Morpeth which ran via Scotsgap Junction.

On the Wansbeck Valley line the initial passenger service was three return weekday trains. Bradshaw's Guide of 1922 shows three trains from Rothbury to Morpeth which left at 8.9, 11.30am and 4.29pm. Three trains returned from Morpeth to Rothbury at 9.45am, 2.15 and 5.55pm, the whole service being provided by a set of coaches and locomotive that were outbased at Rothbury. One carriage off the first morning up service and the evening down service formed a through coach for Newcastle. The Scotsgap to Reedsmouth services started out of Reedsmouth at 8am and ran with the mid-afternoon service extended to and from Bellingham. There was an additional service that ran on Tuesdays only in the early evening.

MORPETH BRANCH.—North British.

Miles	Up.	Week Days only. mrn (Through Carriage to Newcastle, see page 735.)		mrn	(From Bellingham at 4 5 aft., see page 809.) aft		aft	
	Reedsmouth...dep.	8 0	....	1120	4 15	....	6 5	....
3¾	Woodburn	8 10	....	1129	4 24	....	6 14	....
10½	Knowesgate §	8 26	....	1144	4 39	....	6 29	....
14	Scotsgap ‡ ......arr.	8 35	....	1153	4 48	....	6 38	....
—	Mls Rothbury..dep.	8 9	....	1130	4 29	....	Tuesdays only.	....
—	2¼ Brinkburn	8 14	....	1135	4 34	....		....
—	6½ Fontburn Halt	8 26	....	1147	4 46	....		....
—	7½ Ewesley	8 30	....	1151	4 50	....		....
—	9¾ Longwitton....	8 36	....	1157	4 56	....		....
—	13 Scotsgap‡..arr.	8 42	....	12 3	5 2	....		....
—	Scotsgap ....dep.	8 44	....	12 5	5 4	....		....
16	Middleton	8 49	....	1210	5 9	....		....
17½	Angerton	8 53	....	1214	5 13	....	....	....
19¾	Meldon ...[735,745	8 59	....	1220	5 19	....	....	....
25	Morpeth 734, arr.	9 9	....	1230	5 29	....	....	....

Miles	Down.	Week Days only. mrn	(To Bellingham (arr. 3 41 aft.), see page 809.) aft	aft	(Through Carriage from Newcastle, see page 734.) aft	aft	
	Morpeth ....dep.	9 45	2 15	Tuesdays only.	5 55	Tuesdays only.	....
5¼	Meldon	9 58	2 23		6 8		....
7½	Angerton	10 4	2 34		6 14		....
9	Middleton	10 9	2 39		6 19		....
11	Scotsgap ‡ ....arr.	1015	2 45		6 25		....
—	Scotsgap ....dep.	1017	2 47		6 27		....
14¼	Longwitton	1026	2 56		6 36		....
16¼	Ewesley	1031	3 1		6 42		....
17¼	Fontburn Halt ...	1035	3 5		6 46		....
21¾	Brinkburn	1045	3 15		6 56		....
24	Rothbury .....arr.	1051	3 21		7 2		....
—	Scotsgap.........dep.	1022	2 54	5 8	6H32	6 45	....
14¾	Knowesgate §	1033	3 5	5 19	6H43	6 56	....
21¼	Woodburn	1047	3 19	5 33	6H57	7 10	....
25	Reedsmouth 809 arr	1055	3 27	5 41	7H5	7 18	....

H Except Tuesdays. ‡ Station for Cambo (1 mile). § Station for Kirkwhelpington (1 mile).

Above:
Bradshaw's **1922 timetable, Morpeth branch.**

Tables 164 & 164a MORPETH, SCOTSGAP, and REEDSMOUTH, and ROTHBURY

Miles		Week Days only mrn		aft S		aft		
	157 NEWCASTLE ... dep	9 30	..	1A15	..	5 ‖7	..	..
—	Morpeth .... dep	10 15	..	2 15	..	5 50	..	..
5¼	Meldon	10 27	..	2 28	..	6 3	..	..
7¾	Angerton	10 34	..	2 34	..	6 9	..	..
9¼	Middleton North......	10 39	..	2 39	..	6 14	..	..
11¼	Scotsgap D	10 45	..	2 45	..	6 20	..	..
—	Scotsgap .... dep	10 51	..	..	..	6 27	..	..
14¾	Knowesgate.........	11 0	..	..	..	6 38	..	..
21½	Woodburn...........	11 13	..	..	..	6 52	..	..
25½	Reedsmouth.... arr	11 20	..	..	..	7 0	..	..
14¼	Longwitton...........	10 57	..	2 55	..	6 31	..	..
16¼	Ewesley	11 2	..	3 0	..	6 38	..	..
17¼	Fontburn Halt	11 7	..	3 4	..	6 43	..	..
22	Brinkburn............	11 17	..	3 13	..	6F52	..	..
24¼	Rothbury........ arr	11 23	..	3 19	..	6 58	..	..

Miles		Week Days only mrn		mrn S		aft				
	Rothbury......... dep	7 50	..	1135	..	4 21	..	..	..	..
2¼	Brinkburn............	7 55	..	1140	..	4 26	..	..	..	..
6¼	Fontburn Halt	8 6	..	1151	..	4 37	..	..	..	..
7¾	Ewesley	8 9	..	1154	..	4 40	..	..	..	..
9¾	Longwitton	8 15	..	12 0	..	4 46	..	..	..	..
—	Mls Reedsmouth.. dep	7 40	..	..	..	4 15	..	..	..	..
—	3¾ Woodburn.........	7 51	..	..	..	4 24	..	..	..	..
—	10½ Knowesgate.......	8 7	..	..	..	4 39	..	..	..	..
—	14 Scotsgap D... arr	8 16	..	..	..	4 48	..	..	..	..
13	Scotsgap D	8 24	..	12 7	..	4 53	..	..	..	..
15	Middleton North......	8 29	..	1211	..	4 57	..	..	..	..
16¼	Angerton	8 34	..	1215	..	5 1	..	..	..	..
18¾	Meldon	8 41	..	1220	..	5 6	..	..	..	..
24¼	Morpeth .... arr	8 53	..	1230	..	5 16	..	..	..	..
40¾	157 NEWCASTLE ... arr	9 30	..	2 11	..	5 53	..	..	..	..

A Change at Manors. D Station for Cambo (1 mile). F Calls to set down only.
S Saturdays only. ‖ Dep 5 0 aft on Sats.

Above:
LNER timetable, 22 May 1944, Morpeth, Scotsgap-Reedsmouth and Rothbury.

Table 76 MORPETH, SCOTSGAP and REEDSMOUTH and ROTHBURY

Miles	WEEKDAYS	am	am	SO pm	pm	pm
	3 Newcastle .... dep	9 28	....	12 21	5 7	....
—	MORPETH .. .. dep	10 10	..	2 15	5 50	..
5¼	Meldon .... „	10 22	....	2 28	6 3	....
7¾	Angerton .. .. „	10 29	..	2 34	6 9	..
9¼	Middleton North .... „	10 34	....	2 39	6 14	....
11¼	Scotsgap (for Cambo).. arr	10 40	..	2 45	6 20	..
—	Scotsgap (for Cambo) dep	....	10 46	....	....	6 27
14¾	Knowesgate .. .. „	..	10 55	..	..	6 38
21¼	Woodburn .... „	....	11 8	....	....	6 52
25¼	Reedsmouth .. arr	..	11 15	..	..	7 0
—	Scotsgap (for Cambo).. dep	10 43	....	2 46	6 22	....
14¼	Longwitton .. .. „	10 52	..	2 55	6 31	..
16¼	Ewesley .... „	10 57	....	3 0	6 38	....
17¼	Fontburn Halt .. „	11 2	..	3 4	6 43	..
22	Brinkburn Halt .... „	11 12	....	3 13	6A52	....
24¼	ROTHBURY .. .. arr	11 18	..	3 19	6 58	..

Miles	WEEKDAYS	am	am	SO am	pm (Bellingham dep 4.5 pm)	pm
—	ROTHBURY .. .. dep	..	7 51	11 40		4 30
2¼	Brinkburn Halt .... „	....	7 56	11 45		4 35
6¼	Fontburn Halt .. „	..	8 7	11 56		4 46
7¾	Ewesley .... „	....	8 10	11 59		4 49
9¾	Longwitton .. .. „	..	8 16	12 5		4 55
13	Scotsgap (for Cambo).. arr	....	8 22	12 11		5 1
	Reedsmouth .. dep	7 44	..	..	4 15	..
3¾	Woodburn .... „	7 54	....	....	4 24	....
10½	Knowesgate .. .. „	8 9	..	..	4 39	..
14	Scotsgap (for Cambo) arr	8 18	....	....	4 48	....
—	Scotsgap (for Cambo).. dep	..	8 25	12 12	..	5 2
15	Middleton North ...... „	....	8 29	12 16	....	5 6
16½	Angerton .. .. „	..	8 34	12 20	..	5 10
18¾	Meldon .... „	....	8 40	12 25	....	5 15
24¼	MORPETH .. .. arr	..	8 51	12 35	..	5 25
40¾	3 Newcastle .... arr	....	9 29	2 5	....	6 7

A—Calls to set down only. SO—Saturdays only.

Left:
BR NER timetable, 25 September 1950, Morpeth, Scotsgap-Reedsmouth and Rothbury.

By 1944 the service had been reduced, the Rothbury-Morpeth service now being two trains per day but with an extra on Saturdays. The Reedsmouth-Scotsgap service was also reduced to only two trains per day. This pattern of service was roughly the same in 1950.

There were also many specials that ran on the Wansbeck Valley line, as well as many summer troop trains to and from Woodburn for units that went training at Otterburn. These brought in as many as seven to 10-coach trains from all points of the country. Many were hauled to Newcastle from where they would be worked to Woodburn, usually by two 'J21' class 0-6-0s of 52B (Heaton). In addition, 51F (West Auckland) would also supply power, BR Standards Nos 76024 and 76049 being noted on the

Right:
Ex-NER 'J21' 0-6-0s Nos 65033 and 65103 stand at Riccarton Junction with a troop train heading tender-first for Hawick. These two locomotives, based at 52C (Blaydon) were used regularly on the heavy troop trains and other excursions that ran on the line. They were the last two survivors of the class, No 65033 eventually being saved for preservation. *A. J. Wickens*

line. Military specials continued to run every weekend during June and July and until 1956 some came in via Hexham where the pilot locomotive was detached and ran light to Wall, as double-heading was not permitted over the Tyne Bridge, where there was also a 10mph speed restriction. This then rejoined the train at Wall.

Also, diesel excursion trains to Bellingham were run in duplicate in both 1962 and 1963 for the agricultural show. As well as these trains there were 'Garden Special Excursions' which ran from Newcastle via Hexham, Reedsmouth, Bellingham, Reedsmouth, Scotsgap Junction, Rothbury, Scotsgap Junction and thence to Morpeth and Newcastle. These trains stopped to view various station gardens en route and to allow passengers to visit the hostelries in the local towns.

For the enthusiast an RCTS/SLS railtour, the 'Joint North Eastern Tour, York to York', ran via many different lines from Friday 27 September to Tuesday 1 October 1963, taking in Rothbury, Bellingham, Morpeth and Newcastle. Ivatt Class 4MT 2-6-0 No 43129 took the train from Morpeth, and Rothbury which was eventually reached at 7.5pm, over two hours behind schedule. Rothbury was left at 8pm and, as a result, the train did not run on the Bellingham section.

Saturday 9 November 1963 saw the 'Wansbeck Wanderer' operate as the last passenger train to Rothbury and Bellingham. This train left Newcastle at 9.12am with No 43129 again in charge. It ran to Morpeth and then travelled via Scotsgap Junction and Reedsmouth Junction, where the train reversed before going on to Bellingham. On the return there was a photographic stop at Woodburn and then a run to Rothbury, where the train was piped away at 3.15pm. From Morpeth, 'V3' 2-6-2 tank No 67691 took the train forward to Newcastle.

On the Wansbeck Valley and Scotsgap lines, passenger services had been withdrawn on 15 September 1952, but goods services survived as far as Woodburn and Bellingham via Reedsmouth. In 1961 this latter goods service, a Class K, ran from Morpeth to Bellingham MWFO, leaving Morpeth at 8.10am and returning from Bellingham at 11.10am FO or 11.30am MWO. There was also a 10.20am TThFO to Rothbury, from where the train returned at 2.20pm. From 11 November 1963 a freight service existed only as far as Woodburn, a Thursdays-only train running to and from South Blyth.

In earlier years the freight trains were in the hands of 'J21' and 'J25' 0-6-0s, but there were also appearances by Ivatt '2MT' 2-6-0s. Used latterly were 'J21' No 65033, 'J25' No 65663 and Ivatt 2-6-0s Nos 46473 and 46474. On 31 October 1960 Stanier 2-6-4T No 40075 of 55E (Normanton) was loaned to Heaton for trials in the area and was used on the Rothbury & Reedsmouth line on 8 November before returning to its home depot — apparently it was not a success. Following closure of the line

beyond Woodburn, goods trains continued to run, conveying agricultural supplies and products, coal and general merchandise, as well as military stores. In May 1966 the locomotive was nearly always a 'J27', No 65819 from South Blyth. The train ran TThO from Morpeth at 10.20am, while the locomotive came from Blyth at 07.00 and shunted there before departure. This service lasted until 4 October 1966.

In the final two years before closure to freight, a number of specials, organised by the Gosforth Round Table, worked the line. These were usually operated by DMUs and ran on 19 September 1964 (the 'Bellingham Belle') and 1965. 1 July 1966 saw a further special, the 'Wood Burner'. The last train to work the line ran on Saturday 2 October 1966. This was the 'Wansbeck Piper', organised by the Gosforth Round Table, which ran to and from Woodburn hauled by Ivatt 2-6-0s Nos 43000 and 43063. Freight had finally ended on 29 September.

The network of lines in the area was soon removed. By June 1959, track lifting had begun between Riccarton and Kielder, and by February 1960 it was reported that the Tyne Bridge, before Border Counties Junction at Hexham, had been demolished, and track lifting started on that section. By 19 July 1960 the freight-only nature of the traffic had seen a decline in the cutting-back of vegetation and weed-killing, with the track at Reedsmouth becoming heavily overgrown, but the station buildings and signalbox were still tidy. Half a mile south of Reedsmouth the line southbound had been lifted, while that from Tarset to Riccarton had been removed completely. However, Reedsmouth was still connected by rail to Bellingham and in the other direction to Morpeth, the locomotive shed now being used as a coal depot. The 0-4-0 diesel shunters that were employed on the track-lifting trains were also stabled there. A daily demolition train ran out from Morpeth and North Blyth on the Wansbeck Valley line after closure to Woodburn in 1966.

Despite sparse passenger services, the network of lines offered an important lifeline to a rural area. It was useful to be able to reach main-line connections at Newcastle in one direction and Hawick in the other, so shoppers were able to travel there too, as well as Hexham. Following closure, agricultural supplies and produce, military stores, coal and troops all had to be transported by road. As will be seen from the following photographs, most of the places served were remote, to say the least, but Reedsmouth Junction and Bellingham were provided with reasonably large facilities, Reedsmouth being particularly impressive. However, places like Saughtree were served on Mondays, Thursdays and Saturdays only by one train in either direction, and it is hardly surprising that these lines have passed into history in the age of the accountant. It is unlikely that they would have survived today, even with radio-controlled signalling and simplified level crossings.

Above:

Class K1 2-6-0 No 62022 at Riccarton Junction with the 11.10am from Newcastle Central on 13 October 1956, the last day of service. Riccarton Junction was where the Border Counties line joined the important Waverley Route main line from Carlisle to Edinburgh; The junction was immediately to the south of the station platform. Before the track was removed, the stub end of the line at this end was retained for the storage of redundant rolling stock. Riccarton was indeed a lonely place, and as a settlement it grew mainly because it was where the two lines had met. As it was a junction, the NBR built a station based on an island platform, with a bay at the southern end for Border Counties trains.

In reality, roughly two thirds of the Border Counties services ran to Hawick, as most passengers actually wished to end up in civilisation! Accommodation was built for the railway employees, and a railway community soon grew up, with as many as 100 people living in 33 houses. Virtually all contact with the outside world was by means of the railway, the nearest road being two miles away. A Co-operative Society shop was opened on the centre of the platform, together with a telephone box and a post office; there was also a buffet. On the railway side, there were locomotive and carriage sheds for six locomotives and a number of sidings and loops to allow an exchange of traffic between the two lines and for Waverley Route freights to be recessed for watering or held 'inside' for passenger services to pass. It is a little surprising, given that Border Counties passenger services were withdrawn on 15 October 1956, that Riccarton Junction did not become an 'unstaffed' station until 27 March 1967, by then for Waverley Route passengers only. *N. E. Stead*

RICCARTON JUNCTION TO REEDSMOUTH JUNCTION

Left:

Saughtree was served by one train (which ran to and from Hawick) in each direction on only three days a week — Mondays, Thursdays and Saturdays. Seen from a train that actually stopped there — probably the 5.3pm SX, 5.5pm SO Hawick to Newcastle — the station was closed on 1 December 1944 and did not reopen until 23 April 1948. It was between here and Deadwater that a Border signpost was placed in BR days. At this point the railway follows the infant River Liddel that flows eventually to the Solway Firth. Today, rails have returned to Saughtree: the station has been restored, complete with track, and is home to a small Ruston & Hornsby diesel shunter, wagons and a brake van. *H. C. Casserley*

Right:
**BR Standard Class 4MT 2-6-0
No 76049 is seen between
Saughtree and Deadwater with a
ramblers' special on 17 July 1955.
Deadwater station opened in 1880
and was used only on Saturdays.
It was so named because of the
slowness of the stream nearby
which eventually flows to Kielder
and the North Tyne. This spot is
also near the source of the River
Liddel that flows in the opposite
direction to the Solway and is at
the very apex of the divide.**
J. D. Smith

Above:
**A general overview of Kielder Forest, including the local post office, looking towards Riccarton, showing part of
the village and, to the left, the edge of the forest itself.** *Ian Allan Library*

Above:
Class V3 2-6-2T No 67687 at Kielder Forest with the 1.40pm SO to Hexham on 15 September 1950. The signalbox is on the station platform, with a wagon of coal for the station in front. A small ground signal guards the siding from the main line. *J. W. Armstrong*

Right:
A busy scene for a backwater such as Kielder Forest! BR Standard Class 3MT No 77011 arrives at the station with the 11.20am from Newcastle to Hawick, while the 1.40pm SO service to Hexham, with 'V1' No 67641 in charge, waits in the siding to the right. The steps on the platform were used to assist passengers alighting from trains and also visible are the levers in the signal cabin.
J. W. Armstrong

Centre right:
A 'D49' 4-4-0 pauses at Kielder Forest with a passenger train for Hexham in the early 1950s. This view shows how well the station fitted in to the surrounding area and the development of the forest to the rear. Many of the saplings that formed the forest were brought in by train to this station from Aviemore in Scotland.
N. E. Stead

Lower right:
Class V3 2-6-2T No 67639 at Kielder Forest on the last Saturday of operation, 13 October 1956. The locomotive is on the final 1.40pm SO service to Hexham and carries a suitable decoration; it is waiting for the 11.10am from Newcastle, which was running very late due to telegraph problems and time taken to add the extra coaches at Hexham. *N. E. Stead*

Left:
A close-up of the platform area and buildings at Kielder Forest, looking towards Hexham. A wagon load of domestic coal is in the siding. The station was named Kielder until 1948, when it became Kielder Forest as a result of the extent of planting in the area. To the south of here was Lewiefield Halt, opened in the autumn of 1933 for access to a training school for unemployed people, and latterly used by the MoD. *Ian Allan Library*

Centre left:
The remote station at Plashetts (also the local post office) in the early 1950s, looking towards Reedsmouth Junction. Here were the remnants of a siding to the now-closed collieries. It was hoped that the coal here would be of sufficient quality to supply the mills in the Tweed Valley, but in the end it was suitable only for other purposes and provided the Scottish border towns with domestic supplies. It closed in 1926, briefly reopened then shut soon afterwards for the second time. In BR days traffic was very light and the station is now flooded by Kielder Water.
N. E. Stead

Right:
A pleasant view of Falstone station in the 1950s. Similar to Kielder Forest, this had a lever frame, situated in the cabin on the platform, together with a loop and sidings. *Ian Allan Library*

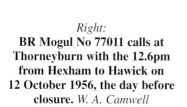

Right:
BR Mogul No 77011 calls at Thorneyburn with the 12.6pm from Hexham to Hawick on 12 October 1956, the day before closure. *W. A. Camwell*

Left:
A view of Thorneyburn, looking towards Riccarton Junction and showing the small station and level-crossing gates, for which there was a crossing keeper.
N. E. Stead

Centre left:
The North Tyne Valley is starting to broaden as can be seen from this view of Tarset, another wayside station. There was a North British drinking fountain here that advised takers to 'Keep the platform dry', as well as a post office situated on the platform. There was a camping coach here in the 1930s. Between Tarset and Bellingham was Charlton, closed after only two years use. *Ian Allan Library*

Lower left:
Bellingham (North Tyne), looking towards Reedsmouth Junction, with a 'J21' 0-6-0 running round a special train for the Bellingham agricultural show. A long rake of covered and cattle wagons are stored in the siding. Bellingham forwarded agricultural produce and livestock and also received coal. Of interest are the shunting signals, situated about halfway up the loop starting signal.
N. E. Stead

Above:
Class J27 No 65819 shunts at Bellingham (North Tyne) on 11 October 1963. Bellingham is a small market town and one benefit that the railway brought was the transportation to the area of slate which allowed the thatched roofs to be replaced by this material after a fire in which much damage was done to buildings.
W. A. C. Smith

Right:
A general view of Bellingham (North Tyne), looking towards Riccarton Junction in the mid-1950s. The line was closed between here and Riccarton for freight traffic on 1 September 1958, roughly two years after passenger services had been withdrawn. *Ian Allan Library*

Above:

On 23 September 1961 Bellingham (North Tyne) was visited by DMU excursions that ran via Morpeth and Reedsmouth, where they reversed. This was for the North Redesdale Show and the trains came from Newbiggin and Blyth. *John Langford collection*

Below:

Bellingham (North Tyne) station on 23 September 1961, before the DMU excursions arrived. This view shows the loading bank, crane and signal cabin, together with a coal merchant's lorry in the yard, right.
John Langford collection

Right:
The last passenger train to traverse the line was the 'Wansbeck Wanderer', which ran on 9 November 1963. This train was headed by Ivatt 2-6-0 No 43129 of 51A (Darlington) and is seen on arrival at Bellingham (North Tyne). Following this date, the freight service was withdrawn between Bellingham and Woodburn. One wonders where the train headboard is today! *Stuart Sellar*

Left:
To mark the departure of the last train on 9 November 1963, a local traction engine named *The Busy Bee* (**Burrell No 3555**) was steamed and was available for enthusiasts and local people to inspect. It is seen at the back of Bellingham station with the 'Wansbeck Wanderer' in the background. *Stuart Sellar*

Right:
No 43129 crosses the fine viaduct over the River North Tyne between Bellingham and Reedsmouth with the 'Wansbeck Wanderer' on 9 November 1963. The other fine viaduct on the line, at Kielder, is now designated an ancient monument. The reservoir has flooded much of the land in this area, together with parts of the Border Counties trackbed. *Stuart Sellar*

REEDSMOUTH JUNCTION

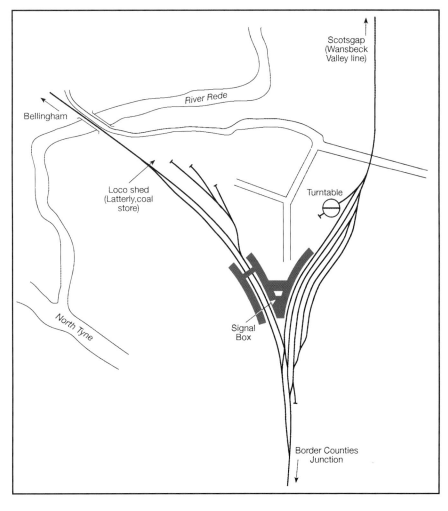

Above:
Class J39 No 64705 at Reedsmouth (always spelt thus by the railway, despite the river actually being spelt 'Rede') with the 4.30pm Newcastle-Hawick on 8 May 1950. Reedsmouth had an interchange platform situated centrally between the Border Counties and Wansbeck Valley lines, the former having an additional platform and loop as trains were more frequent. This necessitated the rather fine footbridge that was put in the LNER. Before this, a subway linked the platforms.
W. A. Camwell

Left:
Track plan of Reedsmouth Junction

Right:
Reedsmouth, looking north, on 7 July 1951. On the right is a Wansbeck Valley-line train for Scotsgap which has arrived behind Class J21 No 65042; on the left Class D30/2 'Scott' 4-4-0 No 62423 *Dugald Dalgetty*, **with a train from Hawick to Hexham, is taking water. Dominating the scene is the signalbox, with the very large water tower to the rear.**
W. A. Camwell

Centre right:
Class J21s Nos 65110 and 65035 take water at Reedsmouth, having arrived from Woodburn with a train of empty stock in 1955. This train had originated in the Midlands with troops destined for the Otterburn Ranges. The 0-6-0s had taken over at Newcastle and had come via Morpeth and Scotsgap to detrain the troops at Woodburn station. The empty stock would end up at Blaydon for servicing for its return journey a week later. *J. W. Armstrong*

Lower right:
Class J27 No 65822 shunts at Reedsmouth with the thrice-weekly goods from Bellingham to Morpeth on 30 September 1963. The locomotive will turn on the small turntable before running to Bellingham having just shunted some loaded coal wagons into the yard. *Ian Allan Library*

Above:

After closure of the line between Reedsmouth and Hexham, Bellingham was served via the Wansbeck Valley route from Morpeth. Seen earlier shunting, 'J27' No 65822 arrives back at Reedsmouth with the thrice-weekly goods from Bellingham to Morpeth on 30 September 1963. The 0-6-0 is passing the former locomotive shed, seen to the rear of the train. Also visible are the somewhat overgrown goods sidings, from where some loaded coal wagons were deposited before turning and proceeding to Bellingham. The shed was used latterly as a coal depot and to house the demolition contractor's locomotive that was used to lift the Riccarton to Bellingham section. It had closed in 1952 and this was where Scottish and English crews changed on BCR services.

Ian Allan Library

Left:

Another 'J27', No 65819, draws forward out of the sidings at Reedsmouth, having deposited some coal wagons on 11 October 1963. It has just retrieved the empties from the former locomotive shed that was now the coal depot. *W. A. C. Smith*

Above:
No 65822 again, here seen from the footbridge at Reedsmouth on 30 September 1963, hauling the thrice-weekly goods from Bellingham to Morpeth though the station, where it has detached two wagons and the brake van. It will then proceed to the stub of the Hexham line, where it will draw forward and then pass through the station once more before setting back onto the wagons and van. The train will then set back down the Hexham line before drawing forward for the run to Morpeth. *Ian Allan Library*

Right:
On the Wansbeck Valley side at Reedsmouth, 'J21' No 65042 waits with the one-coach 7.44am for Scotsgap. In the background, 'Hunt' class 4-4-0 No 62771 *The Rufford* departs with the 6.47am service from Riccarton Junction to Hexham on 7 July 1951. To the left are four through sidings. *W. A. Camwell*

Left:
Class J21 No 65061 stands at Reedsmouth with the empty stock of a special train for the Bellingham Agricultural Show on 22 September 1956. As mentioned previously, there was no place to stable these excursions at Bellingham when the line was open through to Riccarton, so the stock was worked empty back to Reedsmouth. The train is standing in one of the sidings on the Wansbeck Valley side of the station, the line to Scotsgap Junction disappearing behind the train. *Ian S. Carr*

Centre left:
Class J27 No 65819, also seen earlier, is turned on Reedsmouth turntable for the run back to Woodburn and Morpeth on 11 October 1963. The crew are putting their backs into the task. It was normal for the locomotive to work in chimney first and then turn for the run to Bellingham, from where it would return tender first, but on this occasion, the locomotive had run tender first to Bellingham. *W. A. C. Smith*

Below:
An eight-car DMU formation, which has run from Newbiggin to the Bellingham Agricultural Show, at Reedsmouth Junction on 21 September 1961. The train is about to pull forward for reversal on the stub of the Hexham line to run back to Bellingham.
John Langford collection

REEDSMOUTH TO HEXHAM

Below:
Wark station, looking north towards Reedsmouth, with the loading bank and loading gauge on the left. Livestock traffic was also generated here for markets in the Tyne Valley, and the station received a wagon of coal every so often, seen in the siding to the right. *Ian Allan Library*

Left:
The next station was Barrasford, seen here from the south, looking towards Reedsmouth. The wagons in the distance are in store, as the agricultural traffic that had been forwarded and received at Barrasford had ceased by the 1950s. A small ground frame controls access to the sidings and can be seen to the right of the first set of points. A camping coach was placed here by the LNER in the 1930s. *N. E. Stead*

Right:
Chollerton had two sidings with a loading bank and coal depot as well as a platform and a ground frame. In the early 1950s it was still in very presentable condition, as this photograph shows. Note the lamp to the right (and the others), with the station name behind it so as to illuminate the sign. This was a feature of many of the stations on this section, which had neat gardens for the benefit of the 'Garden Special Excursions' that ran past them!
N. E. Stead

Left:
Class K1 2-6-0 No 62073 calls at Humshaugh with the 10am from Riccarton Junction to Hexham and Newcastle on 12 October 1951. This is another neatly planted garden with beehives to the right of the train. A siding can be seen behind the coaches and there is a small loading bank provided to the left which was once used for livestock forwardings. This was the site of yet another camping coach in the 1930s. At one time there was a tramway from here to Brunton Quarry. *W. A. Camwell*

Above:
Class J21 0-6-0s Nos 65110 and 65090 are seen at Wall on an 11-coach troop train in 1952. Although this was a tough load for these two small locomotives, they were regulars on these trains. There were a number of sidings here and to the right of the photograph is the River North Tyne. The pilot locomotive was attached at Wall after having run light from Hexham as double heading was not permitted over the Tyne Bridge at Border Counties Junction. Wall station sold only 138 tickets in 1951, and closed one year earlier than other stations on the line. *J. W. Armstrong*

Right:
Class J21 No 65103 at Border Counties Junction on 14 August 1955 with a 'Garden Special Excursion' which ran from Newcastle to Newcastle via Reedsmouth, Bellingham (North Tyne), Scotsgap, Rothbury and Morpeth, the participants stopping at selected locations to view the station gardens and other delights, no doubt including public houses! The fine signal is complete with shunting arm. The train is about to swing right and cross the bridge over the River Tyne. The cost of repairing this structure was one reason the line was closed. In this view the river is quite low, but it can rise much higher, which would have required the bridge to be strengthened at great cost. There was a 10mph restriction on the bridge and by 1955 a 35mph speed restriction applied over the rest of the line. *R. F. Payne/J. W. Armstrong Trust*

Above:

BR Standard Class 3 2-6-0 No 77011 is seen at Hexham with the stock of a train from Riccarton on 4 August 1956. *Stuart Sellar*

Right:
The 8.51am Newbiggin to Bellingham (for the North Tyne Show), formed of an eight-car DMU, receives the tablet from the signalman at Woodburn for the single line to Reedsmouth Junction on 23 September 1961. Another special from Blyth followed this one. *Stuart Sellar*

REEDSMOUTH TO SCOTSGAP AND MORPETH

Above:
'J27' No 65834 shunts the Thursdays only goods train from Morpeth at Woodburn on 2 June 1966. The line to Bellingham, Reedsmouth from Woodburn had closed in 1963, and the service now terminated at Woodburn. However, there was still a fair amount of military stores traffic, general goods, agricultural traffic and coal transported on the line at this time, and military troop specials also still ran. *Hugh Ballantyne*

Above:
On 28 July 1966 'J27' No 65860 had the Woodburn freight job (the 10.20am from Morpeth) and is seen shunting in the sidings. To the left are the signal cabin, crane and coal merchant's lorry. *Leslie Sandler*

Above:
Class J27 No 65869 at Woodburn in April 1965, having arrived with the freight from Morpeth. The station is in remarkably good condition considering that it is closed to passengers. An Army lorry prepares to receive stores from the train, and there is inward coal — the merchant's lorry can be seen in the background. It has been raining hard, and the crew have rigged up a sheet to keep the water out of the cab while running tender-first.
N. E. Stead

Right:
No 77011 leaves Woodburn for Reedsmouth and Bellingham in the spring of 1963. There is a small siding with rail access and a shed for a platelayers' trolley on the left. The Mogul makes a change from the usual 'J27' 0-6-0. The section from Woodburn to Bellingham closed in 1963.
P. N. Townend

Above:
Class J27 No 65819, seen previously at Reedsmouth, shunts at Knowesgate with the freight from Bellingham to Morpeth on 11 October 1963. As usual it is picking up coal empties, the full ones having been deposited on the earlier run out from Morpeth; the locomotive will position these at the head of the vans seen on the main line, **left.** *W. A. C. Smith*

THE ROTHBURY BRANCH

Above:
Class J21 No 65119 has arrived at Rothbury on another special train in 1954. As well as the 'Garden Specials' there were trains run in connection with race meetings at Rothbury. Regular passenger traffic had been withdrawn in 1952 and the locomotive shed had closed as freight traffic was worked in by a locomotive from Blyth. *J. W. Armstrong Trust*

Centre right:
Rothbury received freight traffic until November 1963. Ivatt Class 2MT 2-6-0 No 46474 shunts the yard on 30 September 1960.
Stuart Sellar

Lower right:
An earlier, 1950, view of Rothbury, looking towards the buffer-stops and featuring a well-filled yard. There was regular freight traffic from Morpeth and stock for the service that ran to and from Morpeth. This was stabled here overnight along with the locomotive, as the first train away was at 7.51am, which took exactly an hour to reach Morpeth. As well as receiving coal and other general merchandise, the station forwarded agricultural produce and livestock.
Ian Allan Library

Above:
The last passenger train from Rothbury, the 'Wansbeck Wanderer', prepares to leave behind No 43129 on 9 November 1963. Was this the only time a buffet restaurant car was worked to Rothbury?
Stuart Sellar

Below:
The first station out of Rothbury was at Brinkburn Halt, which had a siding for goods and freight traffic. This 6 July 1951 photograph shows 'G5' 0-4-4T No 67296 calling with the 5.50pm from Morpeth to Rothbury, where it arrived at 6.58pm. This train had a connection for Woodburn and Reedsmouth at Scotsgap Junction.
N. E. Stead

Above left:
Another halt was passed at Fontburn, before Ewesley was reached, 7¾ miles from Rothbury. 'G5' No 67341 drops off a cattle wagon from the branch freight on 13 September 1952. Livestock traffic still featured on many rural lines, transporting cattle to market and from there to slaughterhouses that were situated in the larger towns in the area. The farming communities also relied on the railway for the inward carriage of other products, such as animal feedstuffs and machinery, as well as the carriage of grain, dairy products, potatoes and beet away from the area. The effect of road transport was immense on this particular part of the railways' business; it did not take long for most of this traffic to be transferred away, and by the 1960s it had virtually all gone.
J. W. Armstrong Trust

Above right:
The wayside Longwitton station in 1950, looking towards Rothbury. An old coach body is used for a store, and by it is a very small 'Gents'. Note that the wooden sleepers have been replaced with concrete ones — the line obviously has a long-term future! A siding is provided for local traffic. At one time, there was a colliery here which provided forwardings for the coast. *A. J. Wickens*

Below:
'J21' No 65090 is seen on its way to Rothbury working a 'Garden Special Excursion' approaching Longwitton on 23 August 1953.
J. W. Armstrong Trust

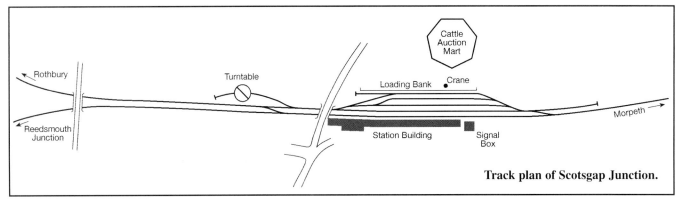

Track plan of Scotsgap Junction.

Left:

Class J21 No 65035 arrives at Scotsgap Junction from Rothbury with the branch freight for Morpeth on 7 July 1951. The train is coming off the Rothbury line, which forks north in the distance by the footbridge; the line to Woodburn is the left-hand road. The gradient away from Scotsgap necessitated an arrester rail on the Woodburn line to stop any breakaways running back into the station. Behind the train, right, is the turntable road. *W. A. Camwell*

Lower left:

The 8.51am Newbiggin-by-Sea to Bellingham (North Tyne) DMU excursion gets away from Scotsgap Junction, where it had called specially for photographic purposes (!) on 23 September 1961. *John Langford collection*

Right:

'J27' No 65819 has reached Scotsgap Junction with a train for Morpeth on 11 October 1963. This train did not work to Rothbury, as this was served on alternate days with Bellingham. The Rothbury freight service ceased from 11 November 1963, the same date as on the Woodburn-Bellingham section.
W. A. C. Smith

Above:

Scotsgap Junction on 23 August 1953 sees 'J21' No 65090 running round the 'Garden Special Excursion' that it has headed in from Reedsmouth. The locomotive will then work the train tender-first to Rothbury. To the left can be seen the long loading bank, while on the right are a number of wagons in the sidings. *J. W. Armstrong*

Above:
**No 43129 approaches Scotsgap Junction from Morpeth with the 'Wansbeck Wanderer' on 9 November 1963.
From here the train visited Rothbury, as seen earlier.** *Verdun Wake*

Right:
**Two miles from Scotsgap Junction
was Middleton North. The station
is seen from the train on
13 September 1952.**
J. W. Armstrong

Upper left:
Class J27 No 65860 calls at Angerton with the 10.20am Tuesdays- and Thursdays-only from Morpeth to Woodburn on 30 December 1965. By this time there was no traffic here, and the station siding had been partially lifted. This train comprises a wagon of military stores and a flat wagon. *David Holmes*

Lower left:
No 65860 seen again at Angerton, this time with the 10.20am Morpeth-Woodburn on 28 July 1966. This time the train is bringing in coal. On the left, an old coach body is in use as a store on the platform. *Leslie Sandler*

Upper right:
No 43129 passes through Meldon running tender first with the 'Wansbeck Wanderer' on 9 November 1963. Of note are the grounded coach body and the wagons stored in the siding on the right. *Stuart Sellar*

Centre right:
The 'J27' 0-6-0s did not have a monopoly on the Woodburn goods; here Ivatt Class 4MT 2-6-0 No 43063 is seen at Meldon on a damp 29 September 1966 with a train consisting mainly of loaded coal wagons. This was the penultimate goods working on the line and the lifted siding and loading gauge can be seen to the rear of the train. *J. R. P. Hunt*

Lower right:
Class J27 No 65819 leaves Morpeth for Woodburn with the 10.20am goods on 30 December 1965. Another short affair, this train had originated at Blyth. *David Holmes*

Alnmouth to Alnwick

Historical perspective

Like Langholm, which had nearly been situated on the proposed main line from Carlisle to Hawick, Alnwick was originally planned to be on a main line, this time the East Coast main line. The scheme had to be changed, however, in this case due to the objection of a local landowner, and, also like Langholm, Alnwick was ultimately served by a short branch line.

The route proposed by the Newcastle & Berwick Railway Company to link Newcastle and Berwick was indeed intended to pass through Alnwick, but the proposal was objected to by the Duke of Northumberland, who owned Alnwick Castle and through whose land the railway would have run. With this rejection, the railway had to find another route — and this was along the coast via Alnmouth, three miles away.

The local people were not pleased with this diversion and a line to link Alnwick with Alnmouth was given Parliamentary approval in 1846 after considerable pressure from the town. Construction took a further four years and it was not until 5 August 1850 that the line opened for freight, with passenger services to Alnmouth starting on 19 August. For the next 37 years trains ended their journey at a rather small terminus, but, with the completion of the line to Coldstream, a new station, built with a large overall roof, was opened. This must have been one of the grandest — if not the most impressive — branch line stations in the whole country.

The line was laid out to double-track standards and left the East Coast main line at Alnmouth, 34¾ miles north of Newcastle. The line ran parallel to the downside of the East Coast main line before passing the turntable which was situated between the branch and the main line. Turning west the line then followed the River Aln, situated to the north of the route. After a mile and a half it crossed a tributary of the Aln at Cawledge Burn, on a fine viaduct. Climbing at 1 in 77, it then passed milepost 2 where a long loop on the up side from Alnwick started.

On the down side was a gasworks with a siding, before the line arrived at the junction with the Coldstream line, where there was a turntable between the lines. As the lines fanned out for the terminus, from north to south was the horse dock, station platform — exactly three miles from Alnmouth — cattle dock, goods shed and a siding for a maltings. Freight traffic was not heavy, but the yard received and forwarded livestock, horses and general merchandise. Coal was also received for the gasworks and merchants for local domestic deliveries. There was a parcels office at the station — vans for this traffic can be seen in some of the illustrations, attached to passenger trains, while newspapers were delivered from Newcastle and London.

Alnwick enjoyed a service 'well beyond its station' and in July 1922, it had approximately 35 passenger trains per day, including those on the Coldstream branch. There was also a Sundays service of eight trains per day. The first major reduction in these came when the Coldstream passenger service was withdrawn on 22 September 1930.

The Winter 1950 timetable showed 15 return services, five of these running to and from Newcastle. Sunday services were still in operation, with eight return trains. Roughly the same level of service continued, and in the summer of 1963 the line had 13 return services per day, four of these being operated to and from Newcastle by DMUs. The line still retained steam power on services from Alnwick to Alnmouth only, these being worked by a variety of power from one of four 'K1' 2-6-0s based at Alnmouth, Nos 62006, 62011, 62023 and 62050, as well as 'J39' 0-6-0, with the occasional 'V1'/'V3' 2-6-2T also used; even Ivatt

Left:
BR NER timetable, 25 September 1950 'Until Further Notice', Alnmouth and Alnwick.

Right:
BR NER timetable, 17 June to 8 September 1963, Alnmouth and Alnwick.

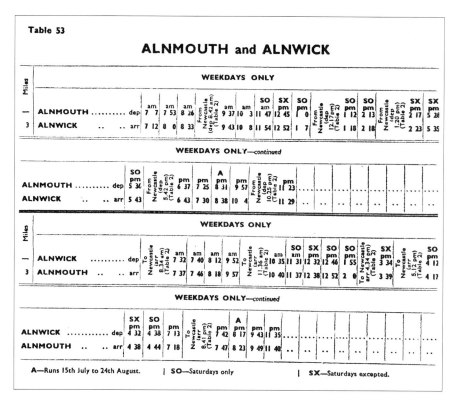

Class 2 2-6-0s put in the occasional appearance. 'K1s' Nos 62001 and 62062 were also used in February 1966, as were BR Standard Class 3 2-6-0s Nos 77002 and 77004. Such was the variety of motive power that even a BR Standard '9F' 2-10-0 worked the Alnwick-Alnmouth line; this was No 92099, which ran on the line on 18 June 1966 to mark the end of steam services.

From June 1966 DMUs took over all the passenger services, but, despite this and track and signalling rationalisation, the line was closed on 29 January 1968. Closure to freight followed on 7 October 1968, this having latterly been limited to coal traffic inwards.

There is currently a scheme to reopen the three-mile branch as the Aln Valley Railway. The station at Alnwick is still in existence, in use mainly as a second-hand bookshop, and the line's formation is in reasonable condition, with the exception of two bridges.

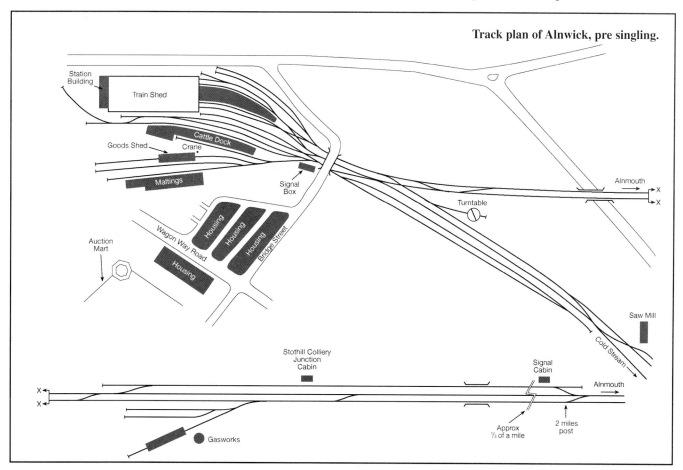

Track plan of Alnwick, pre singling.

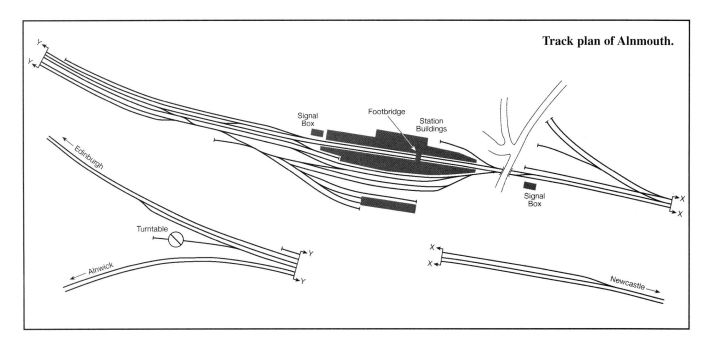

Track plan of Alnmouth.

Left:
**LMS-design Ivatt 2-6-0 Class 2
No 46476 of 52D (Tweedmouth)
shed waits at Alnmouth with the
1.10pm to Alnwick on
25 November 1961.**
David Holmes

Lower left:
**There was a wide variety of
motive power used on the Alnwick
line, Here, 'V3' 2-6-2T No 67656
of 52C (Blaydon) shed leaves
Alnmouth for Alnwick with the
7.14pm service on 17 May 1957.
A 'J39' stands in the loop,
right, with a down freight.**
Roy Hamilton

Right:
Class K1 2-6-0 No 62006 arrives at Alnmouth with the 5.55pm from Alnwick on 19 June 1965. A number of these locomotives worked on the line in the 1960s.
Edwin Wilmshurst

Above:
DMUs formed most of the through trains to and from Newcastle — how useful that service would be today! — and the 3.35pm from Alnwick is viewed one mile west of Alnmouth on 29 May 1962. DMBS No E50221 leads a Metro-Cammell two-car set on the double-track formation, which was later to be singled. *Michael Mensing*

Left:
Class K1 No 62011 crosses the viaduct over the River Aln on 22 March 1966 with the 09.52 from Alnmouth to Alnwick. *John M. Boyes*

Centre left:
Class K1 No 62021 climbs towards Alnwick on a gradient of 1 in 77 with the 16.48 from Alnmouth to Alnwick on 14 May 1966. *Maurice Burns*

Right:
Having left Alnwick, 'J39/2' No 64924 is seen approximately half a mile from the station with the 4.44pm to Alnmouth on 29 May 1962. The double track was still in operation at this time. *Michael Mensing*

Lower left:
The 14.20 DMU from Newcastle arrives at Alnwick on 19 March 1966. Evidence of singling of the line can be seen just beyond the train, where the points now form only a loop. The new colour-light signal, controlled from Alnmouth, guards the route, following closure of the station signalbox. The line to the right, now a siding, once formed part of the route to Coldstream. *Ian S. Carr*

Lower right:
A DMU departs from Alnwick for Alnmouth and Newcastle on 5 September 1964. The fine signal gantry was still in operation before the signalbox at Alnwick closed and the line was singled in the mid-1960s. *Edwin Wilmshurst*

Above:

No 62006 leaves Alnwick on 19 June 1965 with the 16.32 to Alnmouth. The signal gantry controlled the station throat, which until 1952/3 included the line from Coldstream, but it has now lost its signals, as the box is closed, and single-line working to Alnmouth has been imposed in an attempt to cut costs. *Edwin Wilmshurst*

Right:
The 11.30 to Alnmouth leaves Alnwick behind No 62011 on 18 June 1966. The points visible here were hand operated.
M. Dunnett

Centre right:
The last 'V2' 2-6-2 remaining in traffic, No 60836 of 62B (Dundee Tay Bridge), has arrived at Alnwick with the 16.48 from Alnmouth on 1 June 1966 and is setting back the train so it can run round to form the next Alnmouth service. Behind the train is the cutting that once contained the line to Wooler and Coldstream, latterly used for wagon storage. The tall signalbox had a panoramic view of the station and both the Coldstream and Alnmouth lines, but was now closed, and had suffered the indignity of the removal of its nameboard. *Hugh Ballantyne*

Below:
A general view of the magnificent Alnwick station on 1 June 1966 as the train hauled by No 60836, shown previously, arrives from Alnmouth. The station was originally designed by Benjamin Green, as with many other Newcastle & Berwick structures, but was rebuilt in 1887 by William Bell of the NER. The station starter signal gantry has been removed, as seen in the earlier photograph, this having gone when the signalbox was closed. There are still wagons on the yard to the left, and the loading bank and goods shed are visible. *Hugh Ballantyne*

No 62006 waits to leave Alnwick's impressive trainshed with the 16.32 to Alnmouth on 26 June 1965. Today Alnwick station is in use as a bookshop. *David Holmes*

No 62011 waits to leave from the other face of the island platform at Alnwick with the 16.32 to Alnmouth on 12 March 1966. *John M. Boyes*

The exterior of Alnwick station is seen in the mid-1950s. W. H. Smith & Son had a shop, seen in front of the car, and the passenger entrance was through the arch under the awning. *Ian Allan Library*

Alnwick to Coldstream

Historical perspective

At Alnwick, another branch line formed a route to Coldstream on the former York, Newcastle & Berwick line from Tweedmouth to Kelso, where this latter line made an end-on junction with the North British line to St Boswells via Roxburgh Junction.

There were originally two schemes for this line— one promoted by the North Eastern and one by the Northumberland Central Railway. The Northumberland Central wanted the line to pass from Newcastle to Scotsgap, Rothbury, Whittingham and Wooler and thence to Coldstream, while the North Eastern's plan was to build the line from Alnwick only. The latter scheme was to triumph, and the last section of the line opened on 5 September 1887. This could never have appeared to be a profitable undertaking, but was seen as a useful diversionary route for the East Coast Main line, and as such, nearly all the stations had passing loops, although they were not necessarily block posts.

A single-track line, it opened in stages, the first being from Cornhill to Wooperton. Cornhill was situated on the line from Tweedmouth to Kelso and was renamed Coldstream in 1873 and must have been the only station located in England which served a Scottish town. This first section opened for freight traffic on 2 May 1887. The final section, from Wooperton to Alnwick, opened to passenger and freight traffic on 5 September 1887.

The line was 35¾ miles in length after leaving the Tweedmouth to Kelso line at Coldstream and after 3¾ miles, reached Mindrum, the station for Yetholm which was 4¼ miles

away. As with many others on the line, the station here was quite magnificent, consisting of a large house built of red stone, a small lever frame for operating the sidings and a wide platform. There was also a warehouse loading bay. Moving on to Kirknewton, after eight miles, here too was a reasonable station house, a frame housed in what was the upper part of a signalbox that was situated on the platform, together with sidings. Between Kirknewton and Akeld was a level crossing at Yeavering, and although there was no station here, there was a signalbox that controlled the level crossing. After 11 miles came Akeld, the station for Ford, which was over six miles away. The standard station building similar to Mindrum was provided, again with a small lever frame cabin on the platform and sidings for freight traffic. Wooler was the first official passing place for passenger traffic, and as well as the grand station buildings had two platforms, a signalbox that controlled the loop and level crossing, and a number of sidings. This was the first block post and was 13½ miles from Coldstream. From Wooler, the next station was Ilderton, at 17¼ miles, where there was a single platform with a signalbox and a loop.

After 20 miles came Wooperton, another single-track platform, but with a loop and sidings, again with the frame in a small box on the platform. At Hedgeley (22¼ miles) there was another loop and a signalbox, which controlled a level crossing and a number of sidings. After Glanton came the most impressive station on the line, at Whittingham. This had a large island

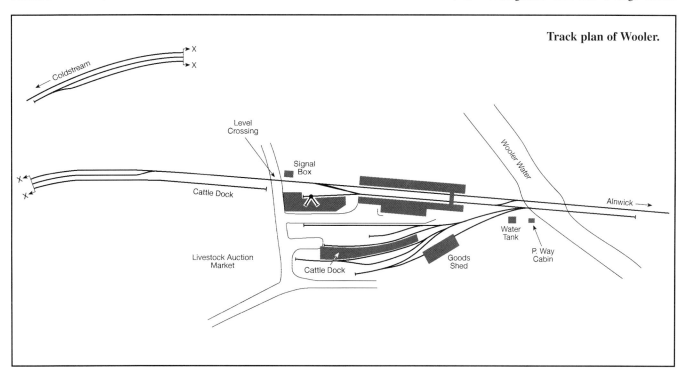

Track plan of Wooler.

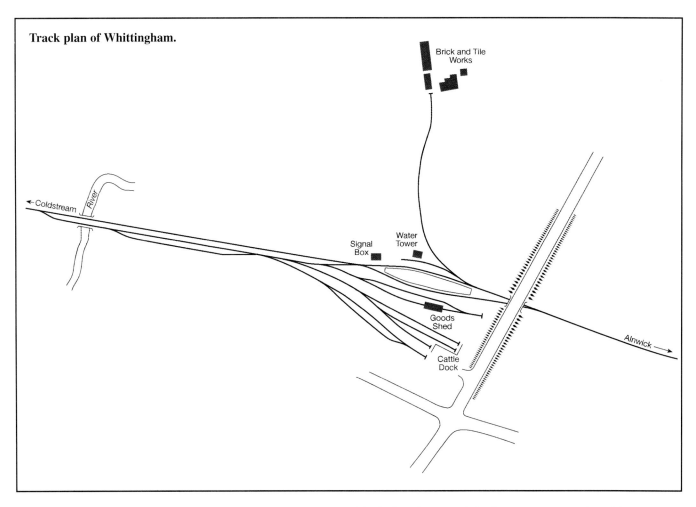

Track plan of Whittingham.

platform, an impressive station building with awnings, a passing loop and a signalbox, water tower, goods shed and yard. It was laid out in rather grand proportions for traffic that it would never have been able to attract. Between Whittingham and Alnwick was Edlingham at 28¾ miles, the junction at Alnwick joining the line from Alnmouth at the station throat.

Train services

Not surprisingly, passenger traffic on the line was not heavy. The initial passenger service was three trains per day, with none on Sundays. By World War 1 this had been increased to four services, the July 1922 Bradshaw showing the line worked by one train set which started at Berwick at 5.55am. This train then travelled via Tweedmouth — it was a Tweedmouth locomotive that worked the train — and then left Coldstream at 6.38am before arriving at Alnwick at 8.10am. The train worked back from Alnwick at 8.27am arriving in Coldstream at 10am. By 10.40am the train would have turned and then ran back to Alnwick arriving at 12.16pm. The return working left at 1.50pm and arrived at Coldstream at 3.23pm from where it departed to Tweedmouth, arriving at 3.43pm. The train then worked back from Tweedmouth at 4pm, arriving back at Coldstream at 4.27, then leaving at 5.29, before arriving at Alnwick at 6.3pm. The final departure of the day left Alnwick at 6.42 and arrived back at Tweedmouth at 8.42pm.

After World War 1 the new motor buses had opened up the area and they were able to serve some of the stations with more convenience. Never a great success, the railway passenger service was withdrawn on 22 September 1930. It is interesting to note that the Coldstream to Tweedmouth portion of the service survived, latterly worked by steam railcars. In the 1930s some of the stations had camping coaches in the sidings in an effort to boost trade.

The line was also seen as important for potential diversions during World War 2, should the East Coast main line ever be

blocked, and many of the loops were strengthened in case they were needed to take heavier traffic. Only one northbound express was noted to have been diverted this way, owing to an incident at Belford.

Freight services had been the line's main source of income and were largely based on agricultural, general merchandise and coal traffic. At Wooler, there was a brewery which attracted inward coal traffic, and the local stations were also served with domestic coal. During World War 2 there was an RAF base at Milfield near Wooler that generated goods and some special passenger workings. In the 1930s, there was significant movement of livestock but this had all but ceased by Nationalisation, and the local daily freight often had only a few wagons and a van for perishables. Latterly, the line saw 'intervention' traffic of sugar and grain, such commodities being stockpiled at remote warehouses in case of requirement in a national emergency.

The August 1948 floods washed away a bridge between Wooler and Ilderton, and the structure was never rebuilt. This section of the line was closed, and the route was operated in two sections — from Alnwick to Ilderton and from Coldstream to Wooler — the northern section being operated by a Tweedmouth locomotive and the southern part by an Alnmouth engine. The southern end was closed on 2 March 1953, and the track was lifted to Alnwick that same year, but the northern end remained open until 29 March 1965, the last freight running from Coldstream to Wooler on 25 March 1965, hauled by BR Standard Class 3 2-6-0 No 77002. A year earlier, a special train, the 'Scottish Rambler No 3', had run on the line from Coldstream to Wooler on 29 March 1964 and this proved to be the last passenger train on the line.

Today, many of the station houses survive as private dwellings and are a fitting tribute to the rather magnificent designs of the time that they were constructed.

Right:
Bradshaw's Guide, **Alnwick and Coldstream, July 1922.**

Below and overleaf (top):
BR NER working timetable 23 May-25 September 1949 showing the passenger service from Berwick to Kelso as well as the freight services.

ALNWICK and COLDSTREAM.—North Eastern.

Miles	Down.	Week Days only. mrn	aft	aft	Miles	Up.	Week Days only. mrn	mrn	aft
—	**Alnwick** ..... dep.	8 27	1 50	6 42	—	**Coldstream** ..dep.	6 38	1040	4 29
7	Edlingham	8 47	2 10	7 2	3½	Mindrum **	6 47	1049	4 38
10	Whittingham	8 53	2 16	7 8	8	Kirknewton	6 56	1058	4 47
11½	Glanton	8 58	2 21	7 13	11	Akeld ††	7 2	11 4	4 53
13¾	Hedgeley	9 2	2 26	7 18	13¼	Wooler	7 10	1114	5 3
15¾	Wooperton	9 9	2 33	7 25	17¼	Ilderton	7 19	1123	5 12
18½	Ilderton	9 17	2 41	7 33	20	Wooperton	7 25	1129	5 18
22¼	Wooler	9 27	2 51	7 43	22¼	Hedgeley	7 30	1135	5 24
24½	Akeld ††	9 34	2 58	7 50	24¼	Glanton	7 35	1140	5 29
27½	Kirknewton	9 41	3 5	7 57	25¾	Whittingham	7 42	1147	5 35
32	Mindrum ** ..748	9 53	3 16	8 8	28¾	Edlingham	7 50	1155	5 43
35¼	**Coldstream** arr.	10 0	3 23	8 15	35	**Alnwick 745** arr.	8 10	1216	6 3

NOTES.

** Station for Yetholm (4½ miles).

†† Station for Ford (6¾ miles).

BERWICK TO COLDSTREAM, KELSO AND ALNWICK

WEEKDAYS

Distance from Berwick	Distance from Coldstream	No.	5084	1300	294	5086	1302	1303	1304	1301	5088	1306	316	5072	5072	5090	5092	5092	5094
		Description	OP		Min	OP	Ety		E & V		OP			OP	OP	Pcls	OP	OP	OP
		Class		B	A		A	D					B			No. 1 Exp			
					SX		MO Q		FO Q		SO			SX	SO		SX	SO	SO
M C	M C		HC am	am	am	HC am	am	am	am	am	am	PM	PM	PM	PM	PM	PM	PM	PM
....	....	DOWN: **BERWICK**	6 30	....	....	9 20	....	....	....	....	11 45	....	....	3 20	3 30	....	6 40	6 52	9 30
1 12	..	**Tweedmouth**	6 33	..	..	9 23	..	..	..	..	11 48	..	..	3 23	3 33	..	6 43	6 55	9 33
....	....	**Tweedmouth**	6 40	7 40	8 45	9 28	11 10	....	*11 30*	....	11 55	1 30	2 0	3 30	3 40	....	6 50	7 2	9 40
5 22	..	Velvet Hall..	6y47	*	..	9 35	..	..	..	..	12 2	*	..	3 37	3 47	..	6y57	7 9	9y47
7 65	....	Norham	6 52	*	....	9 40	....	....	....	....	12 7	*	....	3 42	3 52	....	7 2	7 14	9 52
10 55	..	Twizell	6y57	*	..	9 45	..	..	..	..	12 12	*	..	3 47	3 57	..	7y7	7 19	9y57
13 48	....	**COLDSTREAM** .....Ⓣ	7 4	DD	....	9 52	....	....	*11 55*	....	12 19	....	....	3 54	4 4	....	7 14	7 26	10 4
..	..	UP: **COLDSTREAM**	7 7	..	9 8	9 54	11 35	..	..	Worked by Alnmouth passenger engine	..	*	2 23	3 57	4 7	..	7 17	7 29	..
16 53	....	Sunilaws	7 13	....	....	10 0	....	....	....		....	*	....	4 3	4 13	....	7 23	7 35	....
18 74	..	Carham	7 18	..	..	10 5	..	..	..		..	*	..	4 8	4 18	..	7 28	7 40	..
21 18	....	Sprouston	7 23	....	....	10 10	....	....	....		....	*	....	4 13	4 23	....	7 33	7 45	....
23 40	..	**KELSO**	7 28	..	9 55	10 15	..	..	..		..	DD	3 15	4 18	4 28	..	7 38	7 50	..
17 15	3 47	Mindrum	....	....		....	....	....	....		....	....	....	....	....	....	....	....	....
19 15	5 47	*Kilham Siding*	..	..	..	..	..	..	..		..	..	..	..	..	..	..	..	..
21 44	7 76	Kirknewton	....	....	....	....	....	....	....		....	....	....	....	....	....	....	....	....
24 40	10 72	Akeld .. .. .. Ⓣ	..	..	..	..	..	..	..		..	..	..	..	..	4 28	..	..	..
27 10	13 42	Wooler ....Ⓣ	....	....	....	....	12 10	U	....		....	....	....	....	....	4 35	....	....	....
30 54	17 6	Ilderton	..	..	..	..	SUSPENDED	*	..		..	..	..	..	..	4 47	..	..	..
33 46	19 78	Wooperton	....	....	....	....		*	....		....	....	....	....	....	4 55	....	....	....
35 59	22 11	Hedgeley .. .. Ⓣ	..	..	..	..		*	..	..	..	..	..	..	..	5 1	..	..	..
37 56	24 8	Glanton	....	....	....	....		*	....	....	....	....	....	....	....	5 6	....	....	....
39 33	25 65	Whittingham .. Ⓣ	..	..	..	..		*	..	..	..	..	..	..	..	5 11	..	..	..
42 23	28 55	Edlingham	....	....	....	....		....	....	....	....	....	....	....	....	5 19	....	....	....
44 77	31 29	*Summit*..	..	..	..	..	..	..	..	..	..	..	..	..	..	..	..	..	..
49 23	35 55	**ALNWICK** .....Ⓣ	....	....	....	....	....	*	....	U	....	....	....	....	....	5 38	....	....	....
		Arrives at	St. Boswells 8.1 am		Meadows 12.52 pm	St. Boswells 10.56 am		Alnmouth DD		Alnmouth DD			Meadows 6.10 pm	St. Boswells 4.56 pm	St. Boswells 5.6 pm		St. Boswells 8.16 pm	St. Boswells 8.26 pm	
		Forward Times on Page	W97		W97	W97							W97	W97	W97		W97	W97	

Nos. 5084, 5092, 5094—y No staff in attendance at Velvet Hall and Twizell

No. 1300—Runs forward to Mindrum as required

No. 294—Heaton dep. 5.10 am, page Q65

No. 316—Heaton dep. 9.50 am, page Q67

ALNWICK, KELSO AND COLDSTREAM TO BERWICK

WEEKDAYS

Distance from Alnwick	Distance from Kelso	No.	1308	388	1310	295	390	1312	303	5091	1314	347	5093	396	1305	1316	400	1307	4973
		Description		OP			OP			OP			Pcls	OP			OP		ECS
		Class	D		D	No.3 Unb		D	No.3 Unb		D	A	No. 1 Exp		A	A		B	
		Departs from	Alnmouth 7.15 am	St. Boswells 6.33 am	Alnmouth 8.0 am	Niddrie 7.0 am MO Duddingston 6.55 am MFX	St. Boswells 8.30 am		Meadows 7.0 am		Alnmouth U	Portobello 10.45 am MO Niddrie 10.50 am MSX		St. Boswells 4.0 pm			St. Boswells 7.18 pm		
		Previous Times on Page		W96		W96	W96		W96			W96		W96			W96		
						SX	HC		SX	SO		SX			FO Q	MO Q			SO
M C	M C		am	am	am	am	am	am	am	PM	am	PM	PM	PM	PM	PM	PM	PM	PM
....	....	DOWN: **ALNWICK** .....Ⓣ	7 25	....	*	....	....	....	....	....	DD	....	1 50	....	....	....	....	....	....
4 26	..	*Summit*..	..	..	..	..	..	..	..	..	..	..	..	..	..	..	..	..	..
7 0	....	Edlingham	....	....	....	....	....	....	....	....	....	....	....	....	....	....	....	....	....
9 70	..	Whittingham .. Ⓣ	..	..	*	..	..	..	..	..	..	..	2 16	..	..	..	..	..	..
11 47	....	Glanton	....	....	*	....	....	....	....	....	....	....	2 21	....	....	....	....	....	....
13 44	..	Hedgeley .. .. Ⓣ	..	..	*	..	..	..	..	..	..	..	2 26	..	..	..	..	..	..
15 57	....	Wooperton	....	....	*	....	....	....	....	....	....	....	2 32	....	....	....	....	....	....
18 49	..	Ilderton	..	..	*	..	..	..	..	..	..	..	2 40	..	..	..	..	..	..
22 13	....	Wooler ....Ⓣ	....	....	DD	....	....	....	....	....	....	....	2 52	....	....	5 0	....	....	....
24 63	..	Akeld .. .. Ⓣ	Worked by Alnmouth passenger engine	..	..	..	..	..	..	..	Worked by Alnmouth passenger engine	..	2 58	..	..	..	..	..	..
27 59	....	Kirknewton		....	....	....	....	....	....	....		....	....	....	....	....	....	....	....
30 8	..	*Kilham Siding*		..	..	..	..	..	..	..		..	..	..	..	..	..	..	..
32 8	....	Mindrum		....	....	....	....	....	....	....		....	....	....	....	....	....	....	....
..	..	UP: **KELSO**		7 35	..	9 23	9 40	..	9 50	..		1 25	..	4 40	..	..	7 48	U	..
....	2 22	Sprouston		7 40	....	....	9 45	....	....	....		....	....	4 45	....	....	7 53	*	....
..	4 46	Carham		7 45	..	..	9 50	..	..	..		..	..	4 50	..	..	7 58	..	..
....	6 67	Sunilaws		7 50	....	9 37	9 55	....	10 9	....		1 39	....	4 55	....	....	8 3	....	....
35 55	9 72	**COLDSTREAM** .. Ⓣ		7 57	..	..	10 2	..	..	..		..	..	5 2	..	..	8 10	..	..
....	....	**COLDSTREAM**	....	8 0	....	9 43	10 4	U	10 20	1 25	....	1 45	....	5 5	U	5 35	8 12	*	*10 15*
38 48	12 65	Twizell	..	8 6	..	..	10 10	..	..	1 31	..	..	..	5 11	..	..	8y18	..	..
41 38	15 55	Norham	....	8 12	....	....	10 16	....	....	1 37	....	....	....	5 17	....	....	8 24	....	....
44 1	18 18	Velvet Hall..	..	8 19	..	..	10 23	..	..	1 43	..	..	..	5 24	..	..	8y30	..	..
48 11	22 28	**Tweedmouth**	....	8 26	....	10 23	10 30	DD	10 56	1 50	....	2 10	....	5 31	DD	6 0	8 37	DD	*10 35*
..	..	**Tweedmonth**	..	8 32	..	..	10 35	..	..	1 55	..	..	..	5 37	..	..	8 42	..	*10 41*
49 23	23 40	**BERWICK**	....	8 35	....	....	10 38	....	....	1 58	....	....	....	5 40	....	....	8 45	....	*10 44*

No. 295—Heaton arr. 2.57 pm, page **Q78**

No. 1312—West Ord Siding *. Return of 7.40 am ex Tweedmouth

No. 303—Heaton arr. 3.22 pm, page **Q78**

No. 347—Heaton arr. 5.54 pm, page **Q79**

No. 400—y No staff in attendance at Twizell and Velvet Hall

No. 1307—Calls at Sunilaws to take up watercans for Learmouth Gates

LIST OF SIGNAL BOXES, ADDITIONAL RUNNING LINES, LOOPS AND REFUGE SIDINGS—continued

Description of Block System on Main Lines	SIGNAL BOX	Distance between Signal Boxes		Additional Running Lines*		Loops & Refuge Sidings				Hours Signal Box Open	REMARKS *Broken line indicates lines worked by Permissive or No Block Regulations †PL—Passenger Loop GL—Goods Loop RS—Refuge Siding
						Up		Down			
				Up	Down	Description †	Standage in wagons in addition to E & V	Description †	Standage in wagons in addition to E & V		
	ALNMOUTH AND COLDSTREAM										
Absolute Block	**Alnmouth** North	0	0							See Doncaster and Berwick Table	
	Alnwick East	2	801							As required	
Electric Key Token	Station	0	700							5.35 am until traffic ceases M to S. For passenger trains Su	
	Whittingham Station	9	1315							During running of traffic	
	Hedgeley Station	3	1236							During running of traffic	
	Wooler Station	8	1260							During running of traffic	
Electric Staff	**Akeld** Station	2	983							During running of traffic	
	Coldstream Station	10	1677							See Tweedmouth and Kelso Table	

Below:

Class 'D20' No 62371 stands at Whittingham station with the return daily freight to Alnwick on 27 February 1953, the eve of withdrawal of freight services on this part of the line. By this time, the line was being worked in two sections, and the train is returning to Alnwick after a trip to Ilderton. No 62371 is a 52D (Tweedmouth) locomotive, outbased at Alnmouth. An LNER camping coach was based at Whittingham in the 1930s. There was also a livestock market here as well as grain and other agricultural traffic. A tile works also provided some business. *J. W. Armstrong Trust*

Above:
No 62371 has shunted at Hedgeley on 27 February 1953 and receives the token for the single line before running back to Alnwick. The fine signalbox was far larger than it ever needed to be for the amount of traffic on the line.
J. W. Armstrong Trust

Left:
SLS/BLS 'Scottish Rambler' schedule, 15 April 1963.

Above:
Wooperton station house is one of the fine buildings of the type that featured at nearly all the stations on the Coldstream-Alnwick line. The small extension to the covered canopy is the cabin for the groundframe and the sleepers on the loop are concrete in this 1950s view. *Ian Allan Library*

Above:
Wooler station was second only to Whittingham in having two platforms and was once a block post on the line to Coldstream. It was the biggest generator of traffic. The daily freight arrives from Coldstream with Ivatt 2-6-0 No 46476 in charge on 28 May 1959. Note the large enclosed canopy and fine station house; the points for the yard and other sidings are behind the train. *J. Spencer Gilks*

Right:
No 46482 is seen arriving at Wooler earlier in the day on 18 March, with the branch freight from Tweedmouth and Coldstream. There is a wagon of domestic coal plus two vans for perishables in the train.
Stuart Sellar

Left:
The 'Scottish Rambler No 2' has arrived at Wooler behind Ivatt Class 2 2-6-0 No 46474 on 15 April 1963. This tour had also taken in the line to Duns and would continue over to the West Coast, visiting Kirkcudbright, Garlieston, Whithorn and Stranraer, amongst other destinations, as seen in previous illustrations. *Stuart Sellar*

Centre left:
A close-up of the small ground frame housed in a rather attractive cabin at Akeld, recorded on the occasion of the 'Scottish Rambler No 2' visit on 15 April 1963. *Ian Allan Library*

Below:
No 46482 is seen at Akeld station with the branch freight on 18 March 1961. The loop is in the foreground and the yard was to the left, while the goods store can be seen behind the station sign. *Stuart Sellar*

Above:
Ivatt 2-6-0 No 46475 drifts across Yeavering Crossing, between Kirknewton and Akeld, with the Coldstream-Wooler thrice-weekly freight on 27 February 1963. The train crew are operating the crossing gates. *A. Moyes*

Right:
No 46474 again, this time at Langham level crossing near Yeavering, on 18 March 1961.
Stuart Sellar

Left:
Kirknewton sees the arrival of No 46474 with the 'Scottish Rambler No 2' on 15 April 1963. The platform is now overgrown, but the large structure that looks like the top of a signalbox stands on the platform providing cover for the ground frame. The yard can be seen to the left, behind the train. *Stuart Sellar*

Centre left:
Mindrum was the first station on the line from Coldstream. It was to the line's standard design with loop, and the sidings with a goods storage area are to the rear right. Despite 20 years with no passenger service, there is no sign of vandalism, and things remain remarkably intact.
Ian Allan Library

Lower left:
A photograph taken from the 4pm St Boswells-Berwick service as it arrives at Coldstream at 4.59pm on 7 August 1958. The points under the train show the line coming in from Wooler. The locomotive is 'V3' No 67617.
David Holmes

EYEMOUTH TO BURNMOUTH

Historical perspective

The first branch line 'over the border' from England into Scotland on the North British main line from Berwick to Edinburgh was the short, three-mile line from Burnmouth to Eyemouth.

Eyemouth is situated on the East Coast where Eye Water runs into the North Sea and is a sheltered bay which led to it becoming an important fishing port, that industry employing a large number of the town's inhabitants.

The line from Burnmouth to Eyemouth had been opened in 1891, and was originally built under the auspices of the Eyemouth Railway Company. It was taken over in 1900 by the North British and latterly became part of the LNER. Before the railway was opened, virtually all the fish had to be transported by road to Burnmouth from where it was shipped by rail to the many destinations — as far as Edinburgh or Newcastle. Much the same was for inward traffic, which included commodities, fish bait and coal, these again being transferred by road from Burnmouth.

Such was the desire to link Eyemouth's important fish traffic to the rest of the country by rail direct from the port, that a committee of local people came together and the Eyemouth Railway Company was formed. The company was keen to finance the construction of the route itself, thus keeping independent of the North British, but when the potential investors realised that they would never get a return on their money, as with many railway schemes, support was not forthcoming. Despite the fact that construction had been authorised by Parliament on 18 August 1884, there was still only limited local interest and it looked as though the scheme might fail. Indeed, there were routes proposed other than the one to Burnmouth, which were supposedly cheaper to construct, one of these being a line from Reston via Coldingham — the latter being keen to join the rail network to develop its tourist traffic.

However, the Eyemouth-Burnmouth scheme was saved by Sir James Miller, who purchased 500 shares in the company and thus allowed construction to start — but not until July 1889 (it had taken five years to get to this stage from 1884), and it took until 13 April 1891 for construction to be completed and the line to open. The line was only 2 miles 75 chains long, with a small siding at Biglawburn, and was steeply graded, climbing from nearly sea level at Eyemouth, over an impressive viaduct, to roughly 300ft at the junction at Burnmouth. The journey time was roughly eight minutes and the view was often obscured as the line was frequently covered in fog or sea 'haar'.

The original company had been taken over a year earlier by the North British, which operated the line. With its opening, Eyemouth expanded not only as a fishing port but also as a holiday resort. Fish traffic dominated the freight services, and the 6pm goods was timed to allow local fish merchants to load the morning's catch. Freight income was just over £4,000 per annum.

Above right:
Bradshaw's **July 1922 guide, Burnmouth and Eyemouth.**

Centre right:
LNER 1944 timetable.

Lower right:
BR ScR timetable 1948.

In July 1922 there were six return passenger services on weekdays, with two of these trains extended to and from Berwick, roughly seven minutes being allowed for the journey on the branch.

To cope with the considerable freight traffic there was a goods yard and an 'S'-shaped platform that could cater for large numbers of tourist passengers — and these were significant in the early years of the line's life. Records show that in the early 1920s nearly 38,000 passengers travelled from Eyemouth, but these numbers started to decline in the depression years and never returned, although the late 1930s, before World War 2, saw much local holiday business from the North East. At Nationalisation eight trains a day were timetabled for the line, catering for local journeys which were mainly made to and from Berwick; there were also through services, but generally a change of trains was still necessary at Burnmouth.

Following World War 2, the line was seriously affected by the great floods of 11 and 12 August 1948, when the Eye Water Viaduct, by which the railway entered Eyemouth, had one of its centre piers washed away. Together with this bridge, seven others on the East Coast main line were also washed away, and as mentioned previously, several branch lines were affected. Thus, the line was temporarily closed and with this local people and businesses had to make alternative transport arrangements. Passenger and freight receipts began to fall as road transport made a serious impact on traffic, including both fish and general merchandise. It was perhaps a little surprising that British Railways decided to repair the viaduct at all, but it did, and the central pier was rebuilt on a new concrete foundation, together with attention to the other piers and supports.

With priority being given to the repair of the seven bridges on the Berwick to Edinburgh main line the Eyemouth to Burnmouth line did not reopen until 29 June 1949, the ceremony being performed by no less than the Chief Officer of the Scottish Region, F. T. Cameron, and the Provost of Eyemouth, J. S. Collins.

The passenger service was now eight return trains a day, the 8am from Eyemouth working through to Berwick, returning from there at 8.45am, but by 1953 things had changed significantly.

Despite the expensive rebuilding, the number of passenger services was reduced to one through Berwick service, with only three others to and from Burnmouth, formed of one carriage only. This connected with the stopping service from Edinburgh to Berwick. This was one of Dr Beeching's main targets as he had calculated these services were vastly uneconomic. In 1953 passenger trains departed from Eyemouth at 7.5 and 8am, with a mixed train at 5.15pm. The 8am was a through train to Berwick, where it arrived at 8.18am. Two Class C fish trains also ran — at 3.40pm and at 6.53pm, with wagons being detached at Burnmouth for collection by a pick-up freight service. In the opposite direction, passenger trains left Burnmouth at 7.30, 9.5am (from Berwick depart 8.45), 4.7 and 5.43pm. Fish vans were returned on these services as required on mixed trains — interestingly, there were no official down mixed services as with the up mixed train from Eyemouth.

This sufficed as by this time only an average of five passengers a day were using the service outside the holiday season. So, despite the expensive reconstruction of the viaduct, the line was closed, thus forcing the remaining fish, coal and general merchandise traffic on to road transport, the line not being retained for freight only after withdrawal of the passenger services. The Scottish TUCC finally approved closure at the end of 1961.

Services had been dominated by 'J39' 0-6-0s from Tweedmouth shed during the line's latter years, and it was only fitting that one of these, No 64917, should haul the last train, on 3 February 1962. Like many such trains of the era, this was full, with all the passengers crammed into a single carriage. Formal closure came on 5 February 1962.

Replacement bus services were advertised in the Scottish Region timetable; in the summer of 1964 the connection was given from Berwick upon Tweed — an eight-mile journey by Scottish Omnibuses Ltd.

Track-lifting had begun by July 1962 and was soon completed, with the station at Eyemouth eventually being totally demolished. Burnmouth is now passed at speed by trains on the East Coast main line.

EYEMOUTH BRANCH

UP TRAINS — WEEKDAYS

	No.	32		217	40		42		44
	Description				Fish		Mix'd		Fish
	Class	B		B	C		B		C
M. C.		am		am	PM		PM		PM
2 72	Eyemouth	7 5		8 0	3 40		5 15		6 53
	Burnmouth	7 13		8 8	3 49		5 24		7 0

No. 217—Through train to Berwick arrive 8.18 a.m.

DOWN TRAINS — WEEKDAYS

	No.	69		211			79		81
	Description								
	Class	B		B			B		B
1. C.		am		am			PM		PM
2 25	Burnmouth	7 30		9 5			4 7		5 43
2 72	Biglawburn Siding								
	Eyemouth	7 38		9 13			4 15		5 51

No. 211—Through train from Berwick depart 8.45 a.m.

Above:
ScR working timetable 21 September 1953.

Above:
Eyemouth-Berwick leaflet.

Table 78 — BURNMOUTH and EYEMOUTH

		am	D am	pm	pm	pm	pm	pm	pm									
										WEEKDAYS								
Berwick	dep	7 5	8 45	....	2 27	....	....	7 10	....	....	....	....	....	....	....	....	....	....
BURNMOUTH	dep	7 25	9 8	1 20	2 45	4 7	5 49	7 35	8 30	....	....	....	....	....	....	....	....	..
EYEMOUTH	arr	7 33	9 16	1 28	2 53	4 15	5 57	7 43	8 38	..	..	..	..	..	..	..	..	..

		am	D am	pm	pm	pm	pm	pm	pm									
										WEEKDAYS								
EYEMOUTH	dep	7 5	8 0	12 55	2 25	3 43	5 20	7 0	8 2	....	....	....	....	....	....	....	....	....
BURNMOUTH	arr	7 13	8 8	1 4	2 33	3 52	5 29	7 9	8 10	..	..	..	..	..	..	..	..	..
Berwick	arr	..	8 20	1 24	..	4 10	5 44	..	8 26	..	..	..	..	..	..	..	..	..

D—Through trains between Berwick and Eyemouth.

Above:
BR NER timetable, 25 September 1950 'Until Further Notice', Burnmouth and Eyemouth.

Right:
The main reason for the railway coming to Eyemouth was to serve the fishing fleet and the transportation of fish. Part of the fleet and the harbour can be seen here on 19 October 1961.
Stuart Sellar

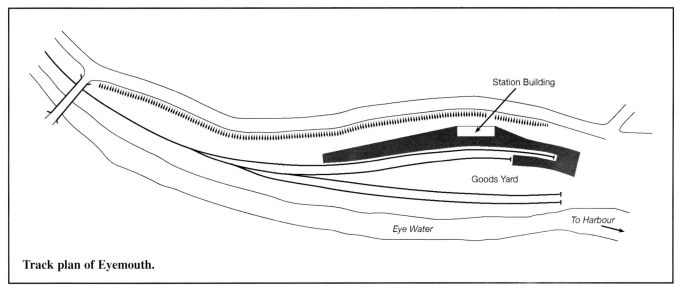

Track plan of Eyemouth.

Above:
Class J39 No 64917 is seen with a train of mostly fish vans at Eyemouth on the last day of service on the line, 3 February 1962. *Edwin Wilmshurst*

Above:
Class J39 No 64843 of 52D (Tweedmouth) shed waits at Eyemouth with the 5.10pm to Burnmouth on 18 July 1959. *W. A. C. Smith*

Above:
A panoramic view of No 64843 earlier on 18 July, this time with the 4pm to Burnmouth, showing the neat station and (on the right) sidings for the fish traffic, complete with a good number of insulated fish vans. Behind the yard is the harbour, with its fishing fleet.
W. A. C. Smith

Centre right:
Class J39 No 64925 leaves Eyemouth with a mixed train for Burnmouth on 26 June 1959. Even at this late stage there were rails alongside the sleepers for re-laying. As there was no 'run-round' loop at Eyemouth, gravity was used to shunt the coach back into one of the sidings to allow the locomotive to then pass it and couple on before placing it back into the platform.
David Holmes

Lower right:
No 64843 climbs away from Eyemouth for Burnmouth on 18 July 1959. The train is passing Biglawburn Siding, about half a mile from Eyemouth, which served a roadside oil-storage tank. *W. A. C. Smith*

Left:
On 3 February 1962 'J39' No 64917 runs into Burnmouth with the 8am from Eyemouth. This train then formed a through train to Berwick, arriving at 8.20am. The Eyemouth platform is to the right, and the train is on the up main line. *Edwin Wilmshurst*

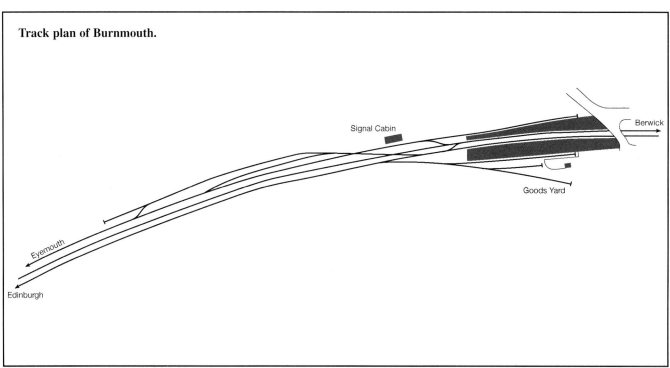

Track plan of Burnmouth.

Berwick

Signal Cabin

Goods Yard

Eyemouth

Edinburgh

Left:
No 64843 stands in the branch platform at Burnmouth with the 4.7pm for Eyemouth on 25 November 1961. Visible through the bridge (and with a fish wagon on the rear), the stopping service to Berwick and Edinburgh, one of Dr Beeching's main targets, pulls away into the distance. *W. A. C. Smith*

CLOSURE DATES

Fountainhall to Lauder
Passengers: 12 September 1932
Freight: 1 October 1958

Roxburgh Junction to Jedburgh
Passengers: 13 August 1948
Freight: 10 August 1964

St Boswells (Ravenswood Junction) to Duns
Passengers: 13 August 1948
Freight (Greenlaw to Duns): 13 August 1948
Freight (Ravenswood Junction to Greenlaw): 19 July 1965

Duns to Reston Junction
Passengers: 10 September 1951
Freight: 7 November 1966

Symington to Peebles
Passengers: 5 June 1950
Freight (Broughton to Peebles West): 7 June 1954
Freight (Symington to Broughton): 4 April 1966
Freight (Peebles Junction to Peebles West): 1 August 1959

Newton Stewart to Whithorn
Passengers: 25 September 1950
Freight: 6 October 1964

Galashiels (Selkirk Junction) to Selkirk
Passengers: 10 September 1951
Freight (Selkirk to Netherdale Siding): 2 November 1964
Freight (Netherdale Siding to Galashiels): 3 October 1966

Beattock to Moffat
Passengers: 6 December 1954
Freight: 6 April 1964

Riccarton Junction to Hexham
Passengers: 15 October 1956
Freight (Hexham to Reedsmouth: 15 October 1956
Freight (Bellingham to Riccarton): 1 September 1958
Freight (Bellingham to Reedsmouth): 11 November 1963

Morpeth to Scotsgap, Rothbury and Reedsmouth
Passengers (Morpeth to Rothbury): 15 September 1952
Passengers (Scotsgap to Reedsmouth): 15 March 1952
Freight (Woodburn to Reedsmouth and Bellingham):
  11 November 1963
Freight (Rothbury to Scotsgap): 11 November 1963
Freight (Morpeth to Woodburn): 3 October 1966

Eyemouth to Burnmouth
Passengers: 5 February 1962
Freight: 5 February 1962

The Peebles Loop (Kilknowe Junction to Rosewell & Hawthornden)
Passengers: 5 February 1962
Freight: 5 February 1962

St Boswells (Kelso Junction) to Tweedmouth
Passengers St Boswells to Kelso and Tweedmouth: 15 June 1964
Freight (St Boswells to Kelso): 1 April 1968
Freight (Kelso to Tweedmouth): 29 March 1965

Riddings Junction to Langholm
Passengers: 15 June 1964
Freight: 18 September 1967

Castle Douglas (junction for Portpatrick line) to Kirkcudbright
Passengers: 3 May 1965
Freight: 14 June 1965

Challoch Junction to Dumfries (junction for Castle Douglas branch)
Passengers: 14 June 1965
Freight: 14 June 1965

Cairnryan Junction to Cairnryan Point
Freight only (War Department line): 30 April 1959

Stranraer to Portpatrick
Passengers: 6 February 1950
Freight (Colfin to Portpatrick): 6 February 1950
Freight (Stranraer to Colfin): 1 April 1959

Alnwick to Alnmouth
Passengers: 29 January 1968
Freight: 7 October 1968

Coldstream to Wooler
Passengers: 22 September 1930
Freight: 29 March 1965

Alnwick to Ilderton
Passengers: 22 September 1930
Freight: 2 March 1953

Ilderton to Wooler
Passengers: 22 September 1930
Freight: 13 August 1948

Above:

No 64614 is seen on the tracklifting train from Peebles West as it crosses the Tweed bridge in Peebles on 14 November 1961. Note the distant signal to the right of the bridge. This section of the line was only ever used for freight traffic and no scheduled through passenger services ran, even in BR days. It was open until August 1959. *Stuart Sellar*

Below:

Humshaugh station, looking north, in February 1960 with a contractor's locomotive engaged in track lifting. *M. Mitchell*

INDEX OF LOCATIONS

Below:
**No 43011 waits at Langholm with the 3.30pm to Carlisle on 6 April 1963. The line in the foreground was one of
the yard sidings, the adjacent one leading to the former locomotive shed, while the next was to the goods shed
followed by two more for other general traffic.** *W. A. C. Smith*

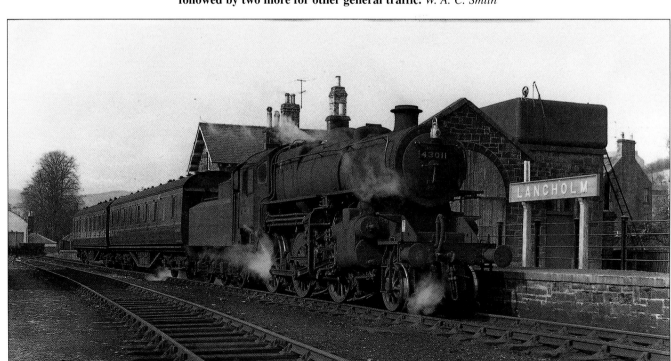